YANKEE THEATRE

Charles Mathews on New York's Park Theatre stage during
his first tour of America in 1822.

YANKEE THEATRE

The Image of America on the Stage, 1825-1850

FRANCIS HODGE

UNIVERSITY OF TEXAS PRESS • AUSTIN

ACKNOWLEDGMENTS

The general subject of this study, of course, has been treated briefly, but with care and perception, elsewhere. Among the earliest and most useful discussions is that of Brander Matthews in *Scribner's Monthly* for July, 1879. Except, however, for Constance Rourke's two volumes, *Roots of American Culture* and *American Humor: A Study of the National Character*, both of which focused the problem with imagination and projection without pursuing it in any extended detail, and whose hints and near guesses have provided springboards for this study, no major treatment of the Yankee on the stage has appeared.

The writer is indebted to all those whose previous study of the subject has contributed to our awareness and understanding of these early developments. The work of the late A. M. Drummond, Jonathan W. Curvin, Portia Kernodle, and Richard Moody is particularly acknowledged (see A Note on Sources). George C. D. Odell's *Annals of the New York Stage*, Charles Durang's *History of the Philadelphia Stage*, Reese D. James' *Old Drury of Philadelphia*, and Arthur H. Wilson's *A History of the Philadelphia Theatre 1835–1855*—all excellent and highly useful local-theatre studies—have been used constantly for records of performances. Special acknowledgment is also made of the kind help of George Freedley of the New York Public Library; of George Nash of the Victoria and Albert Museum; of P. D. A. Harvey of the British Museum, who granted permission to use his unpublished "Bibliography of the Lord Chamberlain's Collection of the British Museum, 1824–1851"; of Frederick Hunter of the Hoblitzelle Theatre Arts Library; of my wife, Beulah Hodge, who gave painstaking care to technical matters; and of The University of Texas Research Institute, which conferred a study grant to aid the author in the completion of this work.

CONTENTS

ILLUSTRATIONS *(with text)*

ILLUSTRATIONS *(following page 132)*

1. "Ancient and Modern Republics"
2. "Box at the Theatre"
3. View of the Bay of New York from the Battery in 1830
4. Park Theatre and Part of Park Row in New York in 1831
5. Frances Trollope
6. Fanny Kemble as Juliet (c. 1830's)
7. George Pope Morris, editor of the *New York Mirror*
8. Thomas Wignell as Jonathan in Royall Tyler's *The Contrast*
9. Charles Mathews in 1818
10. Charles Mathews in 1833
11. Charles Mathews as Agamemnon in *Trip to America*
12. Charles Mathews as Jonathan W. Doubikin and Agamemnon, and the Stage Setting for the Sketch of "All Well at Natchitoches" in *Trip to America*
13. Charles Mathews as Colonel Hiram Pegler, Monsieur Capot, and Agamemnon in *Trip to America*
14. Charles Mathews as Jonathan Doubikin, Miss Mangelwurzel, and Mr. O'Sullivan
15. Charles Mathews in the Many Characters He Played in *Trip to America*
16. Charles Mathews as Jonathan, with the Character of Agamemnon in Richard B. Peake's *Jonathan Doubikins*
17. James Henry Hackett in 1832
18. Mrs. Sharpe, Sister-in-Law of James H. Hackett
19. Catherine (Leesugg) Hackett, First Wife of James H. Hackett
20. James H. Hackett as Solomon Swap in *Jonathan in England*
21. James H. Hackett in His Backwoods Character of Nimrod Wildfire in *Lion of the West*
22. A Caricature of James H. Hackett in His Famous Characterization of Shakespeare's Falstaff
23. George Handel Hill in 1834
24. George Hill as Jedidiah Homebred in J. S. Jones' *The Green Mountain Boy*
25. George Hill as Nathan Tucker in W. Bayle Bernard's *Wife for a Day*
26. George Hill as Major Enoch Wheeler in W. Bayle Bernard's *New Notions*

YANKEE THEATRE

prologue

This book is about the development of American comedy between 1825 and 1850. It briefly follows the emergence of an American-type character in early plays of native authorship previous to this period, and evaluates the immediate stimulus of English comedian Charles Mathews. The major concern, however, is with the work of the four principal American-born comedians who provided its creative energy—James H. Hackett, George H. Hill, Dan Marble, and Joshua Silsbee. These are the famous "Stage Yankees" who entertained audiences with their eccentric New England dialect comedy from Boston to New Orleans, from New York to London.

This book attempts to examine the full range of their theatre activity, not only as actors but also as playmakers, and to re-evaluate their contribution to the growth of the American stage. "Yankee theatre" is therefore used throughout as a composite label to describe these comedians performing American-type characters in plays especially written for their peculiar talents. Unfortunately, the literary evidence available to us today gives Yankee theatre the appearance of gross impoverishment, naïveté, monotony, very poor stuff. One must view it in historical perspective to value it at all. But when it is seen in the light of 1830 America it can be defended as an actor's theatre—as an American *commedia dell' arte*. From this view it was no mean accomplishment. Yankee theatre was not an oddity, a passing fad, or an accident of entertainment; it was an honest exploitation of the materials of American life for an audience in search of its own identification.

Yankee theatre is illuminating as folkloristic anthropology. The delineation of the American character—a full-length realistic portrait in the context of stage comedy—was its projected goal; and though not the only method for such delineation, the theatre form was the most popular and extensive way of disseminating the American image. Novelists and essayists of the period certainly enjoyed a reading public, but it was limited in scope, though probably more highly selective and influential in its contacts than the much broader, more popular audience of the commercial theatres. The Yankee actors openly borrowed from what literary sources were available to them, but because of their special position as actors, who were required to give flesh-and-blood imitations of men for the believable acceptance of others viewing the same men about them, they were forced to draw extensively on their actors' imaginations and to present the American as they saw him. If the image was too often an external one, it still revealed the Yankee as a hardy individual whose independence was a primary assumption; as a bargainer, more clever in his techniques than England's most renowned Yorkshireman; as a country boy, more intelligent, sharper and keener in his dealings, than the city-bred type; as an American freewheeler who always landed on top, not out of honesty, but out of a simple perception of other human beings and their gullibility. All of this was expressed in the eccentric dialect of New England. The Yankee is not often admirable or idealized; he belongs to a race of not-so-pretty bargainers who win because they are more clever, more "slick" than others. If such a portrait is disparaging, if it seems too inarticulate, too naive, too fumbling, too frankly unattractive, it may merely reveal aspects of the American society of the 1830's not much relished by Americans as a view of themselves at any time. By European standards Americans were inarticulate, their culture was as yet crude and undeveloped, and the "refined" audience, as some Americans liked to think of themselves, was not so refined.

We see in Yankee theatre the same folkloristic motifs which were in fashion in Europe during this period, though far more pallid than the creations of Charles Dickens or Nikolai Gogol. But at the base, the impulse was the same. In America, as in Europe, a growing political nationalism with its attendant chauvinism, was forcing the development of a national identity and leading to local treatments that utilized all the elements of the folk—not city folk, but folk in the provinces or country areas. Dialect drama, as the dialect novel, was not American but folkloristic in its natural outgrowth. Realism was the attendant style of these projections, and Yankee theatre followed the main paths of this new interest in the common man. Although it did not approach in any sense the artistic achievement of the Irish literary movement after 1900, the two are comparable in motivations and activities. Essentially the Yankee was always the chip-on-the-shoulder American, proud, chary of his independence and freedom, and cocky in his attitude toward the rest of the world about him, particularly toward England and Englishmen. He revealed a hard core in American character and showed himself as one to be reckoned with and no longer pushed aside as a gawky American cousin, a copyist of English culture. Because the Yankee plays and actors were the first illustrations of American theatre seen in England, what Englishmen thought of them is important in revealing the relationship between Yankee theatre and American life. The large body of English newspaper criticism used as primary source material in this book is a testimonial to their avid curiosity and honest interest. The work of Hackett, Hill, and other Yankee actors, in this view, takes on a significance that the literary remains cannot possibly indicate. The Yankee actors were in no way conscious that they were doing more than making commercial entertainments which would earn them a living, but unknowingly they were participating in a folkloristic pattern highly revelatory of the age in which they were living and working.

What gave the Yankee character such a long life on the stage—he was actively employed as a type for over a century—and made him so popular, not only everywhere in America but in England as well, was his status as a symbol of American democratic society. As has been pointed out elsewhere, America has had a continuous line of symbolic folklore characters—backwoodsman Nimrod Wildfire, the plantation Negro, riverboatman Mike Fink, city-bred Irish firefighter Mose, lumberman Paul Bunyan, and others, to which should be added the type still much with us, the Western cowboy. Yankee Jonathan was not only the first of these, but also, because of the geographic generalization that associated him with many parts of the United States outside of New England, the most important. By the mid-1830's Yankee Jonathan had evolved the Uncle Sam costume, and everywhere he had become the symbol of the new American, new because he was now being recognized as a separate species from his first cousin, Englishman John Bull, who, after two wars to keep Jonathan in the family, now openly disclaimed him, ridiculed him, or, infinitely worse, ignored him.

By the 1830's American political democracy as practicable philosophy had begun to penetrate the English mind as a reality, and dozens of travelers visited America with the intention of reporting at home through their published diaries the successes and failures of this radical new venture and experiment in social organization. Their views play an important part in this study. And at home the expansion of the frontier into the West, with its consequent greatly increased economic and social problems, brought Americans themselves face to face with the enormity of the Great Experiment and to a full recognition of the meanings and responsibilities of this new world of common men. The symbolic image of the Yankee was not accident but an inevitable evolution that brought him to form and meaning out of the context of the times. Jonathan *was* the "common man" in the guise of a New England country boy, with extensions as a trader and slick dealer. The man from the Lower Orders was a distinguishable American in contrast to a man from the Upper Orders, whom English travelers maintained differed little from his counterpart at home. And Jonathan represented the important product of the Great Experiment.

To be seen clearly, he had to be literally displayed on a pedestal, and the stage was the natural show place. Royall Tyler's first Jonathan in *The Contrast* (1787) and those that followed for the next thirty years were the projections of the individualist mind which had absorbed the philosophy intellectually and which, in seeing the new American rising everywhere, had presented the character, half in copy of the English country servant seen on the stage and half as avant-garde expression of American life. But not until the 1820's did the full force of the American political image in Jonathan and his symbolic values present themselves for popular consumption. And then, ironically, it was an English actor in a satirical tirade on American life—*Trip to America* (1824)—performed for English audiences in London, who made American actors aware of the full import of stage exploitation of country Jonathan. From reality to the symbolic life of the stage is the pattern, and we see again the process of myth-making. Yankee theatre thus has philosophical connotations beyond its immediate product, implications which it supports through interpretations of the evolving political life of America from 1820 to 1835. Theatre form is always symbolic; those ideas which survive longest on the stage are rooted in the imitations of men in the real world.

Once the possibilities of the Yankee on the stage were recognized, the move forward was immediate and bustling. It cracked the English-actor tradition by making it possible for young Americans to find a place on the stage in a new form of comedy which Englishmen simply could not act. Once these actors had won a foothold, their popularity had the force of prescribing the inclusion of the Yankee character in nearly all native plays, melodramas as well as comedies. New actors in search of new material strengthened the position of the native playwright and eventually also won for the latter a place in the sun. Yankee theatre specifically illustrates how the first comedians learned their business and how they established a hardy, popular taste for the American product. In the best nineteenth-century–actor tradition the Yankee comedian participated in theatre business and management, procured his own plays by encouraging writers to write for him, arranged the production with the machinists and other actors, designed his own costumes, booked his tours, and trained the companies he performed with. Outside the theatre he was a respected gentleman, except, as in the case of all actors, for the slight taint of his vagabond status. Some Yankee actors managed theatres and acting companies, and their acting won high esteem, which was recognized in theatre benefits, in testimonial dinners, and in public laudations. Though they were of less stature than such stars of the period as Macready, Kemble, and Forrest, the Yankee actors were important men in their theatre. The study of Yankee theatre is therefore the broadest sort of study of the nineteenth-century American stage tradition. The unity of its intention and direction provides a better means of examining theatre in America than does any other aspect of native stage history.

Yankee theatre, then, is an epitome of the emerging America after the Second War for Independence. Emerging nationalism meant emerging national definition. While the cultural transfer from England to America actively continued, the roots of a dis-

tinctively native culture provided the basis for the symbolic portrayal of America on the stage. Yankee theatre thus provided the
stimulus for a critical view of the American abroad as well as at
home. It led to the first cohesive body of American plays, the first
American actors seen in London, and, after it had passed through a
period of change, to a new realistic interpretation of the American
in the "character" plays of the 1870's and the 1880's. The line from
Royall Tyler to James A. Herne is a continuous one, and the core
lies in the rise and flowering of Yankee theatre.

part 1 The Background

chapter 1

The English Traveler's View
of American Life and Theatre

No PERIOD in American history has been more thoroughly described by Englishmen than the 1820's and the 1830's.[1] A small army of curious English travelers descended on America as if it had been made for each of them to discover, and the result was a library of diaries, travel essays, and letters, much of it heavily clouded with prejudiced opinion and not infrequently punctuated with salty, sometimes scurrilous wit about what they saw or imagined they had seen in the busy itineraries that took them from Boston to New Orleans. Today much of this vast wordage is dull reading as we follow each traveler over the same routes in monotonous procession, each wearing his English insignia in dress, manners, and expectations; each trying to record, like any traveler in a foreign land, the curious, the different, the peculiar things he saw about American life. But some of it still makes spirited reading, for English character in its independence and forthright willingness to offer solid and confident opinions on every subject was the same then as now, and the personalities of these travelers emerge to dominate their travelogues with wit, charm, and warmly personal feeling. Anyone well-read in American backgrounds is familiar with the accounts of

[1] *New York Mirror*, XII January 24, 1835, p. 231, mentions that nearly twenty books on the general subject of cultural life in America had been published up to that date. The *New York Mirror* will henceforth be referred to throughout these notes as *Mirror*.

Frances Trollope, Fanny Kemble Butler, Charles Dickens, Tyrone
Power, and Harriet Martineau.[2] But there are also the accounts of
Captain Basil Hall, whose blatant and infuriating statements Mrs.
Trollope openly endorsed, James Stuart, Thomas Hamilton, Charles
Murray, and Captain Marryat, among many others. Actor Charles
Mathews is certainly the most illuminating from a theatre point of
view, and his trip to America will be specifically detailed in a later
chapter in this book. Accounts of America and things American as
a far-off land populated with a curious race of ex-Englishmen had a
ready audience among English readers. The literary taste of the day
was romantic, and America with its Great Experiment had much
potential for lively, escapist reading.

The significance of this body of writing, with its mass of personal
details and opinions, and its reports of American politics, economics,
religion, and social life, lies in the stimulating and provocative,
sometimes maddening "outsider's" view, against which an evaluation of native opinion of American directions and worth becomes
possible. Highly prejudiced as these English travelers often were in
their impatience with customs and manners different from their
own—as any traveler can be—in their suspicious and wary attitude
towards strangers whose reactions could not be readily calculated,
in their fear of the breakdown of a class-delineated and apparently
anarchical society with the hard-to-brook problems of disregard and
imposition of undisciplined lower classes, and prone as they were to
generalizations that might apply to any foreign society wherever it
might be, they still ventured far closer to the truth than contemporary American patriots could stomach. As Fanny Kemble observed,
"Mercy on me! How sore these people are about Mrs. Trollope's

---

[2] Much of the content of this chapter has been drawn from the following
sources: Frances Trollope, *Domestic Manners of the Americans;* Captain Basil
Hall, *Travels in North America;* James Stuart, *Three Years in North America;*
Charles Murray, *Travels in North America;* Harriet Martineau, *Society in
America;* Charles Dickens, *American Notes;* Captain Marryat, *Diary in America;*
X. Y. Z., "Speculations of a Traveller Concerning the People of the United
States," *Blackwoods,* XVI (July, 1824), 92 ff.; A. C., "A Summary View of
America," *Blackwoods,* XVI (December, 1824), 617–651. Three actors recorded
their experiences extensively: Charles Mathews, *Memoirs of Charles Mathews;*
Fanny Kemble Butler, *Journal;* Tyrone Power, *Impressions of America.* Two
companion studies have collected, summarized, and assessed travel in America:
Jane Mesick, *The English Traveller in America, 1785–1835;* Max Berger, *The
British Traveller in America, 1836–1860.*

book. . . . She must have spoken the truth though, for lies do not rankle so."[3] As quickly as the case against America was built up by the persistent English travelers, so was it torn down by the opposite army of enraged Americans who hung Mrs. Trollope in effigy, in words if not in action. An early Yankee play[4]—and these plays usually went out of their way to avoid contentious argument—found her fair game and satirized the sharp-eyed Mrs. Trollope under a pale disguise.

What a paper war it was, with each side flinging literary brickbats at the other: the English aggressive and complacent in their "honest" reporting; the Americans intemperate and desperate in their insecurity and incessant desire to be understood, carrying great chips on their shoulders. These aggressive Americans thoroughly believed, so the travelers reported, that Englishmen were sensitive about losing both wars and their retaliation derived from this unforgivable and embarrassing blow to English pride. Frances Trollope was not likely to win many American friends, no matter how true her statements might be, when she concluded in print that America was "a vast continent, by far the greater part of which is still in a state in which nature left it, and a busy, bustling, industrious population, hacking and hewing their way through it."[5] Even more infuriating was her cool summary of American character: "Jonathan is a very dull boy." She thought the English were by no means so gay and lively as the French, but, compared with Americans, "we are whirligigs and tetotums—every day is a holiday, and every night a festival." She labeled Thomas Jefferson's works "a mighty mass of mischief" and argued that his hot-headed democracy had done "a fearful injury to his country," which, if carried into effect, "would make of mankind an unamalgamated mass of grated atoms, where the darling 'I'm as good as you,' would soon take the place of the law and the Gospel."[6] Another traveler ironically foretold the future when he found the English language degraded. "Unless the present progress of change be arrested by an increase in taste and judgment

[3] Butler, *Journal*, I, 67.

[4] *The Times, or Life in New York*. She was later satirized directly as Mrs. Wollope (sometimes billed as Mrs. Trollope) in James Hackett's famous play about backwoodsman Nimrod Wildfire, *The Kentuckian*.

[5] Trollope, *Domestic Manners of the Americans*, p. 305. Cited hereafter as *Domestic Manners*.

[6] *Ibid.*, p. 306.

in the more educated classes, there can be no doubt that in another
century, the dialect of the Americans will become utterly unintelligible to an Englishman."[7]

Such outspoken criticism was guaranteed to make the American
skin bristle. Some native patriots retaliated with spirited back talk;
others contained their irritation and quietly despaired at the state of
things. "Our periodical literature is never even heard of," poet
Nathaniel Willis reported from England. Washington Irving from
his more or less secure literary position in England argued that although the reporting of America had been done by unqualified
people who had not only failed to supply pure information but had
given a great deal of misinformation and left the great mass of the
British public less informed about Americans than any other people, Americans should not be offended, and above all, should not hit
back in the same vein.[8] So deeply aggravated did the feeling become
that Samuel Coleridge in commenting on Basil Hall's report felt
compelled to say that Hall's writings were too forthrightly impolite,
too hostile and sneering in their attitudes. "A very little humoring
of their prejudices, and some courting of language and demeanour
on the part of Englishmen, would work wonders . . . with the public
mind of Americans."[9] But such tempered points of view were scarce.
The behavior of American audiences toward English actors who
were careless in their publicly stated opinions of Americans—the
Astor Place Riot as late as 1848 is the catastrophic example—under-
scores the feelings between the two countries. "I would not advise
either Mrs. Trollope, Basil Hall, or Captain Hamilton," warned
Fanny Kemble, "ever to set their feet upon this ground again, unless
they are ambitious of being stoned to death."[10]

2

What the roving eye of the English traveler saw in American life
also tells us much about the Yankee actors and the world they were
trying to show on the stage. Both traveled the same routes, experienced the same physical difficulties on the road and in the towns,
and met the same people, the same attitudes, the same popular

---

[7] Hamilton, *Men and Manners in America*, pp. 228–229.
[8] *Mirror*, XII (January 17, 1835), 231.
[9] *Ibid.*, XII (April 18, 1835), 336.
[10] Butler, *Journal*, II, 142.

prejudices. Their common ground was the theatre. Here the English actor-travelers are most informative, but the other travelers were regular theatregoers and together they set down a detailed and revealing image of American stage life that is most useful to the student of the theatre because its outsider's eye drew sharp contrasts with how things were done in the English playhouses. Outside the theatre their views were not far below the surface. Except for Mrs. Trollope, who lived in America for the greater part of two years, a stay long enough to give a much firmer basis for judgments, most travellers tried to see America in a few weeks. Such itineraries were bound to invoke generalizations, false impressions, and superficial conclusions, though much of what they had to say was still valid.

After the long sea voyage to America, with its attendant monotony, sailing adventures, sardine-tight accommodations, poor food, seasickness, and bad weather, the traveler was relieved at the welcome sight of New York harbor and the refinements of the city hotels. From this point he usually took the three major itineraries: to Boston via Providence by boat and stage; to Niagara Falls via the Hudson River to Albany, and Erie Canal packet or private stagecoach west from Schenectady; and the major journey to the South and West via Philadelphia, Baltimore, Washington, Richmond, Charleston, Savannah, and Montgomery, all by water, then by stage to Augusta, where the water journey to Mobile and New Orleans was resumed. Return to New York took the traveler up the Mississippi River to St. Louis, up the Ohio to Cincinnati, then by river, canal, and coach through Pittsburgh or Wheeling to Philadelphia and back to New York. The complaints are always the same: terrible roads with continual jostling and jolting; crowded coaches; salty drivers who insisted that travel begin at two or three in the morning and continue until seven or eight at night; exhaustion; poor inns with greasy, badly cooked food, and dirty sheets. The canal packets were no place for the gentle traveler, crowded and stifling as they usually were, with mass eating and sleeping, no privacy, and clouds of mosquitoes.

New York with its Dutch culture was usually well liked, the general opinion being that it was a more sophisticated city than Philadelphia, which some thought Americans tended to overrate. Opinion was also favorable on American vegetables, which travelers saw in enormous quantities; on steamboat travel; on a few hotels in the major cities; on Saratoga mineral water; on mountain views in the Alleghenies; on the unique qualities of Charleston; on certain aspects of life in New Orleans, and on the Southern plantations; and, of course, on Niagara Falls. But the list of cons was usually much longer. They complained of the absence of literature and painting; of the mud in Washington; of the separation of men and women at parties; of no conversation except with the very best classes; of few eateries where one could enjoy "decent" food; of having to eat great quantities of greasy food very quickly, with meat three times a day and no good wine or conversation to accompany it; of landlords and their ladies sitting at the table; of dining in shifts with industrious eating the main business. The most constant complaints were voiced against the chewing of tobacco and the dirty habit of spitting; against brandy drinkers and rough talkers; against knife carriers, quick to take offence; against substandard English grammar; against nonwalkers and poor dancers. The frequent conclusion: Americans are a hardy and low-class race.

When travelers turned to philosophies and attitudes, they touched the mainsprings of American life. They tended to admire the prison systems but found the slavery markets disgusting and incredible in view of the widely vaunted political credo. They noted the popular religious fervor expressed in the wild revivals of camp meetings, and they longed for an Established Church. All despised the philosophy of equality and were affronted by the freedoms all classes took, with no servants but only "helps." And they held up the "impossibles" of American life as the arguments against its political philosophy: the country could not be rid of slavery without violence; equality will doom America; railroads are impractical for many decades; fine arts cannot develop in such a money-mad context; common religion is absurd, emotional, and primitive; industry cannot replace farming; militia as military protection is worthless. On the whole they found Americans hospitable, but the country still a wilderness only sketchily developed.

With the American character they were more careful of the image they drew but it still looked dubious in its isolation. Americans, they thought, are a race of money-mad, sharp dealers who work constantly. Competition is very great in American life, business morality is low, politics are slippery, and New Englanders are sharpies. Women are incidental and pushed aside. There is no sense of humor, no fun, no leisure time except on the plantations in the South, no refinements except in the very best circles. Americans have no entertainments, for they are not a happy people. And the the final brickbat: American boasting will defeat the advance of America.

If this brief extraction seems to present a bald view of the American life of the 1830's, the reader can begin to understand why native sons were so incensed against such writings. The score was heavily against the American. If he was to improve his poor-cousin status, the American would have to learn to do more than make a living.

3

When the English traveler lowered his sights on the theatre his reporting tended to be more objective and less generalized, although still condemnatory in part. Tyrone Power and Fanny Kemble Butler give us an expert backstage view to balance Frances Trollope's image of the audience side of the house. Their evidence can be further evaluated against that of Francis Wemyss, who, though no traveler, was an English actor who came to America in the 1820's, became a theatre manager in Philadelphia, Baltimore, and Pittsburgh, and set down his experiences in a remarkable autobiography, full of all sorts of theatre information and lore of the period.[11] From these sources the rating of the theatre can be seen quite clearly, for here was a familiar art form *borrowed* from the Mother culture. Except for the traveling actors whose judgments were those of "insiders," what other Englishmen reported on stage matters is of debatable value, more reflective of personal tastes than of objective standards. On the subject of the audience, however, their views cannot be so easily challenged.

Plays in the New York or Philadelphia theatres in the 1830's differed from those in Charleston or New Orleans not in kind but in the artistic level of the performance. New York, as it is now, was the theatrical center, and the Park Theatre, which Tyrone Power judged to be as well appointed as any theatre in London,[12] was the top billing in the country. The American Theatre Bowery—"infinitely superior in beauty" to the Park, according to Mrs.

[11] Francis Wemyss, *Twenty-Six Years of the Life of an Actor and Manager.* Cited hereafter as *Life of an Actor and Manager.*
[12] Power, *Impressions of America*, I, 48. Cited hereafter as *Impressions.*

Trollope—was quite unfashionable, catering as it did to the more common elements of the city's population.[13] Philadelphia's Walnut, Chestnut, and Arch Street Theatres held a secondary position to the Park. In the provinces theatre offerings were much better than might be expected. One traveler thought the theatre at Natchez, the still beautifully preserved ante-bellum city on the Mississippi above New Orleans, so well appointed and conducted that few country theatres in England would gain much in comparison with it.[14] Another saw Mrs. Drake, a leading lady in provincial stock companies, in Louisville and declared her the best tragic actress in America.[15] Fanny Kemble thought the theatre at Boston had the best company she had played with "anywhere outside of London."[16] Opposed to this view was her opinion of the Washington theatre, which she thought wretched in the extreme: "The proprietors are poor, the actors poorer; and the grotesque mixture of misery, vulgarity, stage-finery, and real raggedness, is beyond anything strange and sad, and revolting."[17]

But whatever the level of production might be, the organization was familiar to the theatre-going Englishman. He would have been aware that the stage manager conducted all matters backstage. He usually assigned roles to the actors in consultation with the customary actor-manager, and he supervised rehearsals, including the setting of stage positions. If asked, he would give instructions on how certain roles had been played in the past or suggestions on how to make more effective a current performance. In a stock company, composed mostly of Englishmen who had been hired directly by the manager in London or procured for him through an agent, actors knew their business of acting and performed their creative function directly without the intensively detailed manipulations of the modern stage director. The stage manager, usually a retired actor him-

---

[13] "A few evenings since, they [the orchestra at the Bowery] were performing an overture, which did not exactly suit the cultivated taste of some worthies in the pit. 'Yankee Doodle,' being more in unison with the patriotic ideas of propriety, was loudly called for, and its melting tones forthwith breathed forth in mellifluous harmony. The pit were gratified, and evinced their satisfaction by a gentle roar" (*Mirror*, X [March 9, 1833], 287).

[14] Murray, *Travels in North America*, I, 125–126. Cited hereafter as *Travels*.

[15] Stuart, *Three Years in North America*, II, 330. Cited hereafter as *Three Years*.

[16] Butler, *Journal*, II, 179.

[17] *Ibid.*, p. 136.

self, was the most informed person in the theatre, but in the protocol of the stage he never overstepped boundaries into the actor's realm unless asked to do so. To direct the daily dressing of the stage, required by the constantly changing bill, he had a more-or-less competent staff: a scenic artist, such as Russell, Lewis, Mondelli, Isherwood, or Stockwell, who designed settings; a master carpenter, such as Landers or MacIntosh; assistant carpenters; a property man; and, after 1835, with the introduction of gas for stage lighting, a gasman to supervise the intricate valve system. There was little time for preparing a play in the modern sense, although once a basic repertory had been arranged, new pieces were regularly added without a production breakdown. The extremes of production are too often cited by theatre historians as evidence of the haphazard rat race of a stock theatre.

However, with actors trained and experienced in the business of getting up their own parts, together with a highly skilled group of craftsmen on the scenery and effects, the continual alteration of the stage and acting piece, as in modern European state repertory theatres and all opera theatres, was a disciplined and orderly business, even routine if the manager was not erratic. Wemyss mentions the bill for the 1827–1828 season at the Chestnut: two hundred nights of performance with thirty-four new pieces and eleven revivals. His examples of extremes show the pressure put on theatre: "Got up a long part after the performance concluded at 12:30, and had lines by 4 A.M."; "Get up a new farce for Monday—you will have all week to rehearse it—"; or playing, as did Wemyss, sixteen parts on twenty-two consecutive nights.[18]

There was no costume problem unless the piece was an unusual spectacle, in which case the manager arranged for the extra dresses. The customary procedure required the actor to furnish his own wardrobe, as did Wemyss, who spent three hundred pounds sterling on a new stage wardrobe before coming to America. The major problem was the stage spectacle, the baroque imitations of the Renaissance masque, which no theatre could do without because they brought in the mass audience. Spectacular melodrama, romantic to a high degree in its scenes of far-off lands, of ships on the sea, of falling bridges above rushing torrents, of burning cities, of stage

[18] Wemyss, *Life of an Actor and Manager*, pp. 195, 134, 85.

battles and the fall of fortresses, required the highest coordination
from the production staff. When the spectacle was successful, as in
the sinking of the *Caroline* in *Red Rover*, which many in the
audience declared absolutely real, the staff's expert craftsmanship
was fully apparent. When the spectacle failed and caused laughter,
as it did in one piece where a shower of rain enveloping a boat was
suddenly terminated and the thin gauze curtains that made it were
inexplicably hoisted into the flies, the production staff were still
admired. An occasional stage accident indicates the dangers of
stage machinery and the haphazard movement on the part of the
actor. "Mr. Tryal Deves was accidentally shot in the Battle of
Waterloo," writes Mr. Wemyss, "and died." A benefit was given
for the wife of this volunteer actor and his nine children. Even the
experienced professional was not safe from harm. By a thrust of the
sword from Edwin Forrest, Wemyss lost two front teeth in a mimic
fight. Forrest always took his stage business very seriously, and this
fight, to Wemyss, was "too real for fancy."[19]

The stock company, in which actors were hired for a season to
play in whatever theatre or theatres the manager desired, was the
standard business arrangement. The actor knew his character line,
and the rehearsals were used only to set the business. The curse that
was to haunt the theatre for most of the century began during the
1820's: the rise of the star system. Before this time the stock company had been the only form of operation. Only a few theatres had
regular bills, and these were concentrated in the cities along the
Atlantic coast. Transportation was limited, and seasons were of
relatively short duration. But after 1820, with rapidly expanding
cities on every side, with steamboats in operation on the rivers, with
the West open to movement through the Erie Canal and other
linking transportation, the star system—a traveling star actor moving from city to city and performing his roles with each local stock
company in the rest of the characters—became highly profitable.
By 1830 it was common theatre practice, but it soon became apparent to managers, who at first had welcomed its "grander" entertainment, that the high cost of star performers could mean financial
ruin. The practice continued, however, and star actors traveled the
major circuits—Cooper, Booth, Forrest, Macready, Kean, Charles

[19] *Ibid.*, p. 166.

Kemble, Fanny Kemble, Charlotte Cushman, Josephine Clifton in the serious characters; Mathews, Power, Dowton, Vestris, Rice, and, of course, the Yankee actors (Hackett, Hill, Marble, and Silsbee) in the comedy roles. This was the theatre the Yankee actor knew, and he played a large part in shaping it.

When the English traveler attended the theatre he was probably aware of the theatre smell, a composite of "oil, powder, rosin, and other villainous odors which mingle at the entrance to theatres."[20] He may have seen the "grease," as the lamplighter was called, or after gas had been introduced he might have noticed that the stage light came from the borders instead of the ladders behind the wings. He was aware of the upstairs saloon where alcoholic drinks were served, a familiar place to him in England. If the season was winter and he was early for the performance, he probably felt the cold in the unheated room; if familiar with backstage life, he envied the actor who had a fire in the greenroom, where he gathered with other actors to warm himself before and during the performance. He saw a house that was redecorated yearly to attract business; that was arranged in eighteenth-century style, with three tiers, in the third of which sat the gallery gods and the prostitutes. In the boxes of the first two tiers were the ladies and their escorts, and in the pit the male audience—theatre critics to a man. The house was lighted by chandeliers, a method which Wemyss scornfully objected to because it exposed to view "that very portion which should be kept as much as possible in the shade, and which has contributed more to the downfall of the drama, than all the other causes put together . . . the third tier of boxes, where licentiousness prevails in its worst form."[21]

Before the performance began and between the acts the English playgoer heard an orchestra, largely recruited from Germany, play selections from the body of "national airs" constantly in demand in American theatres. Again Englishman Wemyss cannot conceal his irritation when he is accused of suppressing the national music, an accusation which he met by inserting in the program: "So far from forbidding them, I have frequently given orders that one or more should be played every evening. . . . Between the play and the farce

[20] George Hill, *Scenes from the Life of an Actor*, p. 49. Cited hereafter as *Scenes*.
[21] Weymss, *Life of an Actor and Manager*, p. 73.

each night, the time will be exclusively devoted to National Airs."
His real feelings sided with orchestra leader Bram, who could not
endure the frequent repetition of "Yankee Doodle" to the exclusion
of Mozart and Weber.

After the opening music and before all set changes the theatregoer heard a bell ring. This served as a warning, not especially for
the audience, but mostly for the actors and stage hands, particularly
at the opening and closing of a star engagement. If the traveler had
attended the theatre on certain nights, he would have participated
in a "benefit" performance, a managerial arrangement which gave
an actor the proceeds of a certain performance beyond fixed management costs. The actor so "benefited" could program it in any
way he could arrange with other actors and he could solicit extra
payments from patrons who supported him in this personal bid for
money and popularity.

Theatre programing of this period located the position of the
Yankee plays in the general context of theatre fare. The usual
evening's performance consisted of two or more plays, a serious
drama first, followed by an "afterpiece"—a comedy or farce.
Dances, songs, and other light entertainment were performed between pieces. In this arrangement an audience could be kept fully
occupied from seven-thirty to after midnight. A playgoer like Mrs.
Trollope, who always left before the afterpiece, had the opportunity
of seeing only what parts interested him. A five-hour bill is long by
modern standards, but it was kept alive by its variety in textures
and types, by its fresh performers in each piece, and by its frequent
changes of scenery. The Yankee actors occupied the afterpiece
position until they won star status, when a full evening of Yankee
plays became a possible managerial offering.

What the playgoer saw in the period 1830–1835, the core of the
Yankee-theatre period, was a heavy programing of Shakespeare,
together with highly rated serious drama of the day by Sheridan
Knowles and others of less importance; romantic melodrama, which
included spectacular adaptations of the novels of Sir Walter Scott
and found large audiences; and the equestrian drama which with
melodrama began the breakaway from the older traditions of theatre
fare as the make-up of the audience shifted. The classical eighteenth-
century comedy of Sheridan and Colman was played less and less,
and the new writers of comedy, such as J. B. Buckstone, J. R.

Planché, T. Morton, J. R. Poole, R. B. Peake, W. B. Bernard, D. W. Jerrold and others, occupied prominent positions. The important thing to recognize here is that the American stage was completely dominated not only by English actors but also by English drama and comedy. During the next few years Yankee theatre would alter this direction by shifting audience demand toward the American product. But, except for the new American comedy and an occasional Indian drama like John Augustus Stone's *Metamora*, the English traveler saw the same fare he would have seen at home. He therefore took no pains to set down much detail about this aspect of the stage unless it involved American characters or actors.

4

What the traveler had to say about the audience he met in the theatre is highly significant. Here he noticed a strong difference in manners and tastes. All travelers more or less agreed that theatres were poorly attended, a proof in their eyes of the inferior position of American culture and a detriment to its progress. They noted that the audience was dominantly male—"too cold," thought Power— with the ladies attending in numbers only on special occasions. When women came they occupied the first row of boxes in a concentration which did not make the best audience distribution throughout the house. Tyrone Power and Fanny Kemble, as we should expect because of their wide experience, give us the most balanced judgments. Both noted the quiet attentiveness with which the play was watched. Audiences did not applaud, hammer sticks, shout "bravos," or show their appreciation of "points" as often as did English audiences of the day, though such an occasion as the Kemble opening at the Park found as immense a reception as it would have in London, with the audience getting up, waving their hats and handkerchiefs, and shouting welcome. Both found American audiences sensitive to the theatre experience, with Power going out of his way to protest the charges of insensibility. Fanny Kemble explained such performance failures as those with *The School for Scandal* and *The Provoked Husband* by writing them off as not only thoroughly English in tone and manners, and thus highly removed from American life, but also as too exquisite and witty even for most of the English audiences of the day. What seemed of prime importance was the "size" of the playing, the level of exaggeration, and the nature of illustration which the actor could supply. "You must not be so quiet: give them more bustle," Power was advised. "You must point a little broader, my dear fellow," said another. "You're too natural for them: they don't feel it," said a third. And to this noted difference and contrast in taste levels, Power could only reply: "If it's natural they must feel it. . . . Each of my characters are, according to my ability, painted from nature; they are individual abstractions with which *I* have nothing to do; the colouring is a part of each, and I can't change it, as I change my audience:—'tis only for me to present the picture as it is; for them to like or dislike it."[22] What a remarkable statement this is in support of a growing theory of realism on the stage and what the audience was expected to see. Not many months later one of England's finest comedians, William Dowton, toured the theatres of America and met failure everywhere, even to being deposed as the best Falstaff in a final New York appearance by the American Yankee comedian, James Hackett, on the same charges that his (Dowton's) characters were too subtle, too small, and not vigorous enough for American theatregoers.

Fanny Kemble noted with enthusiasm the "new" audience attending the theatre. The older, more refined, highly educated, upperclass playgoer had been superseded by a new, more crass theatregoer. It was much the same in England. "I would rather a thousand times act . . . to a set of Manchester mechanics than to the most select of an aristocracy, for they are 'nothing if not critical'." But she turned with indignant and scornful horror at the American practice of refusing entrance to Negroes: "Here's aristocracy with a vengeance." On this point, the Fanny Kemble who was later to marry a Southerner, live in the South, and see its race problems with keen perception, was not far removed from other English travelers. Thomas Hamilton notes seeing a "Haytian" attempt to enter a theatre in New York only to have his money tossed back at him "with a disdainful intimation that the place for persons of his colour was the upper gallery." With barbed amusement Mrs. Trollope points out that the Negro theatre in New York provided gallery seats for whites who chose to visit it, "following in this, and equal justice," the arrangement of the white theatres. When "Jim

22 Power, *Impressions*, I, 48.

Crow" danced onto the stage, as he did during this period in the person of T. D. Rice, it was a white actor impersonating the Negro. The minstrel tradition which follows close on the heels of Rice's work is a "white man's theatre" exploiting the American Negro and his way of life.

The infrequent theatre-going English traveler set down the extremes of his experience. James Stuart was glad to escape from the Bowery Theatre, though a handsome house, because it was filled to suffocation on one of the hottest evenings he ever felt. In Boston, contrary to expectations, he found the Puritan audience loudly applauding French dancers: "The more outré the dancing, the more the applause." He found in Charleston the theatre ill-attended, even in Race Week, and in Louisville a separate entrance provided for ladies "who are not received in society."[23] Charles Murray, in mourning the low state of literary interests among young men in America, scornfully notes that they have time to give to the dance, the race-courses, the billiard table, the tavern bar, and the theatre. But he also reports after attending the theatre in Natchez that the audience was a fine one, neatly dressed, without any pretension or display of finery, with the men in the usual evening attire, with noisy and merry fellows in the pit, and with a gallery "in possession of some dozen swarthy goddesses wearing upon their heads and persons all the several colours which nature had denied as ingredients in their complexions."[24]

Frances Trollope, as she does in almost every other phase of American life, gives the most complete picture. She went to the theatre regularly, and her criticisms ring with the authority of the experienced playgoer who sees the stage as a necessary instrument for the instruction and improvement of manners in society. Like all amateur critics, however, her recorded judgments of what she regarded as bad far outnumber those she may have thought good or at least passing. In New York's Chatham Theatre she observed in the front row of a dress box a woman nursing a child. At the Park, where she did not admire Edwin Forrest (he "roared . . . very unlike a nightingale"), she saw many men with mustaches colored with the grim tinge of tobacco juice, and heard, without ceasing, the continuous spitting of the chewers. In Philadelphia, as she con-

23 Stuart, *Three Years*, pp. 132, 330.
24 Murray, *Travels*, pp. 125–126.

tinually notes everywhere, she saw a man "deliberately take off his coat and sit in his shirtsleeves," while other men kept their hats on, and spat continuously on the floor. In Washington, one man in the pit was seized with a violent fit of vomiting, which appeared "not in the least to surprise his neighbors." She also notes that not one in ten of the male part of the audience, made up of legislators, sat in the usual manner, but had their legs thrown over the front of the box, or were stretched out at full length on a bench, or sat on the front rail. Here, too, the spitting was incessant. In Cincinnati, where she lived for many months and went to the theatre frequently, she again mentions the shirt-sleeved men, the smell of onions and whiskey, continuous and distracting noises, and applause expressed by cries and thumping with the feet. Such demonstrations increased to pandemonium when the audience were taken with a "patriotic fit" and called for "Yankee Doodle" as though their reputations as citizens depended on the noise they made. In general, so exaggerated was Mrs. Trollope's description to James Stuart that he felt compelled in his book to argue vigorously against Mrs. Trollope's view. He maintained that he had never seen rudeness on the part of the male audience, nor would any persons have been tolerated in sitting on the edge of the box enclosure.[25] But Mrs. Trollope's opinion held sway once it had been set in print, and no amount of denial or evidence offered to the contrary could shift the opinion that American theatre audiences were of the crude sort which reflected the general pattern of everyday American life. Her view was underlined by such publicly posted rules and regulations as those of the Cincinnati theatre which forbade numerous uncouth activities: loud talking in the bar; altercations in the house; standing or sitting on the railings; cracking nuts during the time the curtain is up; throwing nutshells, apples, etc. into the pit; or boisterous conduct in the gallery, including whacking sticks on the seats or banisters.

In spite of all this, perhaps because of its overt nature as diatribe, one is forced into a logic, largely supported by newspaper criticism of the artistic merits of performances in the large eastern cities, that Mrs. Trollope's view needs a great deal of tempering with accounts of what was right and proper in American theatre. There is prob-

[25] Stuart, *Three Years*, p. 576.

ably no question that American audiences, particularly in the West, differed in matters of manners and taste from those in England, but the level of theatre maintained in the States would not have been possible without a large measure of discipline and forbearance on the part of the audience.

The English traveler in America had stated his case fully and all too frankly as to what was wrong with American life. That he had stirred up a great deal of controversy there is no doubt. His highly personal reports, in the long run, may even have been beneficial, for they set many minds to work at discovering what was wrong and what could be done to correct the error. To see the image of America in a fairer perspective one must balance the English traveler's outsider's look against the native critic's more subjective insider's opinion. Mrs. Trollope's view of an America entirely devoid of gaiety and too tight-fisted to indulge in theatregoing requires rebuttal. Out of insecurity comes self-examination and creative remedy. The Great Experiment had to battle with its own inner conscience.

chapter 2

America's Self-Examination: A Changing Culture, the Stage, and a New Audience

F THE REPORTING of American life by English travelers seems harsh and external, much of it can be attributed to the usual travel errors: too little time and lack of perspective. Their opinions were still hot with the confused emotions stimulated by strange places, by different ways of doing things, and by certain aspects of the new democracy abhorrent to them. On the other hand, Americans looking at themselves had no such disadvantages. They were in a well-known environment; local customs were familiar to them; their democracy was deliberately chosen, hard-fought-for, and greatly prized. But their reaction to foreign criticism was strong, sometimes extreme. They either struck back with blind patriotic diatribe, or, as men of conscience, became seriously concerned and sought ways to improve things. Just when the American needed to build his own self-confidence, when he needed to show John Bull that he had a strong independent personality with creative capacity and imagination, when he desperately needed to sell American worth at home to his fellow citizens who paradoxically preferred outside products, then the native American patriot, in an ironical defense, frequently lashed out against his own sterility, ineffectiveness, and failure in a continuing self-conscious examination, presenting himself in a role far from that of the boaster. "The principal formation must be within itself, or it cannot possess our individual and national character"[1] applied not only to the making of an American literature but to the critical attitude itself. This point of view the English traveler could not easily see, for he had little time to examine the unpublicized opinions of America's own critics, which were beginning to appear in literary journals ostensibly for the few, though these few were the core of the new literary leadership. Had he been able to look more deeply into American life he might have become aware of this conscience at work. Had he been unusually perceptive he might also have noted the major facts of American life: the tremendous importance of the opening of the West and its significance to the developing American democracy; and the industrialization and growth of eastern cities in parallel to what was happening in England. The English traveler reported on America during a most extensive period of fluctuation and change; and much of the deeply significant was obscured by the outward show.

The 1820's and 1830's, the years reflected in Yankee theatre, are fascinating to study because they nurtured the seeds of American economic growth with its eventually dominating materialistic philosophy of scientific progress and its accompanying social and political problems that came to full maturity in the Civil War and its aftermath.[2] It was an age of advancing frontiers and western settlement; of canal, road, and railroad building; of rapid growth and dominance of eastern city life with its "new" sociological evils and frustrations; of revolution in manufacturing methods and knowhow that began a conversion of natural resources into wealth and power and nursed the beginnings of the labor-union movement; of advanced shipping, fishing, and whaling industries that expanded contacts with other continents. In 1830 the United States was predominantly a nation of independent farmers, with less than seven percent of the population living in cities of 8,000 or over, but by the end of the decade the conversion to city life was earnestly in progress. At the same time the movement westward had shifted twenty-five percent of the population to the trans-Allegheny region and made the Mississippi and Ohio Rivers great avenues of com-

[1] *Mirror*, IX (September 10, 1831), 79.

[2] Background works of particular interest here are: Arthur M. Schlesinger, *Political and Social History of the United States;* Clifford and Elizabeth Lord, *Historical Atlas of the United States;* D. S. Muzzy, *History of the American People;* Arthur M. Schlesinger, Jr., *The Age of Jackson;* Frederick J. Turner, *The Frontier in American History.*

merce. The building of the Erie Canal in 1825 and the development
of a railroad system from a scant twenty-seven miles in 1830 to
several thousand by 1840 threatened to depopulate Eastern manufacturing centers. A ready unity appeared in the expanding econ-
omy, which resembled a torn spider's web still clinging to old
anchor points while new ones were secured and patterned firmly to
the nucleus. Swelling frontiers meant increased trade, which in turn
demanded increased manufacturers. This called for factory labor,
city growth, and new markets for Western farm produce and
natural resources. It comes as no surprise to find Western section-
alism in conflict with already existing Northern and Southern
differences.

It is in this brief period that the new utopia of government
directly in the hands of the governed ran the gamut of discovery,
battle, and partial realization, only to smother temporarily in
reaction and to disintegrate for lack of education, vigorous belief,
and courageous leadership. Democracy in the 1830's is partially
defined in the action of a Dorr rebellion, with its cause in universal
manhood suffrage; in the birth of labor unions and the realization
by workingmen that the right to a living wage can be insured only
in proportion to the amount of organizational pressure forced on
employers; of Geneva "justice" with its verdict that workers can be
fined and imprisoned for conspiring to withhold labor so that they
can coerce employers into better wage and working-condition bargains. For the first time "small" men were in a position to argue
their rights in political assemblies and on lecture platforms. The
day most feared by the Federalists and conservative Republicans,
the day when the many secured enough power to control property
interests, had already dawned. Above all, the issue that had forced
the earlier separation between conservative and radical elements,
the issue that was summed up much too simply as the poor against
the rich, "the house of Have against the house of Want," was
gradually becoming clearer.

Andrew Jackson, war hero and Westerner, was the leader and
symbol of the age. His fight against Nicholas Biddle and the Bank
personified his liberalism and belief in a strong central government;
but, at the same time, as plantation owner and slaveholder he was
intimately tied to the much larger controversy of Negro slavery.
The thirties fostered the first weak and unorganized stirrings against

this social and economic sore, slowly festering in the public conscience. Politically the subject was only indirectly open for discussion, although the farseeing knew that it would eventually have to
be faced and resolved. Jacksonian idealism steeled men's minds to
the problem, and slowly the belief that slavery was not only im-
moral but incompatible in a democratic society began to arouse men
to action. And the rapid westward expansion undoubtedly hastened
the inevitable conflict of interests which culminated in the Civil
War.

The English travelers could not resist pointing out the great paradox of the American political creed and the American political
reality, and like everyone else they could not know how it would
end. The most advanced in their thinking could see the great surge
in America, and in the thought of Americans, not as Englishmen
removed to a new country but as a distinct race who were determined in their desire to stand on their own feet. As the travelers
took their trips through the Erie Canal to Niagara Falls, or up the
River from New Orleans to St. Louis and Cincinnati, they could not
help seeing the tremendous expansion in American life. Yet, without
knowing more of what it had been like before they came, or without
the vision of the American pioneers, who could see a great future in
the vastness of America beyond the Appalachians, their judgments
were too often small, confined to the material problems of their
everyday lives as travelers. It is revealing of their characteristic
English thoroughness that they discovered as much as they did.[3]

2

The determined drive for native American expression in the arts
and the "new" American criticism behind that drive—the conscience and the pressure—the English travelers missed altogether.
So little understood was it even among Americans except for a small
group—a sort of American avant garde—actually participating in
it, nothing more could be expected. When N. P. Willis made his
wry comment that American periodical literature had never even
been heard of abroad, he should have added that the situation was

[3] Harriet Martineau and Alexis de Toqueville should not be included in the
group of ordinary travelers. Their approach to the American experiment was
far more informed and serious in intent, and their reports were much more
perceptive and penetrating.

little different at home. The general mass of Americans were too busy making a daily living in a bustling, highly competitive world to worry much about literature. Yet these periodicals displayed a concern and exercised a leadership and influence far beyond their immediate circumstance. The state of the American arts was their primary worry, and they were determined to do something about it. Of the dozen or so literary magazines that were published in the 1820's, a list which includes *The Albion, The American Monthly Magazine, The Museum of Foreign Literature and Science, The United States Review and Literary Gazette,* and *The American Quarterly Review,* it was *The New York Mirror* and its editor, George Pope Morris, that led the way, especially in matters of the theatre. A study of the *Mirror* from this one point of view alone provides enough evidence to establish it as a primary and most active instrument in the campaign to foster the American arts.

From its first issue in 1823 and during its life for the next two decades, with such associate editors as Samuel Woodworth, Theodore Fay, N. P. Willis, John Inman, and Epes Sargent, Morris' premise was always the same: "The Character of this work is intended to be, *literally* and *emphatically,* American . . . in accordance with our national habits, patriotism, and mode of thinking."[4] In matters of the theatre Morris rushed in headfirst as a critic, won his free pass at the Park after arguing in his column against his exclusion, and undertook the grave responsibility not only of arbiter of critical taste in theatrical matters but of instigator and pressureman in the development of American drama and theatre in accordance with the basic tenets of the *Mirror.* Nor could American theatre have found a better advocate, for General Morris, poet, song writer, and on two occasions a playwright of sorts,[5] possessed that remarkable "spirit of *bonhomie*" that assured his success as an editor highly capable of attracting other talents and exciting their interests and enthusiasms along the lines of his own thinking. Scarcely five feet two or three inches in height, with short, crisp,

---

[4] *Mirror,* I (August 2, 1823), 1.

[5] See *Poems* by George P. Morris. A brief memoir details his work. For another treatment see William Northall, *Before and Behind the Curtain,* pp. 185–204. The two plays were *Briercliff* (1825), a play in five acts founded on the American Revolution, and *Maid of Saxony* (1842), an opera written for Mr. C. E. Horn. The first was played for forty nights and returned an estimated $3,500; the second was performed fourteen nights at the Park.

dark, curly hair and twinkling black eyes, this composer of the song "Woodman Spare that Tree" was a dynamo of energy, a forthright journalist with just the right amount of bullishness for success anywhere in the newspaper profession.[6] That he had chosen to defend the arts and had taken his stand as a literary orator on that platform was most fortunate. A critical judgment of his creative work as poet and playwright would doubtless assign him a very minor position, even condemn him as a superficial, rather empty literary fancier, but his aggressive and imaginative work on *The Mirror* won him a prominent place in the hierarchy of nineteenth-century American journalists.

Morris was not the only theatre critic of his day, but such writers were scarce in the 1820's, and he was among the best. His enthusiasm was projected on the level of a dedicated missionary, so determined was he to improve the American stage at all costs. In the late twenties he gave over the heavy responsibility of theatre reviewing to William Cox and others, but he still participated actively in theatrical matters. His point of view and the directions he established were maintained in the dozens of theatre articles in the subsequent pages of the *Mirror*, articles which ranged from local and provincial reports to theatre history, the contemporary English and French theatre, and theatre theory.[7]

General Morris pulled no punches in his aggressive attack on the New York stage, and his strong stand as champion of the American product was apparent from the first. "The good old legitimate drama is laid on the shelf" in favor of popular entertainment, he began.[8] "The Theatre, indeed, has of late been allowed too loose a rein. . . . The grand object appears to be making money. . . . There is not sufficient attention paid to the cultivation of a nice taste."[9] He vigorously condemned actors for ad libbing obscenities from the stage and castigated managers who allowed it. On the occasion of the opening performance of Samuel Woodworth's *The Forest Rose*, when only

[6] *Dictionary of National Biography*, XIII, 207.
[7] The scope of theatre pieces is so broad and the reporting so continuous that the *Mirror* is easily the most important primary source of theatre activity in New York from 1823 to 1835. William Dunlap, Mordecai Noah, W. C. Bryant, and J. K. Paulding, and many others wrote for Morris' weekly. Dickens also was published here, in serial form.
[8] *Mirror*, I (October 11, 1823), 86.
[9] *Ibid.*, III (March 25, 1826), 279.

a hundred people had turned up at the Park to see it, he carped vigorously at the audience for its depreciation of American creative efforts, and he fumed with indignation that an English actor could be vigorously applauded, when his superior, if he were an American, would be hissed. After the first performance of an adaptation of Fenimore Cooper's *The Spy*, he lacerated the manager for producing it so poorly and for letting it be "literally *murdered* by the performers." And with the help of Cox the campaign was stepped up. "It is a scandal and disgrace to our play-going public, that the refuse and trash of the London theatres, minor as well as major, attract . . . crowds, while the highest efforts of our own countrymen are neglected."[10] None would be foolish enough to devote long hours to playwriting, he argued, if they were poorly produced by managers and snubbed by cold and neglectful audiences.

But not all was castigation. Much perceptive, analytical criticism, as detailed as any by Hazlitt or Hunt, and as highly descriptive of acting as it was lengthy in its recounting of plots and analysis of structure, appeared week after week. When praise was merited it came in great quantities, for Morris was essentially an enthusiast about plays and actors. But he saw his job as a theatre custodian, and at that he worked industriously. When it was rumored that another new theatre would be built in New York, a note of professional despair was sounded at the prospect of having to review more bad entertainment: "Sirs, sweet sirs, no more theatres at present, if you please." The whole object of dramatic criticism, he maintained, must be to preserve the theatre as a place of refined entertainment —"as pure and undefiled as the bright icicle glittering in the sunbeam," was his florid simile. The theatre should mirror good taste and politeness, and the function of *Mirror* criticism was to point out to actors and managers where they were deficient or neglectful in this respect.[11]

From this it is clear that Morris extended his notion of criticism beyond the point of objective viewing for the benefit of his reading audience to the more important function of riding herd on managers and actors. He set himself up as a one-man censorship board and declaimer of bad taste, all for the public good. Frequently he felt compelled to lash out against the empty and meaningless exploita-

[10] *Ibid.*, IV (December 30, 1826), 183.
[11] *Ibid.*, III (March 25, 1826), 279.

tion of stage spectacle, against cataracts of real water, explosions of powder magazines, and murders. "We have a hearty hatred of cataracts . . . and should rather see one good play or opera decently got up, than be wearied with the stupid vulgarities of a 'Wilderness of Monkeys'." He also railed vigorously against puffs, arguing that actors of real merit were injured and disgusted by seeing the poor praised equally with the good. Nor did he hesitate to criticize the critics and fashions in criticism. He ridiculed jargon and pretensions as he hammered away at his own definition of what criticism meant to him. "If criticism is just, it ought to be bold and unshackled," he maintained; "if unjust, it will fall to the ground of itself."[12] If today we seriously question what Morris thought was good theatre art, it is important to remember the artistic levels and the aesthetic of the period in which he was writing. In the overview his personal judgments, as well as those of his reviewers, are not too dissimilar from the opinions of serious London critics on the same subjects.

With American materials, Morris' enthusiasms were more lonely ones. Yet he had the pioneer's vision and the bullish character to pursue what he thoroughly believed to be America's inevitable and necessary direction. "There is no other country whose records present more abundant matter, more various character, or more interesting scenes and events for dramatic exhibition or general exaltations," he argued with fired-up patriotic oratory. And he hoped that "the honest prejudices of ruder or less enlightened times" would no longer retard "the efforts of the republic in her generous and intellectual contest with the civilized states of Europe."[13] But even if the American world seemed ready for a thrust forward, how this could be expedited was a serious matter for consideration. Action was needed, not merely enthusiasm or railing against the lack of support elsewhere. The least the *Mirror* could do would be to help create the right atmosphere for this action by setting it in the most positive critical light and encouraging its reception.

From many points of view Morris' direct, actionist attack was enough to help get things started. He could see clearly that if native Americans were to learn the art of acting, it was the *Mirror's* responsibility to foster, encourage, and praise the best actors from England in order to hold them up as "studies" for young actors to

[12] *Ibid.*, VI (February 28, 1829), 271.
[13] *Ibid.*, III (October 15, 1825), 93.

copy. He maintained that, because other professions had become crowded, no time had ever been so ripe as the present for the development of the theatre arts. For the first time young Americans were encouraged to look to acting as a possible career.[14] So he threw the critical weight and reputation of the *Mirror* behind native professional effort, and almost single-handedly fought the case of new American plays and actors. Yankee actors James Hackett and George Hill were given extensive biographical-critical treatments, with accompanying lithographs, side-by-side with Washington Irving, when they achieved stardom in their performances at the Park Theatre in the early 1830's. The *Mirror* subsequently followed their activities very closely, and in the process it set the pace as the best single reporter of the expectations and growth of American comedy.

General Morris and the *Mirror* were not the only supporters of the American on the stage, however. In three major critical treatments of the state of American drama published in the *American Quarterly Review* in 1827, 1830, and 1832, the whole case was examined extensively, with special attention given to the causes for the lack of American dramatists of note.[15] One article identified the scapegoats as unsympathetic managers, the starring system, and poor taste in American audiences. Another blamed the machinists and scene painters, who had turned the English stage, from which America derived its energies, to a blatant, empty spectacle-stage, with theatres in which no voice lower than a scream or a roar could be distinguished. The third railed against such mediocrity as the Forrest-Stone Indian play *Metamora* as an example of the depths to which the American drama had fallen, and expressed doubt whether it could ever quite recover from such a blow. When William Dunlap published his *History of the American Theatre* in 1832, he could point to a body of some 275 titles, including some translations and some unperformed plays, about half of which had been written in the 1820's, as evidence that an American theatre did exist. Dunlap's personal works numbered over fifty, which made him the most prolific; but he also recognized other writers: J. N. Barker, John Burk, Joseph Hutton, M. M. Noah, J. H. Payne, Richard Penn Smith,

[14] *Ibid.*, VII (October 31, 1829), 135.
[15] The three articles in the *American Quarterly Review* are: "American Drama," I (June, 1827), 331–357; "Dramatic Literature," VIII (September, 1830), 134–161; "Dunlap's American Theatre," XII (December, 1832), 509–531.

J. A. Stone, J. O. Turnbull, and Samuel Woodworth.[16] Of the plays on his list scarcely a quarter had American themes or native characters. Nevertheless, despite this small number, Dunlap's evidence clearly indicates that an American theatre was on the move. In a forecast of the future, Dunlap maintained that American theatre must be measured by the drama it had and would create; yet, as he looked ahead, the subjects for the continuation of the study are largely the actors who dominated the stage. No playwrights are included. Was this merely a careless omission on Dunlap's part? It is certainly a curious prophecy, because no American playwrights of any strength emerged until after the Civil War.

Other Americans who set out their views on what was happening to American arts in this period could not subscribe to the record of accomplishments of American theatre as reported by Dunlap or wax enthusiastic with General Morris over the bright prospects. James Fenimore Cooper stated flatly that there were no American dramatic writers "or next to none"; that there was too much foreign competition and too much domestic employment in other pursuits to encourage this sort of marginal work.[17] In trying to be honest with America and to judge the case fairly, he concluded that the American stage was composed of foreigners and exerted "little influence on morals, politics or anything else."[18] The strength of this statement made in 1828 by one of America's most respected and successful authors was to be tested in the strenuous theatre activity by Americans in the next few years. The question as to whether American theatre could free itself from the stranglehold of English actors on the American stage, as General Morris in his most enthusiastic moments hoped it might, still had to be answered. Yankee theatre would give part of that answer.

3

The composition of the theatre audience and the position of the native actor were greatly altered by westward expansion and city growth. The opening of the West meant greatly increased opportuni-

[16] William Dunlap, *History of the American Theatre*, pp. 407–410. Charles Durang (*History of the Philadelphia Stage Between the Years 1749 and 1855,* Series I, Chapter LXXV) notes an extensive list of American plays acted in Philadelphia before 1822. His intention is to correct Dunlap.

[17] James Fenimore Cooper, *Notions of the Americans*, I, 148.

[18] *Ibid.*, p. 166.

ties for the acting profession because it greatly increased the number of theatres which required new actors to supply local stock companies. It also established new circuits for star actors. Samuel Drake, Noah Ludlow, Sol Smith, James Caldwell, and others had moved into the West as theatre managers in the forefront of the migration, and they had brought to Cincinnati, Louisville, New Orleans, Mobile, and St. Louis, much of the same theatre fare one could see in the eastern cities. Francis Wemyss, from his vantage point on the edge of the West in Pittsburgh—three hundred miles and four and a half days by coach without a single stop from Philadelphia—could well advise the inexperienced actor to "go west for practice," and many did. England could no longer supply all the actors that were needed, though the actor migration to America was still at its height. In this void the American actor found a place not only in the West but in the formerly "closed" stock companies in eastern cities. Yankee actors Hackett and Hill were in this latter group, while Marble and Silsbee, coming somewhat later to the stage, learned their profession on the stages of Western theatres. There was not much idealism among theatre managers: theatre was a commercial enterprise like any other business, and it followed the ready economic laws of supply and demand.

The most significant change in this reorganization of the theatre on a much broader pattern was the shift in audience composition. This had become noticeable early in the 1820's in eastern cities, where industrialization required large numbers of workers. As young men moved to the cities for employment the theatres found a new audience whose craving for entertainment was not easily satisfied, and whose receptive enthusiasm Fanny Kemble readily noted. The older, more solidly established audience stopped going to the theatre in large part after 1820, and it was the new city migrants whose interests had to be considered. The development of the Western theatre audience, much less refined and coarser in its tastes as Mrs. Trollope had noted, could not help but act as a modifier, a leveler of the whole American theatre pattern.

Much of this change can be seen in theatre programing, which had shifted away from what was regarded as classical theatre fare —the eighteenth-century comedy of manners and sentimental tragicomedy of Sheridan, Goldsmith, Colman, Home, and others—to the new theatre spectacles and romantic melodramas. Because the same

sort of city development and shift in theatre audience was underway
in England, a body of machine-made drama was readily available
to American theatre managers for their new theatregoers with
nonliterary backgrounds. And buried in all this was a theme that
appears over and over again—the merit and worth of the common
man. Here is a major shift in dramatic emphasis, without doubt the
most significant movement in English play structure since George
Lillo's break from the classical themes of the seventeenth century.
George Barnwell and the solid middle-class businessman's morality
has given way to William of His Majesty's Navy (*Black-Eyed
Susan*) and honest Luke (*Luke the Labourer*). Here are the new
representatives of the lower orders.

But Americans in search of native stage fare did not have to look
to England for inspiration in this direction; there was even more of
it at home, where the air was full of democratic feelings and faith
in the destiny of the common man. Furthermore, the audience could
determine much of what it saw on the stage. Actors, playwrights,
and managers were under constant pressure to reflect popular ideas
and feelings, for the expression of disapproval was actively in the
hands of the audience through the tradition of "hissing." Here was
a direct declaration of audience likes and dislikes which was not
only allowed but actively encouraged. The audience was therefore
in a position to determine what it wanted to hear, not by staying
away from the theatre to express its disfavor as it would today, but
by forcing an open battle, with the actor in the center of the abuse.
The dictates of the audience, with all their potential goods and evils,
were heeded.

In this context the appearance of native American character types
would seem to have been inevitable. With the shift to the new audience and its dramaturgical demands, with the opportunity for employment and training in the theatres of the West, with the expansion of theatres and the loosening of organizational control of theatres in the eastern cities, with the active support of such critical
groups as those around the *New York Mirror*, the most favorable
circumstances for the development of Yankee theatre were created.
The real problem confronting American actors was not so much
whether they would be allowed to perform, but *what was suitable*
to perform once they had the opportunity. The search for stage material of the right sort, together with dramaturgical devices for pre-

senting it and writers to put it into stage form, was the most baffling problem which they tried to solve. That it led, through their weakness as creative artists, and through their desires as businessmen and performers to court public favor, to confusion about what was truth and what was merely romantic claptrap, should not be surprising. In this attempt to bring real American life onto the stage they were fighting the popular style of the day; that any reality at all peered through this tight mold of Romanticism is a testimonial to the need for such reality and the aesthetic pleasures that such reality could give.

chapter 3

The Yankee as a Symbol of American Life

HE DELINEATION of the Yankee as a geographical type with definable character traits did not attract public notice until after the Revolutionary War, when he became the subject of factual and literary study. As a real-life American his identity had undoubtedly been taking shape for many decades, but it took the shaking-up process of the war years and the resulting intermingling of Colonial Americans from New England to Virginia, as well as the presence of the "outsider" in the English occupation forces who was looking objectively at his "different" American cousins, to bring the Yankee into focus as a recognizable entity. Once the primitive image had been established, the Yankee found himself in essays, poetry, songs, novels, almanacs, and a body of plays. For the next forty years before the beginnings of Yankee theatre writers of all backgrounds and talents joined fact and myth into a slowly emerging, recognizably American type with an inherent identity, an identity something like that of the Irishman, or, more aptly, the Yorkshireman, with whom the Yankee was not infrequently compared.[1]

By 1820, his image was more definite in form, but he did not fully take his place as the major American of the century until he had passed through the hands of Yankee theatre and such writers of humorous essay-fiction as Thomas Haliburton, Seba Smith, and James Russell Lowell.[2] After mid-century he reached literary prom-

[1] See John Bernard, *Retrospections of America, 1797–1811*, pp. 37 ff., for a comparative picture. Note also M. C. F. Morris, *Yorkshire Folk-Talk*, pp. 64 ff.
[2] Although the work of these writers is mentioned only in passing in this

inence in the serious novels of Melville and Hawthorne, and, in a new realistic image, he held a place on the stage for the remainder of the century. The fact that he was so widely employed in all kinds and levels of literature attests not only his reality but the intensive need of Americans to look at themselves self-consciously in the literary mirror to see what they had become or could be. That by mid-century a good many Americans were dismayed and heartily annoyed with the fantastic appearance of this symbolic American as he strayed too far from reality seemed to affect the situation very little; he was merely recast closer to the "new" idea of what the Yankee had become, and continued his literary and stage life.[3]

The origins of the word *Yankee*,[4] shrouded as they are in half mystery, offer a good example of nationalistic myth-making. Investigators variously ascribe the word to a language carry-over from a fierce tribe of Indians who were named "Yankoos"; to a Cambridge farmer named Jonathan Hastings, who first used *Yankee* in 1713 as an adjective of excellence; to the Cavaliers, who used it as a term of derision when referring to Cromwell's Roundheads; or to Massasoit, who used it in reference to the Pilgrims as invaders. *Yankee* may have come into the language from Dutch or German sources, or at least from Continental usage.[5] A credible and widely accepted derivation is the theory that *Yankee* appeared in an abortive attempt on the part of the Indians to pronounce *English*, or the French version of it, *L'Anglais*.[6] Whatever its derivation, by Revolutionary War times the word was in wide use in reference to New Englanders. It is reported that the British soldiery took up the name as a term of derision, flinging it at the New England colonials with

------

study, it forms an important, contributing background. Of major interest are Seba Smith's *Letters of Major Jack Downing* and *The Life and Writings of Major Jack Downing*, Thomas C. Haliburton's *Traits of American Humor*, James Russell Lowell's *The Biglow Papers*. See Walter Blair, *Native American Humor*, pp. 38–62, for brief samplings.

[3] Note the Gardener in the opening scene of Eugene O'Neill's *Mourning Becomes Electra*; also the Stage Manager in Thornton Wilder's *Our Town*.

[4] This word has been variously spelled: *Yankie, Yankey, Yanki*. It has been used as a noun, adjective, and verb.

[5] For a detailed treatment see Oscar Sonneck, *Report on the "Star-Spangled Banner . . ."* The *New English Dictionary* maintains that perhaps the most plausible conjecture of the derivative of *Yankie* is from the Dutch *Janke*, diminutive of *Jan* (John), applied as a derisive nickname by either Dutch or English in the New England States.

[6] See Cooper, *Notions*, I, 72; also Bernard, *Retrospections*, pp. 37 ff.

sarcasm, only to find it reconverted by the ingenious "Yankees" into a word of staunch pride. The American version of "Yankee Doodle," as we know it, was probably composed at this time by a British officer who set it to a tune familiar throughout the Colonies, and American troops quickly appropriated it as their own.[7] Later, in its wide use in countless variations, the song became the personification of the New Englander, particularly in stage versions.[8]

Yankee had scarcely been established as a New England nickname when it began to take on broader meanings.[9] Shortly after the Revolutionary War, British travelers used it indiscriminately to refer to all inhabitants of the United States, and though the Yankee character was formally associated with New England in literature, the broader use of the word continued despite frequent sectional protests. More careful travelers pointed out that *Yankee* should be applied only to those sections of New England isolated from the large coastal cities, and that the American city-dweller looked at his country cousin with a contempt similar to that held by the English. During Civil War times Southerners and Englishmen attached the label to all Northerners, and this usage remains in practice today, though both Europeans and South Americans employ the word, often derisively, to refer to all citizens of the United States. Because of its extensive political and literary interpretations carrying connotations of both the good and the nefarious, *Yankee* is among the most significant American words of the nineteenth century.

In 1828 Fenimore Cooper thought that both the national and the local meanings of the word were in general use. Since it could easily move in one direction or the other, there was no simple way to pin down its meaning. In this study of Yankee theatre, the more specific geographical designations of "down-East" and "down-Easter" will

---

[7] Sonneck, *Report,* p. 109. Since Colonial times hundreds of verses have been composed to this simple melody for which Sonneck lists sixteen different theories of origin. It became so popular that South Carolina banned it along with "Hail Columbia" and "The Star-Spangled Banner" during the Civil War.

[8] One of the earliest pre-"Yankie Doodle" versions to the tune has been variously labeled nursery rhyme and simple explanation of sex discovery:

> Lucy Locket lost her pocket,
> Kitty Fisher found it;
> Not a bit of money in it,
> Only binding 'round it.

[9] Even the state of Ohio was labeled "the Yankee state" (*Dictionary of American English,* IV, 2515).

occasionally be used. Their connotations are rather complicated, but in general usage they refer to that geographical area north and east of Boston, especially the State of Maine, and thus are highly restricted meanings of *Yankee*.[10]

To define *Yankee* is one thing; to pin down the character of the New Englander is quite a different matter. Today there is no American about whom we know more, so continuously has he been described since Revolutionary War times. But this total picture of the New Englander is not valid here. Rather, we shall be considering that fragmented, vague Yankee of the 1820's, still nebulous and evasive, a mixture of fact and fantasy. What we see from our long view seems to be excessively oversimplified and utterly naive, so broadly is the Yankee defined. From the first he is not a city type, who might be the same in Boston as in New York or Philadelphia, but a country fellow whose uniqueness in dress, substandard speech, and country dialect was readily discernible. He was a mixture of amiable rustic simplicity and hardy independence, with which he threw his adversaries off guard, and a shrewd and cunning intelligence, with which he unfailingly won his bargains. What was commendable in the character, Cooper remarks,[11] was claimed in kind by other Americans the country over; what was unflattering, even despicable, was labeled Yankee eccentricity and looked down on, for other Americans were ashamed of his reputation for duplicity, trickiness, sharp bargains, and "cute" dodges. In his journals, John Bernard wryly commented, with characteristic good humor, that there were no Jews in New England because the competition was too great for them to exist. Frances Trollope, who did not go to New England during her stay in America but met Yankees elsewhere, praised their industry and singleness of purpose, but she also declared that she had never met anyone who did not paint the New Englanders as "sly, grinding, selfish, and tricking." Such traits, she remarked, were avowed by the Yankees themselves, with a complacent smile and a boast that no people on earth could match them at overreaching in a bargain. When Americans praised the New Eng-

---

[10] Distinctions among a *down-East* Yankee (north and east of Boston), a *Varmount* Yankee, and a *Connecticut* Yankee frequently appear in literature. Although geographical delineations are usually made in Yankee-theatre plays, the fine distinctions are not developed.

[11] Cooper, *Notions*, I, 72 ff.

landers as the most moral people in America, Mrs. Trollope was forced to conclude that moral character there was greatly lower than it was in Europe.

After 1790 the Yankee became generally known outside of New England as he migrated from western Massachusetts and Connecticut to New York, Pennsylvania, and Ohio.[12] He was never better known than in the guise of the Yankee peddler who worked up and down the land, never far behind the latest boundary of the frontier. With him he took the New England reputation for hard dealing, slipperiness, and peculiar humor. Occasionally he settled in a small town and opened a shop, but it was still the same independence and fatal stubbornness in the art of the bargain that made others avoid as well as seek him. A "smart, enterprising man" was the best neighborly commendation one New Englander could make about another; and this demanded industry, contrivance, thrift, and a wise understanding of the human race. As the Yankee sat quietly and calmly, whittling at his block and spitting tobacco juice in the dust, his wisdom was a bit hard to estimate. But one knew better than to challenge it without first having the intelligence of also being born a Yankee.

2

Early native comedies featuring the Yankee character played a significant role in the attempt to show something of this image to other Americans.[13] It should be pointed out at once that Yankee theatre does not derive directly from these plays, which hover in the background, but rather from other more immediate stimulations affecting American actors in the 1820's. Nevertheless, any study of Yankee theatre must consider them, because they reveal the first primitive developments in this stage type.

Of the several extant plays which made early attempts to show native character, three are of more than passing interest: Royall Tyler's *The Contrast* (1787), James Nelson Barker's *Tears and Smiles* (1807), and A. B. Lindsley's *Love and Friendship, or Yankee Notions* (1809). *The Contrast* is, of course, the first play to use the

[12] The central New York town of Penn Yan was named for its principal immigrants—Pennsylvanians and Yankees.

[13] No attempt is made in this section to give a full treatment to early plays with Yankee characters. This would be a major study in itself.

Yankee as a major character. Twenty years before, Andrew Barton's *The Disappointment* had brought a character (Racoon) on the stage in a version of Yankee Doodle,[14] and Captain Stanley had mentioned some Yankee types (Jonathan, Jemima, Tabitha, and Yankee) in a prologue written for Howe's Thespians at New York's John Street Theatre in 1777,[15] but only Tyler's play set out a clearly drawn character.[16] *Tears and Smiles* and *Love and Friendship* follow Tyler's influential lead, and show variations on the idea.[17] In 1805 Hugh Brackenridge declared that he could not use an American character in a novel because the American, as yet, had no character, neither clown nor gentleman.[18] Such a view apparently did not deter lesser writers, who continued to work on the coarse image of the Yankee.

Royall Tyler was Boston-born, but like many young men of his day he saw much of New England during the shake-up of the War years as he traveled from one point to another in Massachusetts, Rhode Island, and Connecticut, as aide-de-camp to General Lincoln, and again in Shay's Rebellion in 1786. When he wrote *The Contrast* in New York in the spring of 1787 he had not been outside New England, but his city-country experience was quite sufficient to help him draw the contrast presented in the play. With the spirit of Yankee Doodle riding high in the surge of postwar feeling, country-boy Jonathan and Colonel Manly, the latter possibly something of Tyler himself, were highly relevant to him, and he proceeded to model his play after the Sheridan-Goldsmith-Colman school, with

[14] O! How joyful shall I be,
       When I get de money,
    I will bring it all to de;
       O! my diddling honey.
[15] George Seilhamer, *History of the American Theatre*, II, 27.
[16] The subsequent history of *The Contrast* after its initial opening at the John Street Theatre on April 16, 1787, illustrates the immediate popularity of Tyler's rustic Jonathan. Hallam presented the play six times in New York, twice in Baltimore, and once in Philadelphia, Alexandria, Georgetown, Frederick, and Boston. When actor Thomas Wignell, who played Jonathan, published the play, 658 copies were sold, with a patronage list from Boston to Barbadoes, including George Washington, Henry Knox, Edmund Randolph, Robert Morris, and many other prominent Americans.
[17] For a listing see Perley Isaac Reed, *Realistic Presentation of American Characters in Native American Plays Prior to 1870*, pp. 46–49.
[18] Quoted in Blair, *Native American Humor*, p. 14.

its interest in the contrasts between city and country life. From our view today, Tyler's comedy has an unpretentious charm and warm humor, but William Dunlap, when he first saw it played, thought it extremely deficient in plot, dialogue, and incident. Nevertheless, with a sharp eye toward what would go on the stage, Dunlap apparently could not forget Jonathan. The next year he penned a comedy of his own with a Yankee—*The Modest Servant, or Love in New York*—which closely resembled *The Contrast*.

Tyler's famous comedy about Jonathan and Colonel Manly's trip to New York is extensively discussed elsewhere, and the only intention in mentioning it briefly here is to show its position in the overall context. Jonathan the first is our principal interest in this play. When he is compared with the Yankee of a half century later, he looks like a skeleton standing beside his own fully matured exterior. He is primarily a simple country rustic, a far cry from the sly, ingenious, horsetrader type of the later Yankee plays. Yet he seems to possess the potential of these later traits, for he is not easily fooled and he frequently gives better than he receives. As a rustic type he seems to be as much English as American. If it were not for the few bits of dialect that Tyler has added to his speech, he might easily be taken for his English cousin.[19] Jonathan's independence is illustrated in the distinction he makes between a waiter, which he is, and a servant, which he distinctly is not, and his origin in America is particularized when he sings "Yankee Doodle". "I can't sing but a hundred and ninety-nine verses; our Tabitha at home can sing it all." It is largely the dialect, however, that gives him a native American appearance and the Yankee label.

We know a bit more about how Tyler's Jonathan looked on the stage from the descriptions of Thomas Wignell in his first playing of the role—an Englishman trying to be a Yankee.[20] The only primary piece of evidence of this "English" Jonathan is an engraving

[19] The differences from regular speech indicated in the printed version of the play (1790) are mostly in the line of expletives: I vow; by the living jingo; dang it all; tarnation; the dogs; Gor; maple-log seize it; the rattle; swamp it; dang'd. Other language differences were apparently not clear enough to Tyler to be recorded, or were left entirely to the actor.

[20] See Dunlap, *History*, p. 71, for comment on this performance; also Laurence Hutton, "The American Play," *Lippincott's Magazine*, XXXVII (March, 1886), 289–298. Hutton probably much overstates Wignell's development of the role.

made by William Dunlap a few months after the première of *The Contrast*. If Dunlap's print is accurate,[21] Wignell played Jonathan after the fashion of the English country rustic. A darkish uncombed wig, a long coat, knee breeches, plain linen to contrast with the fancy linen of the city characters, and black stockings constitute Jonathan's costume as Dunlap saw it in the last act. This bears little resemblance to the bright comedic costume sported by the later Yankee-theatre actors. Dunlap also tells us that Wignell was a small person, well formed and muscular. "His large blue eyes were rich in expression, and his comedy luxuriant in humor, but always faithful to the author. He was a comic actor, not a buffoon." From this we can project that Wignell's acting was probably related to the light comedy style required by Colman and Sheridan, and far from the vulgarity and broad humor of the later Yankees. Wignell probably had none of the individualized, particular touches of the Yankee eccentric. It is likely that he carried Tyler's country dialect onto the stage, where it sounded more like a stage Yorkshireman or other English county types, rather than a New Englander, even though Tyler may possibly have suggested details. Wignell was first an Englishman, then an actor, and he could not be expected to tell an audience much about genuine native Americans.

Tears and Smiles (1807) is a curious addendum to the stage Yankee because it was written by a Philadelphian and acted by an Englishman, both of whom professed never to have seen a Yankee when they brought out the play. It is of specific interest here because it so thoroughly illustrates the attitude toward the reflection of native character on the stage. How can "outsiders" possibly delineate New England character? We will continually face this question throughout the whole course of the Yankee theatre. In *Tears and Smiles*, Barker, who later worked much more extensively and knowledgeably with New England types, pointed to a few native differences, but they are all of the general-American sort. He tries to show the upper order in General Compden, a kind of undeclared middle order in Sidney, and the lower order in Nathan Yank. For contrast he adds an American fop in Mr. Fluttermore, a Frenchman in Monsieur Galliard, and an Irishman in Mr. O'Connor. The plot

---

[21] McKee believes that the inferior workmanship of the engraver makes it of little value as likenesses. See Royall Taylor, *The Contrast*, Dunlap Society Edition, p. x.

is a simple, worn one. A father tries to force a daughter to marry a fop against her wishes, but she is saved when her hero returns home from the Tripoli campaign. Like Tyler's Jonathan, Nathan Yank is a waiter and country rustic who seems to have come from no particular place. He spends his time aiding and abetting others, but has no scene in which he is the center. His dialect is indicated in the playscript by an occasionally mispronounced word, bad grammar, and odd word order: e.g., mortal sorry; 'tarnal; who do you count I seed go in a door; 'twer; sartain; ater; purtyish; sich; cute; afear'd.

We know even less about Joseph Jefferson's Nathan Yank in *Tears and Smiles* than about Wignell's Jonathan.[22] As an English actor familiar with the general line of classical low comedy in the same tradition as Wignell, his character could have been scarcely more credible than that of the first Jonathan. His task was undoubtedly even more difficult than Wignell's, for the latter probably had Tyler's advice, drawn from his experience with New England rustics, while Jefferson was left to his own resources because the playwright's own background was utterly deficient in firsthand knowledge. "Such a Yankee as I drew," wrote Barker twenty years later. "I wonder what Hackett would say to it." In referring to Jefferson's acting he notes that the audience was kept awake by "the expectation of seeing that funny fellow, Jeff., again! Never did I hail a 'funny fellow' with so much glee as on that eventful night." As in the case of Wignell, how much Englishman Jefferson could reveal of native Americans is a pertinent question. It seems likely that at the time the play was presented, neither Barker, only twenty-three at that time, nor Jefferson intended to draw a Yankee directly from life, but they approached the character more in the line of making an artificial, low-comedy stage device. Only later when the "real" type was on the stage was Barker fully aware of his skimpy, undeveloped contrivance.

Love and Friendship, or Yankee Notions (1809) was written by a nineteen-year-old Englishman, A. B. Lindsley, who acted in his own play when it was first presented at the Park Theatre.[23] Unlike

---

[22] Undoubtedly English actor Joseph Jefferson, who played Nathan Yank and for whom Barker had expressly written it, added a good deal more in the playing than appears on the printed page. Barker thought him a great hit in the part.

[23] Very little is known about Lindsley's life. T. Allston Brown (*History of the American Stage*, p. 221) indicates that a Mr. Lindsay (sic) joined the Park

the former plays, which were content with one Yankee apiece,
Lindsley's comedy was drawn with three Yankees: Captain Horner,
Jonathan, and Jack Hardweather, the last a nautical Yankee. And
apparently not considering this sufficient for the comedy scenes, the
playwright tossed in two Negroes, Phyllis and Harry. Where previous writers had found difficulty in discerning the characteristics
of only one Yankee, Englishman Lindsley now attempted to delineate three. The strong influence of *The Contrast* is again obvious in
Love and Friendship. The plot concerns a tyrannical, money-con-
scious father intent on marrying his heiress daughter to foppish
Dick Dashaway, who blames all his vices and bad manners on his
college days. After a series of involved incidents, with the help of
the Yankees she finally wins her true love. The scene of the play is
Charleston, South Carolina. The Yankees are even less attached to
the plot than in the other plays, and except for the comedy-relief
scenes, they are employed mostly for carrying messages. There is
no subplot; all the characters are joined, sometimes vaguely, sometimes directly, to the main plot.

However badly constructed the play may be, *Love and Friendship*
still evidences some development in the Yankee. Jonathan, the most
important of the three Yankees and certainly the only one in direct
line with Tyler's Jonathan and Barker's Nathan Yank, is again a
servant type. This time, we can note, he is involved with Captain
Horner in trading Yankee notions. Although barely mentioned,
Jonathan is a peddler, and this is what has brought him to Charleston. This is the first time the Yankee-trader idea has been introduced
in a play. Also used for the first time is a Yankee story in a fully
developed dialect. Later on, we will find this an important device in
Yankee theatre. The story appears near the beginning of the play
when Jonathan relates his adventures with Captain Horner on the
first night aboard ship. Though it is not developed to any great degree, Jonathan's story has a number of the identifying marks which
distinguish this peculiarly native comic device so important two
decades later: general theme, deviations, peculiar style of delivery,
dialect, exaggerations, and lack of specific point. Lindsley's antici-

---

Theatre company in 1808. Odell (*Annals*, II, 299) lists Lindsley in one cast for
that season. Lindsley's detailed knowledge of America and Yankees in particular
would indicate an extensive American background. Could he possibly have been
an American by birth?

pation of the Yankee story is a surprise in this dull play. Says Jonathan:

But it beets every thing twew see capun Horner git intewe such a tarnal passion. Jest as it was the fust night we left Boston; and all for nothen at all as a body may say, only 'caze I a axt um (for I jest cum from Suffield, where they makes wooden dishes, and never went to sea 'fore) as 'e lay acrost the door what goes down chamber 'f 'e was goen tewe driver the whul enduren night and how 'e'd stop her, with all that are cloth flyen top on her. Darnation! says 'e, in a torne down passion— don't swear so, capun, says I, (cool as a Keowcumber) git out 'f my sight Jonathan says 'e, hot as a nettle; never fetch me 'f I dewe, says I, (brushen up tewe 'um you may be sartan) darnation! agin says 'e, you're 'nough tewe make the devil mad, Jonathan . . . it beets all nater, capun, says I tewe think friends'll fall out so like the deuce, and quarrel enamost for jest nothen at all, says I; so make it up, and let me sop some 'f our burnt punken 'lasses, capun, says I:—you may sop hell, Jonathan, says he—'bliged tewe you capun, says I, but I knows what's duty and good manners; so, arter my commander, 'f you please. So chargen um not tewe swear so, I told um tewe unbutton his collar, and cool it, for I was sartan it must be warmish arter swearen so hot; and off I goes sing'n and hoppen, like the very rot.

A few verses of "Yankee Doodle" are then used to carry this maturing Jonathan off the stage. Two decades later the Yankee story will embody the character traits of shrewdness and hard dealing, but as yet this distinguishing "wit" of the Yankee has not been exploited. Only in a brief speech does Jonathan indicate a half vision of his subsequent dominating label when he says, speaking of Jews, "Folks says the're keener than Yankees for all they aynt hafe the wit; yit a poor luberly country cracker stands no more chance with um, 'thout he's a brother Jonathan."

In spite of the overly involved plot, the rambling scenes, and a failure to draw the Yankees more tightly within the play, *Love and Friendship* marks a significant stage along the main stream of Yankee growth. Bits of incidental humor, such as Jonathan's description of how to kiss a girl, are also revealing.

O'ny 'e don't dewe it right; 'e don't kiss the place we Yankee boys dewe, but I spose 'e dewes it arter the fashion 'f the place, though I don't much like it, by gum! and guess the Yankee gals wouldn't nuther. I am

sartan they ruthur have the lips 'f a handsome young man like me
touch theirn than the back 'f their hands.

In this passage, probably the first really serious attempt to record
the language in a play, it is notable that the Yankee dialect is well
developed. The speech of both Captain Horner and Jonathan is fully
indicated, though Jack Hardweather speaks a sort of seaman's dialect
composed chiefly of nautical expressions instead of the phonetic
modifications indicated in orthography for the other two characters.
This points a specific contrast in convention between the land and
sea Yankees. The latter has always appeared as a separate specimen,
and seldom in conjunction with a land Yankee as in this play.[24]

3

The two plays that most directly affect Yankee theatre are David
Humphreys' *The Yankey in England* (published c. 1815) and
Samuel Woodworth's *The Forest Rose* (1825). The first provided
an enormously useful reference book for Charles Mathews in the
development of his Yankee characters, and very likely also influenced Hackett. The second provided a multiple stimulus: it fired
George Hill with the ambition of becoming a Yankee actor when he
saw Alexander Simpson play Jonathan Ploughboy at the Chatham
Theatre in 1825, and he later acted the role himself; it stimulated
James Hackett to tell his first Yankee stories, for they followed
within a few weeks after Simpson's first performance; and it gave
Joshua Silsbee an acting piece for a hundred-night run in London at
mid-century. Both plays were written by New Englanders who saw
unusual possibilities in native-character drama. Any evaluation of
that drama would certainly credit their significant contribution.

Though it was not printed or performed until six years after
Lindsley's comedy, Humphreys had drawn *The Yankey in England*
in rough outline many years previously, probably under the direct
influence of *The Contrast* and other plays with Yankees printed during the 1790's.[25] The principal interest in Humphreys' play lies not

[24] See J. S. Jones, *The Usurper, or Americans in Tripoli* for another play of a
later date with similar use of the two Yankee types.

[25] Humphreys' first play, *The Widow of Malabar*, was published in the same
year as *The Contrast*, 1790. *The Yankey in England* was begun as early as 1792,
and Humphreys worked at it off and on until 1814, when plans for a celebration
called it forth from obscurity. See Leon Howard, *The Connecticut Wits*, p. 294,
for more detail on this subject.

in its plot, or even in its two Yankee characters, Mr. Newman and Doolittle, but rather in its notes on real-life Yankee character and its seven-page glossary "Of words used in a peculiar sense, in the Drama; or pronounced with an accent or emphasis in certain districts, different from the modes generally followed by the inhabitants of the United States." Humphreys' word list[26] was undoubtedly much more widely used in the composition of Yankee plays than has generally been acknowledged. Charles Mathews confessed that he loaned R. B. Peake a copy when that English playwright was in the process of drawing Jonathan Doubikins for his farce of *Jonathan in England*. This also implied that Mathews had *Yankey* at hand when he and James Smith and possibly Mrs. Mathews worked out the different Yankee parts in *Trip to America*. We strongly suspect that James Hackett, as well as other actors and writers, found its glossary most useful, if only to compare it with their own efforts.[27]

Whether General Humphreys used any other source material than his own observation, we do not know. Probably none would have been necessary. As a native resident of Connecticut,[28] he had a firsthand knowledge of the country people, particularly of their speech forms. These he had listened to closely, and he set them down in the most complete list compiled up to that time. He was not a linguist in the scientific sense, but his observation was keen and his interest in local habits and customs was intense. He had something of the amateur anthropologist about him in his zeal to delineate Yankee character.[29]

General Humphreys is not only extremely careful about the speech of the Yankee, he is also very specific about his geographical location. Doolittle is not a "general" American, nor even a New England man in the broad sense, Humphreys points out, but he comes from the interior of New England and can be distinguished by "a peculiar idiom and pronunciation, as well as by a peculiarity

[26] See Chapter 4 of this study for details. The entire word list has been reproduced as Appendix B of this book.

[27] John Neal, *The Down-Easters*, I, iv, maintains that Hackett and Hill borrowed heavily from Humphreys' piece, and that it is the only genuine Yankee play.

[28] Humphreys lived at Humphreysville, Connecticut.

[29] For example: chaunce=chance; chares=chores; clus=close; coad=could. The list also includes a large number of merely low-colloquial forms common throughout the States. See Appendix A for a general discussion of Yankee stage speech.

of character."[30] Humphreys thought the Yankee's good qualities more than compensated for his singularities and failings. In his view, the Yankee was made up of contrarities: simplicity and cunning.

Inquisitive from natural and excessive curiosity, confirmed by habit; credulous, from inexperience and want of knowledge of the world; believing himself to be perfectly acquainted with whatever he partially knows; tenacious of prejudices; docile, when rightly managed; when otherwise treated, independent to obstinacy; easily betrayed into ridiculous mistakes; incapable of being overawed by external circumstances; suspicious, vigilant and quick of perception, he is ever ready to parry or repel the attacks of raillery, by retorts of rustic and sarcastic, if not of original and refined wit and humor.

What a perceptive and detailed picture this is. One wishes that Humphreys had been more of a playwright, for when we turn to the script we are disappointed in what he did with Doolittle.

The production of *The Yankey in England* is revealing because of its peculiar circumstances. In a note appended to the play we learn that it was presented in January, 1815, by an amateur acting group in Humphreysville, Connecticut, in accordance with "a general, legal provision for watching over the education, health and morals of children and others employed in such establishments."[31] The play was attended by clergymen, magistrates, selectmen, and other respectable citizens, and the delineator of Doolittle won "universal admiration." Was Doolittle the genuine article itself? This is the only recorded performance of the play. Its triteness and rambling construction tell us why it was never considered for professional production.

The second play which directly affected Yankee theatre, Samuel Woodworth's *The Forest Rose, or American Farmers* (1825), is a transition play, being at once a summation of the Yankee's development on the stage up to this point and a foretaste of what it is to become. One of the first indications that the *New York Mirror* intends to support American drama is its defense of Woodworth's play. George Morris did not review this work of his former colleague

---

[30] In the play Doolittle claims that he was born "Sumwheres in Varmount, between Brattleborough and Bennington." He was a cooperer by trade until he was impressed into the British Navy as a seaman.

[31] The Humphreysville manufacturing plant.

on the *Mirror*. Nevertheless, when he noticed a slim audience at one performance, he made it an occasion for lashing out at the failure of Americans to support their own native writers. Later, he noted that it had been performed twice to overflowing houses.[32] Had he done a bit of puffing as a devoted missionary in the field? Morris is affronted, perhaps along with Woodworth, at Manager Wallack's refusal to allow Woodworth to appear on the stage after an early performance. But whatever the situation may have been, *The Forest Rose* marks the entry of the *Mirror* into the battle for the development of a native theatre. Woodworth's play undoubtedly paved the way for what was to follow. Since Woodworth is the first of what can be labeled Yankee-theatre playwrights, a brief look at his background can help our image of this new movement in American theatre.

Today the author of *The Forest Rose* is remembered, if at all, through his brief poem "The Hunters of Kentucky,"[33] celebrating Jackson's victory over Packenham at New Orleans, and his famous song, "The Old Oaken Bucket." He was born a New Englander on January 13, 1785, at Scituate, Massachusetts, the son of Benjamin Woodworth, a soldier in the American Revolution, and Abigail (Bryant) Woodworth.[34] His formal education was limited, and soon we find him apprenticed to a printer, Benjamin Russell, the editor and publisher of Boston's *Columbian Centinel*, where he began his career as a writer.[35] In 1809 he moved to New York, married Lydia Reeder a year later, and during the war years occupied himself with publishing a weekly paper titled *The War*. From that time forward his poems, essays, and other writings appeared regularly in newspapers and magazines, frequently over the signature "Selim," occasionally over his own name. Several of Woodworth's poems were first printed in "The Complete Coiffeur; or an Essay on the Art of Adorning Natural and of Creating Artificial Beauty" by J. M. D. Lafoy, Ladies' Hair Dresser, 1817. Subsequently, Woodworth helped George Morris found and edit the first issues of the *Mirror*, a contact which tied him to the important literary figures

[32] *Mirror*, III (October 15, 1825), 95.
[33] Samuel Woodworth, *Melodies, Duets, Trios, Songs, and Ballads*, pp. 221–223.
[34] One of the best accounts of Woodworth's life and work is Oral Coad, "The Old Oaken Bucket," *The Sewanee Review*, XXVII (1919), 163–175.
[35] Oscar Wegelin, *Early American Plays, 1714–1730*, p. 101. See also the *Cyclopaedia of American Literature*, I, 71.

of the next two decades. Though he remained in the employ of the *Mirror* for only one year after its founding, he continued one of its favorite sons until his death on December 9, 1842. Favorable notices and reviews of all his literary activities appeared regularly in its pages. Among the several plays that Woodworth prepared for the stage during his period of theatre activity between 1822 and 1836, only *The Forest Rose* and *The Foundling of the Sea*, which will be mentioned later in this study, can definitely be labeled Yankee plays.[36]

The Forest Rose is a pastoral comedy with songs, constructed around the typical Yankee themes of proving country over city worth, and the superiority of the native American over the imported Englishman. Its romantic sentiments are nowhere more clearly expressed than in Woodworth's lyrics for which John Davies provided the music.

> Ye fair, who seek a splendid lot
>   Behold content, a richer prize
> Within the humblest ploughman's cot,
>   That rank and pride dispise.
> And palace or cot, whatever your lot,
>   The farmer your table supplies, my dear,
>   The farmer your table supplies.
>
> CHORUS:
> For Lords of the soil, and fed by our toil
>   American farmers are blest, my boys
>   American farmers are blest.

The single plot of *The Forest Rose* is the model for Yankee theatre plays. All the characters are necessary, and all are involved in the complications of the romantic story, with the Yankee not appended to but directly involved in the plot. The simple love story revolves around the attempts of Bellamy, an English city slicker, to seduce Harriet Miller away from William, her rustic intended. Miffed because Sally Forest tricked him while blindfolded, into kissing Rose, the Negro maid, Jonathan Ploughboy arranges to take Harriet instead of Sally to the country dance. Meanwhile, the seduc-

[36] Other titles include: *The Deed of Gift* (1822); *Lafayette, or The Castle of Olmuty* (1824); *The Widow's Son* (1825); *King's Bridge Cottage, a Revolutionary Tale* (1826); *The Cannibals* (1833); *Blue Laws, or Eighty Years Ago* (1833).

tion plot thickens. Bellamy decides to abduct Harriet and pays Jonathan five guineas for assistance, but Jonathan and Sally outsmart him by substituting Rose, in disguise, for Harriet. At the end, all the lovers are happily united, even Jonathan and Sally. Woodworth's word picture at the beginning of the first scene illustrates his intention in the play as a whole.

The overture expresses the various sounds which are heard at early dawn, in the country, commencing at the hour of silence when even the ticking of the village clock is supposed to be heard. It strikes four, and a gentle bustle succeeds, indicating the first movements of the villagers. A confused murmur swells on the ear, in which can be distinguished the singing of birds, the shepherd's pipe, the hunter's horn, etc. etc. etc. until the united strength of the band represents the whole village engaged in their rustic employments.

Why did Woodworth locate *The Forest Rose* in the northern part of New Jersey? Jonathan Ploughboy says that he comes from Taunton, Massachusetts, which certainly qualifies him as a Yankee. With his New England background, Woodworth certainly knew what he was doing. Did he choose New Jersey because of its familiar meanings to New York audiences? Did he intend to set Jonathan apart from the other "Jersey" farmers in the play? In a later decade Dan Marble occasionally titled Woodworth's piece: *American Farmers, or the Yankee in Jersey*.

The character of Jonathan Ploughboy shows a wide advance over any previous delineation. Not only has he become an important part of the main plot, but he is also a more completely drawn personality. He is a shopkeeper, a small business man, which in itself is a promotion over his former state of servant or "waiter." And his cleverness as a hard dealer is given ample illustration.

BLAND. So you are a shop-keeper, then?
JON. A little in the merchant way, and a piece of a farmer besides.
BLAND. What do you sell?
JON. Everything: whiskey, mollasses, calicoes, spellingbooks and patent gridirons.
BLAND. With which you try to shave the natives.
JON. No, sir; everybody shaves himself here. There is no barber nearer than Paris.
BLAND. You don't understand me. By shaving I mean making a sharp

bargain, or what your parson or deacon might denominate cheating.

JON.   Me? I wouldn't serve a negro so. But as to the parson or deacon, folks say they are pretty cute that way themselves.

And again later when confronted with the problem of whether he should keep Bellamy's bribe, he argues with himself:

I don't calculate I feel exactly right about keeping this purse; and yet I believe I should feel still worse to give it back. Twenty-three dollars is a speculation that a'n't to be sneezed at, for it a'n't to be catched everyday. But will it be right to keep the money, when I don't intend to do the job? Now, if I was at home, in Taunton, I would put that question to our debating society, and I would support the affirmative side of the question.

Has his new position as a businessman created other problems? A rude note has crept into this play in the constant epithet, "I wouldn' sarve a negro so," and his opinion of Rose as a "garlic-eater." This seems to be the beginning of a comedy line involving the abuse of the Negro servant. We will note in the next chapter that Mathews used it in his two pieces a year before Woodworth wrote his play. *The Forest Rose*, as a title, has two implications: one refers to country girl Sally as a rose—"of all the flowers that bloom, I love the Forest Rose the best"; and the other, which is obscure and unrevealing of what Woodworth intended, lies in the Negro woman whose first name is Rose, and, since she works for Deacon Forrest, she would be known as Rose Forrest, a reversal of Sally's epithet. Buried in *The Forest Rose* were more inherent thoughts and feelings of Americans than had appeared in any of the play with Yankees up to this time.

Alexander Simpson as Jonathan in *The Forest Rose* has the distinction of being the first native-born American actor to play the Yankee on the stage in a fully developed play featuring the type. Noah Ludlow notes that Simpson's Jonathan Ploughboy was "simply a comic New Jersey boy, without any of the more eastern peculiarities."[37] Did Simpson know any Yankees firsthand? Was he related to any himself? He was born in Albany, New York,[38] and

[37] Noah Ludlow, *Dramatic Life as I Found It*, p. 433.
[38] H. P. Phelps, *Players of a Century*, p. 55. Brown (*History*, p. 335) reports that Simpson died in Poughkeepsie in 1827. Simpson was a printer by trade and

this would have put him close to the Yankee home base of interior New England. Though Simpson's playing of the part was undoubtedly more American than any stage Yankees before him, he cannot be considered in the class of New England eccentrics that developed in the few years following the first performance of Woodworth's pastoral opera.

------

went to New York as an actor by way of an apprenticeship in the Albany Theatre.

chapter 4

Actor Inspiration: Charles Mathews
and Satire on America

NGLISH ACTOR Charles Mathews (1776–1835) is the pater-familias of Yankee theatre. As the model and instructor of James Hackett, who was copied by the others, Mathews set the pattern for low comedy in America. At first glance there is something amusing in this paradox of an Englishman showing Americans how to put themselves on the stage. Yet it makes very good sense from a practical point of view, for only a celebrated comedian of Mathews' stature could have given dignity and importance to such a stage novelty or provided acting style and script content of imaginative enough proportions to excite young American actors to the stage possibilities of the Yankee. Through the strength of his position in the theatre, he gave them courage to flout the accepted repertoire and try native materials.

Trip to America and *Jonathan in England* are Mathews' major contributions to the Yankee theatre canon. It was through them that he gave Hackett specific actable content and performance know-how that clearly set the direction of the young American, for Hackett copied him, not exactly but so closely that the borrowing was obvious to those Americans who had seen Mathews on his American tour in 1822–1823 or to Englishmen who saw Hackett on his visit to London in 1827. But there was no other way for the Americans to learn the business of the stage, which was also the business of the box office, except by imitating the popularly accepted forms and styles. Audience critical dictum was far more open and direct at that time than now, and a freewheeling innovator could be howled down from the stage in a matter of minutes.

It was Charles Mathews' art of mimicry that Hackett followed so closely. The English comedian had not made his fame and fortune in acting the standard comedy of the day, but in his satirical take-offs of national peculiarities which he brought on the stage in his celebrated annuals, *At Home with Charles Mathews*. In his one-man, vaudeville-type performances he had lightly ridiculed through songs, skits, and monologues the Scots, Welsh, Irish, many of the English county types, and the French, German, and Dutch. His shows were galleries of realistically conceived national types, women as well as men, which he brought off with quick costume changes and ingenious continuity. But he was much more than a vaudeville performer. The artfully contrived satirical content gave imaginative extensions to his character creations. At the base Charles Mathews was a dialect comedian of wide versatility, and this was what stimulated James Hackett. Later on, the American would copy Jonathan, Uncle Ben, Mallet, and others, at first using some modification of the same script material, later devising new content of his own. But Mathews always hovers close in the background. Hackett will even try to improve on the Mathews' original, with the unspoken but obviously indicated argument that an American should know more about native manners than an Englishman. Firsthand knowledge of the real thing, however, often leads not to art but to confusion on the stage; talent, intelligence, imagination, and critical capacity in the actor-improvisor are much better qualifications. Mathews invented and Hackett copied; and only when he had learned what to do, did the American pursue his own original ways. By teaching Hackett how to become a dialect comedian, "actor-wrighter" Mathews was the progenitor not only of the Yankee but of all native American dialect comedy.

2

When Charles Mathews played his *Trip to America* at the English Opera House in London on March 25, 1824, the American scene came vividly to life in a stage travelogue for the first time. Mathews had made a tour through the American provinces and had taken home what he regarded as an authentic report.[1] But unlike other travelers who published their journals or made occasional lectures, Mathews presented his views from the stage in anecdotes, colorful imitations, patter songs, and monologues. Here was England's top comedian capitalizing on the vogue for travel reports by providing a delightful evening of comic entertainment at the expense of the Americans. Mathews was perfectly suited for the job. He excelled in mimicry—Leigh Hunt called him "a genius"[2]—and this gave dynamic life and variety to his entertainments. Washington Irving awarded him top honors,[3] and Coleridge pictured him as "a comic poet acting his own poems."[4] Macaulay believed him to be "the greatest actor I ever saw, far greater than Kean. . . . I admired him and laughed my sides sore whenever I saw him."[5] Even the seldom complimentary Charles Macready thought the characters which Mathews invented by himself were both admirable and inimitable and his talents for mimicry most exceptional.[6] Alfred Bunn, manager of Drury Lane during the 1830's, labeled Mathews "the most extraordinary actor that ever lived."[7]

Mathews' ability as a mimic is graphically illustrated in Leigh Hunt's account of a weekend with the comedian. Hunt was awakened one morning by the noisy splashings and extremely vocal protestations of a small boy having his face washed. Since he had seen no child the night before and this was a very real and noisy one, Hunt asked his host at breakfast where his son was. He was

---

[1] For detailed accounts see *Memoirs of Charles Mathews*, ed. by Mrs. Mathews; also *The Life and Correspondence of Charles Mathews*, abridged by Edmund Yates. The content of this chapter is based on an article by the author, "Charles Mathews Reports on America," *Quarterly Journal of Speech* 36 (December, 1950), 492–499.

[2] Leigh Hunt, *The Autobiography of Leigh Hunt*, p. 118. For a comparison of Mathews with other comedians in 1807 see Leigh Hunt, *Critical Essays on the Performers of the London Theatres*.

[3] Pierre Irving, *The Life and Letters of Washington Irving*, I, 401.

[4] Henry Barton Baker, *English Actors from Shakespeare to Macready*, II, 231.

[5] Henry G. Paine, "Charles Mathews," *Actors and Actresses*, ed. by Brander Matthews and Lawrence Hutton, IV, 2.

[6] *The Diaries of Macready*, ed. by William Toynbee, I, 239. Macready did not hold Mathews the man in such high regard—"not high souled" or a "gentleman" in the strict sense. He also thought him dull as a companion because he talked mostly about himself.

[7] Alfred Bunn, *The Stage: Both Before and Behind the Curtain*, I, 58.

astonished to learn that the small boy was none other than Mathews himself having fun with his stage character of "the schoolboy with shining morning face."[8] Hunt's admiration increased when the comedian gave him a special rendition of the infant character "nothing to the age of an hour and a quarter."

Another of Mathews' admirers was Charles Dickens, who had seriously thought at one time of taking up acting as a profession. In his journals Dickens tells us how he went to the theatre nightly for nearly three years, and always to see Mathews when he played.[9] Even the discriminating William Hazlitt, who thought Mathews weak in conventional stage characters, admitted that were the ingenious Mathews to show his unusual gallery of eccentrics "he might exhibit it every night for a month and we should go every night."[10] So constantly favorable is the criticism of Mathews' art of mimicry that we must set him down as unusual in his own time and certainly among the very best comedians of the nineteenth-century stage.

Before looking at *Trip to America*, we should catch a glimpse of Mathews the traveler, since he claimed that his entertainment was an authentic picture of what he saw during his professional visit to this country in 1822–1823. Most of his views are recorded in detail in the series of delightful and personally revealing letters he sent to his wife and James Smith, the literary friend who later helped prepare the unique entertainment. From his first arrival at New York in September, 1822, Mathews set about discovering and noting the individual quality and distinct flavor of America and its inhabitants. That his view proved to be superficial and for the most part revealed only the externals of that life which he had hoped to individualize is no particular discredit to him. Few had yet examined the native American with any thoroughness and Mathews' glimpse was as good as most. Here was a traveler who saw America through the eyes of an aristocrat, a pessimist, and a potential yellow-fever victim. Imagine the consternation and literal fear of this nervous tourist on learning while still aboard ship that New York was fever-swept and that to be safe he must go ashore at

[8] Hunt, *Autobiography*, p. 167.

[9] John Forster, *The Life of Charles Dickens*, p. 380.

[10] A. R. Waller and Arnold Glover (eds.), *The Collected Works of William Hazlitt*, VIII, 433.

Hoboken. He soon became convinced that the United States was still uncivilized (and in his own telling his pessimistic comments encourage sympathy), that it was an uncomfortable wilderness "where miserable disappointment has followed enterprise and industry." In letter after letter he frankly reveals his dissatisfactions, his candid shock at the unbelievable state of affairs, his British snobbishness, his plain fear and discomfort. The democratic order of things seemed to harry him most. "It appears to me that the lower orders must necessarily prevent a European from being comfortable, if he has not made up his mind resolutely to look on, laugh, and thoroughly despise. If this must be the effect of a republican form of government, give me a monarch, even if he be a despot."[11] And again:

The want of cheerfulness and civility is striking, and the egregious folly of the middle and lower orders in their fancied independence, is calculated to produce a smile of thorough contempt rather than anger. It consists in studied sullenness, the determination never to be civil or apparently kind to a fellow creature, and not to bow, or say thank ye, to a person they know to be their superior. . . . The upper order . . . either like it, or are compelled to submit to it. . . . The manager of a theatre tells me that it is not in his power to induce the lamplighter or carpenter, when he walks into the greenroom before the ladies to take off his hat, and this is allowed, and must be submitted to, they tell me.[12]

The troubled Mathews presents the amusing paradox of the professional stage comedian, whose business it is to point the finger of ridicule at others, seriously involved in what is essentially a comic situation. How pathetically humorous he becomes in his own telling as we see him pitted against the complexities, the nearly insurmountable discomforts, of what he chose to regard as frontier life. Mathews in America is a movie reel of staggering events with the odious yellow fever constantly lurking on his trail. "It is next to an affront to say it is dangerous," he sputters. His irritation increases with transportation difficulties, peculiarities in bed and board, and freezing weather in Boston that prevents him from washing because there is an inch of ice in his washbowl. How ridiculous he must have looked attending rehearsal with his nose stuffed with cotton to

[11] Yates, *Mathews*, p. 261.
[12] *Ibid.*, p. 264.

prevent his smelling the "d—— American mutton chops!" So vociferous was Mathews in his blunt and heartless criticism of America that manager Price "followed him like a shadow and nursed him like a baby" to insure that his discordant comments would fall on sympathetic ears and not on those of an oversensitive public.

But in spite of the tortures that afflicted Mathews on his American visit, he did return a fair report on the people he saw about him. Personalities in all walks of life were his daily bread and butter, and his keen eyes searched everywhere as he traveled back and forth between Baltimore and Boston by stagecoach, steamer, or sailing packet. Conversation with travelers, coachmen, innkeepers, waiters, and journeymen of all kinds, often as not culled more as an eavesdropper than as a participant, gave him the native flavor of manners and talk. Often he was discouraged about collecting useable material, for he found it extremely difficult to pin down the "real" American. "If I enter into conversation with a coachman, he is Irish; if a fellow brings me a note, he is Scotch. If I call a porter, he is Negro. I can't come at the American without I go to the porterhouses and that I cannot condescend to do." Instead he searched for character and situation in lawcourts, in churches, and in the public rooms of wayside inns. He noted that all people seemed to be dressed alike, with nobody well dressed, no one shabby. The judge, the barrister, the shopkeeper, the President, the members of Congress, the mechanic, the servant—all wore the same clothing.

Despite the difficulties of putting his finger on what he wanted, Mathews' American began to take shape. "I am driven to boarding in the home with Price," he writes, little realizing that this would provide him with some of his most entertaining material. He was much amused with the inordinate love of military titles: "Why are we so long changing horses, Colonel?—This was addressed to our coachman—a fact." He thought landlords were the most independent people in America: "He can't be caricatured: I won't spare him an inch. He is, too, the most insolent rascal I ever encountered. . . . I have already three or four distinct specimens of the same species. The effect will depend more on matter than manner." We can almost see Mathews rubbing his hands in anticipation of the stage fun to come. The comedian was much disappointed, and so are we when we read his letters, that winter weather and difficult travel made it impossible for him to go to Washington when Congress was in session.

What he could not discover firsthand, he filled out through probing conversations with the many personalities he met during the course of the tour, for whether it was Baltimore, Philadelphia, New York, or Boston, he encountered eager responsiveness from the "well informed, polite, hospitable, unaffected" leading citizens of the upper order. "He's a very correct, gentlemanlike man in private life, and at times the life of a dinner-table by the specimens of characters of the day," Washington Irving had written, and Americans who sought his companionship found him all of this. William Dunlap and James Fenimore Cooper took him on a vacation cruise up the Hudson River to Albany so that he could see more of America and American manners than New York would reveal.[13] We learn through Dr. Francis, who accompanied them, that Cooper's recent novel about American colonial life, *The Spy*, which had appeared recently in a stage adaptation, was the leading subject of discussion. They sat on deck and talked through an entire night because the sensitive Mathews could not endure sleeping in the common cabin with the rest of the male passengers. Cooper was greatly excited by the colorful Mathews,[14] and Dunlap marveled at the comedian's unusual ability as a raconteur. Undoubtedly Mathews learned as much from these natives as he learned anywhere on his travels in the States.

3

Less than a year after Mathews arrived back in England he introduced his satirical travelogue to London audiences. It won immediate favor with a public eager for any and all comment on American life. In his entertainments of previous years Mathews had had considerable fun at the expense of the Scotch and Irish,

[13] Dunlap, *History*, p. 386. See also J. F. Cooper, *Gleanings*, II, 214. Cooper took Mathews to the belfry of the Capitol in Albany that he might get an accurate notion of the localities. He stood gazing at the view a minute, and then exclaimed, "I don't know why they make so much fuss about Richmond Hill." Cooper's remarks to his readers is not without a bit of sly wit: "Mr. Mathews did not recollect that they who *do* make the fuss scarcely ever saw any other hill."

[14] See Mary Phillips, *James Fenimore Cooper*, pp. 320–322, for an account of the trip.

and they had themselves enjoyed the satire. His garrulous Scotch-woman had nowhere been more successful than in Edinburgh. Now it was America's turn to take a ribbing. In spite of Mathews' deliberate toning down of the satire, he soon found himself involved in a vigorous literary controversy with Americans who claimed this was an unfair and inaccurate report of American life. English theatregoers of 1824, however, found it bright and gay, and the eccentric manners of their American cousins vastly amusing. Jonathan was as ridiculous as an Irishman or a Scotchman who, of course, were nothing at all like Englishmen.

For three and a half hours the clever Mathews kept his audience laughing with a magic hatful of characters, alive and breathing, from his American experiences. What was remarkable about the entertainment was that Mathews was the sole performer, acting the dozen or so characters one after the other and often simultaneously. Unfortunately the comedian never published his original and fully detailed version of *Trip to America*, and we are forced to depend on abbreviated, partially narrated treatments which do not reproduce his chatter in its entirety.[15] The peculiar Mathews flavor, however, is readily recognizable, and we can catch the spirit of this unusual performance. Early in the piece he defines Yankee in its broadest sense: "what you may call an American and of course an American is what you must call a Yankee." Mr. Pennington, a quiet, temperate American, explains that *Yankee* is the Indian for "English" and that it became associated with all Englishmen; therefore it is English in nature.

From his first entrance on the stage with a lively explanation of why he went to America, Mathews skips gaily through his adventures in New York, Elizabethtown, Baltimore, Washington, Philadelphia, Boston, and Providence, interspersing his account

[15] The writer has used two versions in this discussion: *Mathews in America, or the Theatrical Wanderer*, and *Sketches of Mr. Mathews's Celebrated Trip to America*. Both are fairly complete in detail. Neither is an exact reproduction of Mathews' script, but narrated and edited accounts of the performance. Frequent bits of Mathews' talk and business are included. The lyrics to the songs are complete although the wordage may possibly vary from Mathews' originals. Colored illustrations of the costumes are included, and in one version (J. Limbard) Robert Cruikshank, brother of the famous Dickens illustrator, is acknowledged as the artist. For a brief summary of the published program and illustration of the characters in *Trip* attributed to Mathews himself, see Mathews, *Memoirs*, III, 442–443.

with colorful mimicries, jokes, and patter-songs—half song, half
dialogue. His stagecoach driver is a Major Grimstone, "a stiff, formal, consequential, and deliberate master of the whip" who bullies
his passengers as so much luggage. "Why, forsooth? because he is
nothing more nor less than a major in the American army." The
grim, humorless Major is filling in his spare time with writing a
book on comedy. Imagine the scene at Mrs. Bradish' Boarding
House with its salty chatter about the boarders.

> "I *guess*," and "I *calculate*," here they're
>   exclaiming,
> But still we can't blame them for that I will
>   show;
> And "I reckon" the Yankees we musn't be blam-
>   ing,
> For we have expressions in England, "You
>   know."

Then there is the Militia Muster song-monologue about a troop of
"irregular regulars" with umbrellas, swords, and fishing rods for
muskets. James Hackett will later develop this into a full-blown
sketch. No number on the program could have been more amusing
than the visit to the African Theatre with Mathews skillfully
mimicking a Negro actor.

"To be, or not to be? that is the question; whether it is nobler in de
mind to suffer, or tak' up arms against a sea of trouble, and by
oppossum end 'em." No sooner was the word *oppossum* out of his
mouth, than the audience burst forth, in one general cry, "Oppossum!
Oppossum! Oppossum!" and the tragedian came forward and informed
them, that he "would sing their favorite melody with him greatest
pleasure."

> Oppossum up a gum tree,
> Have no fear at all;
> Oppossum up a gum tree,
> Him never tink to fall.
> Oppossum up a gum tree,
> Him hop and skip and rail;
> But Nigger him too cunning,
> So he pull him down by de tail.

Mathews describes a visit to Bunker Hill, performs a sketch on the

Boston Post Office, and relates an anecdote about sleigh-riding with a conversation between Brother Jonathan and an Englishman.

JON. There's a sleigh, I guess.
ENG. You shouldn't say "I guess," you know.
JON. But you say "you know," I guess.
ENG. But if I say "you know," you say "I guess" you know; but I don't say "you know," you know.

Mathews' most successful hit in *Trip to America* was the character of Jonathan W. Doubikin,[16] a "real" Yankee. This, of course, is the first time an English audience had seen such a character. Here was Mathews' "authentic" American, and a peculiar fellow he was. Jonathan "the doubtful"—I guess, I reckon, I calculate—becomes in Mathews' mimicry the homebred American prototype: a country fellow, unpolished and a hard bargainer. Mathews has his Jonathan tell a Yankee story about his Uncle Ben which points a sharp satirical barb at American liberty and freedom.

"Uncle Ben," says I, "I calculate you have a Nigger to sell?" "Yes, I have a Nigger, I guess. Will you buy the Nigger." "Oh, yes! if he is a good Nigger, I will, I reckon; but this is a Land of liberty and freedom, and as every man has a right to buy a Nigger, what do you want for your Nigger?" "Why, as you say, Jonathan," says Uncle Ben, "this is a land of freedom and independence, and as every man has a right to sell his Niggers, I want sixty dollars and twenty-five cents."

Later on, Mathews, with the help of Richard Peake, will develop the satire in this brief sequence into a full-length farce and call it *Jonathan in England.*

Another type-character of importance introduced in *Trip to America* is the American Negro in the persons of Maxmillan and Agamemnon. "I shall be rich in black fun," Mathews had promised in his letters from America. "I have studied their broken English carefully. It is considered the real thing even by the Yankees." Mathews maintained that his character of Agamemnon was drawn from real life: "a very fat Negro, whom I met, driving a stage-coach, and urging his horses by different tunes on a fiddle, while he ingeniously fastened the reins around his neck."

---

[16] A final "s" was later added to this name. Note the comic fun in the original form: Doubikin=Do-be-kin; this paints the ironic relationship in the same way as does Jonathan, the nephew of John Bull.

To conclude his piece and at the same time show his best characters in one scene, Mathews performed what he called a "monopolylogue," a burlesque skit titled *All Well at Natchitoches.* Where did he run across this Indian name? His cast included Colonel Hiram Peglar, a Kentucky shoemaker; Agamemnon, a poor runaway Negro; Jonathan W. Doubikin, a real Yankee; Monsieur Capot, a French emigrant tailor; Miss Mange Wurzel, a Dutch heiress; and Mr. O'Sullivan, an Irish improver of his fortune. Certainly no better display of his versatile talents could be found to round off the evening.

Mathews' method of presenting *Trip to America* was highly individual. The general notion of this intimate style of comedy came down from Garrick's contemporary, Samuel Foote, the best mimic of the eighteenth century,[17] with whom Mathews was often compared, but such entertainments as *Trip to America* were his own invention. The only stage properties were an armchair and a reading lamp, to provide the atmosphere of an evening "At Home." Against this intimate background Mathews recounted his adventures in mimicry, anecdote, and song, and spiced them with comic dances, lightning off-stage costume changes, and an occasional bit of ventriloquism. A good deal of the novelty in *Trip to America* derives from the use of Yankee, Negro, Dutch, Irish, Scotch, and French dialects. The American tones, pronunciation, and phraseology, critics reported, were amusing to English ears: "The way in which the assent of 'O Yes,' and the dissent of 'O No' were given by genu-ine Yankees, always told; and the being 'pretty particular considerable damned' over everything, never failed to excite that sound so pleasing to an actor's ear—bursts of laughter."[18] In addition, each character had its individual costuming, usually copied from life. Mathews declared that Jonathan's dress, which consisted of a large straw hat, a sealskin waistcoat, and a heavy greenish-brown cloth coat reaching to his feet, was a replica of clothing worn by a New England farmer he had seen aboard a Hudson River packet.

The characters in *Trip to America* take on additional life when we understand more of Mathews' individual style of acting. His face was heavily lined, accenting strongly his inner character and

[17] Percy Fitzgerald, *Samuel Foote*, pp. 61–65.
[18] *The Literary Gazette*, March 27, 1824.

feeling. His manner was dry, intimate, and familiar. Although Hazlitt characterized Mathews' performance as "manually dexterous," as more dependent on the external characteristics of gait, facial expression, and catch phrases than on any subtle appeal to the mind,[19] Leigh Hunt thought even his commonest imitations were not superficial. "Something of the mind and character of the individual were always insinuated, often with a dramatic dressing, and plenty of *sauce piquante.*"[20] Hazlitt believed Mathews' best imitations were based upon something characteristic or absurd that had caught his fancy. The comedian was adept at the "loutish stare of rustic simplicity" and "the artful leer of vulgar cunning" so often seen in his low-country characters such as coachmen, landlords, and probably in Jonathan. Mathews' acting style would probably be characterized today as vaudeville technique combined with a realistic mimicry of people he found in everyday life. It is difficult to imagine the versatility of such an actor as Mathews. To give a dozen diverse characters a distinct identity in a single evening is indeed no mean accomplishment.

The significance of *Trip to America* is twofold. Mathews drew a satirical picture of the American scene at a time when we had scarcely begun to realize our distinctive differences. As an outsider looking in he had caught with imagination much of the outward show of American life of the 1820's, and had pointed the finger of ridicule in the best comedy tradition. But equally important is the rare opportunity he gives us to look at his two selves—the actor and the man. Seldom have we had this relationship so nicely set out, for through this sequence of an actual trip and then the report on it, we are able to distinguish this double personality and we can see both sides more clearly. A great comedian on stage can tell us much about life, but knowing him off the stage—knowing his weaknesses, his fears, his good and bad humors—gives his work double focus.

How accurate was Mathews' image of America? Certainly the sketches appear to follow closely the observations in the letters, although he had greatly softened his views of the lower classes. With allowances made for the exaggerations of vaudeville humor, Mathews himself assuredly thought he was presenting an honest

[19] William Hazlitt, "Mr. Mathews at Home," *London Magazine*, 5 (May, 1820), 179–183.
[20] Hunt, *Autobiography*, p. 166.

view that would help, not hurt, relations between the two countries.
How wrong he was! He had unquestionably disturbed many Americans. Was his pointing too broad, too obvious? Washington Irving
records attending a performance and finding it "stupid and tedious."[21] When Mathews played *Trip* during his second tour of
America in 1834 the high tension of the 1820's had largely abated.
On that occasion the *Mirror* reported that people laughed at the
jokes, good, bad, and indifferent, and yawned where they found it
dull.

4

Jonathan in England, the second piece culled from Mathews' American tour, first performed at the English Opera House later the
same year (September 3, 1824), is quite a different matter. Mathews
put it together in collaboration with Richard Peake. Here is no
gentle, friendly satire, but a barbed, finger-pointing, overt travesty
of American democratic life. Its hard look not only outraged Americans, keenly wounded at what they regarded as Mathews' unfairness, but engendered so direct a protest in London that Mathews
withdrew the piece and never played it again, despite his thinking
it only a "harmless laugh" at Americans. In 1833 James Hackett
disinterred this play, removed the offensive sections, and turned it
back at the English as a countersatire.[22] In 1824, however, with the
Second War for Independence only a few years removed, it was
simply written off as bad taste. Were the sentiments expressed in
this play a more accurate statement of how Mathews really felt
about Jonathan? *Trip* was full of the same good fun and friendly
laughter he had evoked with the Irish, the Scotch, and the French
in the other *At Homes*, and only the supersensitive took it poorly.
But there was something mean in this second piece, something not
quite laughable, because it pointed out too blatantly the sharply

---

[21] When Irving went backstage afterwards, sending word ahead to Mathews
that an American wished to see him, the actor came rushing out of his dressing
room in a state of nervous excitement. He was greatly relieved to discover that
his visitor was only the American writer. "My God! Irving, is it you, my dear
fellow? I am very glad to see you." Irving smilingly acknowledged Mathews'
relieved welcome and chided him, "Confess that you expected to find a tall
Kentuckian with a gun on his shoulder."
[22] See Chapter 8 of this study for Hackett's use of this play.

defined incongruity between the idealistic expression of American freedom of the common man and the blight and ill-conscience of Negro slavery. Here was the dichotomy of American life, and the subject was too torridly controversial to handle on the stage. By rubbing the American sore, Mathews' love of the real thing on the stage violated the code of the day that allowed only good fun and spurned problem plays. His strong feelings burst the bounds of satire and emerged as political diatribe. Was this his conclusive statement on his disenchantment with American democracy? If so, could the play have succeeded had Peake been more subtle, less overt, in the dialogue?

Mathews tells us much about how *Jonathan in England* was put together.[23] The intention was to recast Jonathan Doubikin in *Trip* into conventional play form, with the Mathews' travel notes again the basis for the ordering of incident and dialogue. R. B. Peake, regarded by many as the best writer of farce in England at that time, set to work under Mathews' guidance, employing the word list from the glossary in Humphreys' *The Yankey in England* which Mathews had brought home with him. The musical-farce that emerged[24] showed bumbling, country Jonathan just arrived in Liverpool from America with his Negro slave Agamemnon. He is met by Mr. Ledger, a Liverpool merchant, who gives him a letter of recommendation to Sir Leatherlip Grossfeeder, a Common Councilman in London. During the night before Jonathan starts for the city two postilions rob the larder in his room; when they are discovered they rush off in their haste with Jonathan's letter, leaving behind them their own recommendations as lackeys, which Mr. Ledger has also written. Jonathan goes to London, shows the wrong letter, and is taken for one of the postilions. The usual mistaken-identity game now begins, with Sir Leatherlip thinking his new servant most insolent. After a series of shenanigans Jonathan is finally identified. In a subplot an American settled in London, Mr. Delapierre, finally wins Mary, the ward of Sir Leatherlip. The plot is thus entirely conventional. But this is not the life of

---

[23] Mathews, *Memoirs*, III, 583 ff.
[24] The play was published under the original title in the late 1820's. The version used for discussion here is the original manuscript version approved for performance by the Lord Chamberlain on September 1, 1824.

the piece. It is the Jonathan-Agamemnon controversy over slavery and freedom that gives the play significance for us. This may well be the first antislavery play.

Only by examining the dialogue in detail can we see why the Mathews-Peake satire seemed so belligerent. The comedy begins with Mathews smiling at himself as Jonathan resolves to keep a revenge diary on English manners. "I'll touch 'em up in an atarnal manner that's what I will. My blud is up. I'm pretty considerable darn'd mad about that Mathers[25] who I hear has taken me off at the playhouse, but I'll make the whole kingdom smart for it when my book is published." And he makes his first exaggerated and overly simplified entries from what he sees in the Waterloo Hotel: "Hotel . . . havn't got no bars; no comfortable chairs throughout the whole kingdom of England. All head waiters in England are called Tidys." He refers to the Uncle Ben story which Mathews had used in *Trip to America*, notes that tobacco is not used in England, and exits singing "Yankee Doodle." Jonathan is soon back again, however, and this time with Agamemnon, who sings "Possum Up a Gum Tree," another *Trip* song. Jonathan now declares to Mr. Ledger his intention of selling Agamemnon to the highest bidder. "It hurts my feelings to part with him, but durn it, I want the dollars, and perhaps he will get a Boss that won't thump him so much as I have done. Uncle Ben leathered him pretty considerable more than I did tho." When Ledger mildly protests, Jonathan, thinking he is being insulted, goes into a tirade: "We Yankees have got hard heads. We wan't brought up in the woods to be scart at an owl in an ivy bush. You can't scare me so, nor make me not luv my country, with all its forts. Its a notion deal better than eny other I know'd on." When Ledger denies insulting him, Jonathan replies, "I don't mistake; you mistake yourself. You've got the wrong sow by the ear. I'm a free-born American, father was a free-born American, Uncle Ben was a free-born American, and wont I stan by em too stiff as a poker." When Ledger argues that Jonathan is unreasonable to become so angry over nothing, Jonathan replies, "I guess I b'ent, I'm glad I b'ent, and I don't incline to when everything mads me so." Then he notes in his diary that English people are so passionate

[25] A reference to Mathews in *Trip to America*.

they don't mind offending their best friends. Jonathan tries to sell
Agamemnon to Tidy, a waiter in the hotel, in exchange for a horse,
and the Negro pleads with Tidy to buy him. The Yankee gets so
noisy that Tidy asks him to leave, which occasions an example of
Jonathan's stubbornness. "I won't budge, if I hant a mind ter."
So he is pushed out. That night at the inn when Mrs. Lemon asks
if the "black gentleman" wants a bed, Jonathan laughs at her
polite name for the Negro and her solicitude for a slave who sleeps
on the ground.

When Mathews and Peake confuse Jonathan with the postilion,
there may have been more than simple plotting in mind. As we
watch him in the next scenes he is shown in comparison as more
vulgar, more insolent, more crude than the lowest of the English
servant class. Sir Leatherlip is disgusted with his insolence. Later,
Jonathan is specifically contrasted with the Butler in Sir Leatherlip's household when he accidentally enters the Butler's room and
mistakes its occupant for a friend of the family. The Butler has been
kidding Blanche, the Negro maid, about her color, but it is light
banter compared to what follows. In discussing politics with the
Butler, the Yankee has a chance to further express his ideas on
liberty and freedom, and when he sees the Negress at the table he
notes in his diary, "English members of the Congress drink tea
freely with their female niggers." When Agamemnon appears and
the Butler shows sympathy toward him, Doubikins is again outraged. He argues that the Butler should buy Agamemnon, and, to
make the offer more attractive, he explains that under Virginia law
any little Agamemnons will become the property of the Butler.
After Jonathan departs Blanche tells her Negro friend, "Dere be no
slave in dis country. Moment you put you foot on shore here, in
England, you free!" Agamemnon questions this. "Free? Free? What
is dat? We hear de name in America, but we don't know what it is."

BLANCHE.   You Massa is not you massa. No more. If he tump you, you
            tump again.
AGA.   Oh! Oh! Oh! I cry wid joy. (Cries. Stops.)
BLANCHE.   Hush! Don't make noise. You free gentleman now.
AGA.   O, but if I cussed, Jantan beats me again?
BLANCHE.   If he beat you, catch him beat you here. You swear de salt

> peace against him and constable take him up to public office
> in Bow Street.
>
> AGA. Oh nice country England. God sake de King! Rule Britannia!
> Give me kiss you sweet moonshine sun flower. (Kisses her.)

In the last scene of the play Sir Leatherlip discloses that Mary's
fortune has been wiped out in a bank failure in New York. Sir
Leatherlip is again outraged when Jonathan enters with a cigar in
his mouth and starts talking economics with him. When the Yankee
lights the cigar at the gasometer Lady Grossfeeder has set up to
help society with scientific experiments, the equipment explodes.
The police arrive to arrest Doubikins, and in the flurry of a farce
ending the mistaken identity is revealed. A crash in the closet discloses Agamemnon and Blanche together. But when Jonathan
threatens to beat his slave, Agamemnon talks back: "You punish!
Pooh! Massa boss, I free, I put my foot in it." American deception
and dishonesty are given one last thrust when Jonathan reports
that Mary's money is not lost, that the company did not fail, that
Uncle Ben put it in the paper because he wanted to buy stock at a
cheap price in Baltimore. Delapierre, who proposed to Mary when
he thought she had lost her money, is now able to piously denounce
Uncle Ben's trick as fraudulent and to argue that it is a mistake to
assume that all men in America are dishonest.

Jonathan in England was an "ingenious" farce to Mathews. He
could see nothing in it that was not considered in America a fair
subject for laughter. But he was quick to shift some of the blame
from himself to Peake by crediting him with the plot and "every
sentence in the other characters." Did he imply by "other" that
Jonathan's dialogue was his own invention? He had also invented
Agamemnon. And to disperse the blame even further he points a
rude finger at General Humphreys, whose Yankee word glossary
had been used as a speech model. And he had also exploited
Humphreys' definition of the Yankee character.[26] "Wicked man,"
writes Mathews with sly innuendo, "to caricature his own countrymen in such wretched style and clumsy fashion, and to lead the
English into error! Fie, fie, Humphries!"[27] Yet try as he would to
throw responsibilities on others, there was no question that *Jonathan*

[26] See Chapter 3, Section 3.
[27] Mathews, *Memoirs*, III, 540.

in England was Mathews' bald statement on American life and manners. He had found little to complain about in the upper orders who, he asserted, were very little different from people he knew at home. And this he represented in the play through the character of Delapierre. But the lower orders, as we see constantly in the diaries, were an entirely different matter. Jonathan was an uncouth, stupid, witless, dishonest, stubborn, easily insulted, unmannerly braggart, lost in a civilized society, a Negro beater, and a mockery of true democracy.

Jonathan in England reflected Mathews' deep pessimism about the Great Experiment. What a contrast this play made with the mildness of *Trip to America*, which had been designed to generate good feeling between England and the United States. Jonathan in small, superficial doses was harmless; on an extended scale—oversimplified and exaggerated—he took on a new, harsh reality. The grave and severe objection to the Mathews-Peake farce may have been partially credited to the truth it spoke. Mathews had two reports to make on America, but only one was palatable from the stage of the times. Realism or Romanticism? The battle of styles in the nineteenth century is well underway.

part 2 Borrowing and Innovation

James H. Hackett: The First Native
Yankee in London

WHAT WAS the contribution of James Henry Hackett (1800–
1871) to Yankee theatre? In the decade of his creative activity from
1826 to 1836 he established the Yankee as the significant American
character type on the stage. As the first native comedy actor of
prominence, he took his incentive, direction, and something of his
style from Charles Mathews; but once he saw the possibilities of
what he could make of it himself, he moved quickly in original
directions. Without the eccentric, creative imagination of a first-
line artist, but with more of a businessman's practical hardheaded-
ness of what would go, Hackett plunged headlong into fashioning an
indigenous form of comedy for a stage that still looked almost entirely to England for its product. He wrote himself, encouraged
other Americans to write for him, and dared the tradition and awe
of the London stage as no American actor had done before. He
pursued the Mathews' line of satire and capitulated to the growing
desire for romantic story plays only when competition and practical
concerns forced him to turn in that direction.

Hackett was no New Englander. To him a Yankee was an American with the mask off. Like others in the New York coterie of which
he was a part, he saw the stage type as a means of telling others
about this new race of people only recently descended from Europeans but quite different in manners, mind, and spirit. James
Hackett's Yankee was the American common man of the 1830's

raised to the artificial, caricatured level of farce comedy. As a living comic-strip character he had more reality than the real thing. And Hackett gave to Englishmen, as he gave to Americans at home, a not very commendable image of what the new man was like. That the Americans of his time found it highly amusing, that Englishmen were disturbed, even outraged by it, is adequate testimony to the force of the image he created. Undoubtedly it made a difference that it was an American handling this tender subject. George Hill would surpass him in authenticity, and Marble and Silsbee would carry his image much farther afield, but it is to James Hackett that we must turn for that first, crude, native image of Americans, living and breathing in the person of a live actor on the stage.

If James H. Hackett's guest-star appearance at London's Covent Garden Theatre on April 5, 1827, in the first performance by an American actor in London as an American character, could be considered an augury, Yankee theatre was certainly doomed to total failure and oblivion. So utterly complete was the rejection of Hackett's Yankee by both audience and newspaper critics that anybody with less character than Hackett would have abandoned this low-comedy device then and there. The theatre reviews of that evening, which incidentally provide the first body of criticism on Hackett's work as an actor, paradoxically made the American comedian the villain and Charles Mathews the hero. While they mercilessly tore Hackett's performance to shreds in ostensibly reporting the reactions of the audience, they lauded the English comedian for his American characters. Though perhaps not as accurate as Hackett's, they thought the art Mathews had shown in putting them on the stage with animation and delight an illuminating contrast to Hackett's utter dullness as an impossible bore. Here was the overt warning that was to hover near Hackett in his second appearance in London in 1832, a warning to which he might have listened had it not been for his Yankee stubbornness and determination.

Much of Hackett's character is revealed on this important occasion in 1827, at once a summation point from which to see what he had done as an actor up to this date and a point of departure for his development of the Yankee character in the years following. London could not know that James Hackett would become the principal American comedian for the next half century, and would make famous on the stage not only the Yankee, but the backwoodsman

Nimrod Wildfire, the Dutchman Rip Van Winkle, and Shakespeare's Falstaff.

It was a confident Hackett who went to London in the fall of 1826. There is no evidence to tell us why he made the trip, but we can conjecture that he wanted to learn more about the business of comedy acting by watching the best of the English in this line; to find comic material he could perform; and, one can imagine knowing Hackett's ambitions, to get an engagement in London which, whether it was successful or not, could help greatly in bolstering his growing reputation at home by giving him the London label, so important if a native actor was to make any headway against the enveloping tide of English actors coming to America. What he took with him that could encourage a London manager to stand sponsor was a somewhat spotty record garnered from a few performances at the Park Theatre after his debut there only a few months previous (March 1, 1826), a few positive mentions in the press, and a sense of opportunism that was to be strongly characteristic of his long life on the stage.

How he finagled his evening at Covent Garden we do not know unless we accept the explanation offered by the *London Examiner* that he had volunteered for the evening "purely for his own amusement" and without a view to any engagement, with the time of his departure for America previously fixed before arrangements were concluded.[1] Other reviewers seemed to take for granted that he would again appear, perhaps as a regular member of the company. Hackett's reception undoubtedly put a quietus on this, however, even had it been in the offing if he were successful. Perhaps his most effective drawing card was his status as the first American actor who had visited London.[2] Moreover, he was not only capable of giving a firsthand view of the American character, but he could also satisfy London's curiosity about what Americans were doing in the field of acting. Few Londoners of the time knew any Americans and very little about America. Here was an opportunity to put both on show. One reviewer of the evening preferred to look at

[1] *London Examiner*, April 8, 1827.

[2] John Howard Payne had, of course, appeared on the London stage in 1813. He was not advertised as an American until his second performance, nor did he perform anything that could be labeled an American play. The fact that he shortly afterwards abandoned acting for a career of writing leaves to James Hackett the honor of first consideration as a serious American actor in London.

Hackett's performance as a specimen of free trade which ought to
be productive of good feelings between Englishmen and Americans.
Had communications been in that day what they are now, and
Americans at home had discovered how Hackett was treated, instead
of consolatory feelings, Hackett's reception might have provoked an
international crisis. When the Yankee comedian went to England in
1826, he was a representative American, and before that fatal night
London audiences had been ready to give him a hearing.

2

James Hackett's background merits some detailed treatment at this
point because it gives us a clear picture of how the early native
actor found his way to the stage. He was far from being an established star when he made his first excursion abroad, for he had been
acting only a few months and had scarcely begun to know his business. Like other young Americans who went on the stage during
this period, Hackett did not come of an acting family. His background was solid middle class, a circumstance that would ordinarily
have led to a much different professional career. Hackett's lineage
was a good one.[3] The family roots derived from one of the Norman
barons under William the Conqueror and the title, now dormant,
had been passed down as Hackett of Hacketts'-town, County Carlow,
and Shelton Abbey, County Wicklow.[4] He was descended on his
mother's side from the Reverend Abraham Keteltas of Jamaica,
Long Island, a native lineage that afforded him indirect connections
with the Duanes, the Beekmans, the Roosevelts, and the DePysters.[5]
Young Hackett could hardly have had better connections in a city
still controlled, as was also a good deal of the upstate area, by Dutch
families. His father, who had moved to New York from Holland,
where he had been a lieutenant in the Life Guards of the Prince of
Orange, died when the boy was scarcely three, and he was brought

[3] Hackett's early background has been rather thoroughly treated elsewhere. See
Montrose Moses, *Famous Actor Families in America*; R. Osgood Mason, *Sketches
and Impressions*, II, 259–268; William Winter, *The Wallet of Time*; John
Durand, "Souvenirs of Hackett the Actor," *Galaxy*, XIV (October, 1872), 550 ff.;
Joseph Ireland, *Records of the New York Stage*; "Mr. James Hackett," *Tallis's
Drawing-Room Table Book* (1851), pp. 36–37; James Hackett, *Notes, Criticisms,
and Correspondence upon Shakespeare's Plays and Actors*.
[4] See *Mirror*, XVII (November 16, 1839), 167, for James Hackett's actual
assumption of the title on the death of his cousin.
[5] Moses, *Famous Actor Families in America*, pp. 144 ff.

up by his mother and her family. He began his schooling at Union Hall Academy. Later, he attended Columbia College, but after a serious illness he left school, began reading law with General Robert Bogardus, and shortly thereafter became a clerk for Abraham K. Fish, a wholesaler in groceries. At nineteen he married Catharine Lee Sugg,[6] an ingenue in the Park Theatre company. So begins his direct association with the stage. When Hackett later turned to acting, she was an important asset, and they played as a team for many years. She acted roles in all his new stage pieces and accounted in no small degree for their success. "Her merry, romping country lasses," writes Ireland, who held her in high regard, "have never since been equalled, and her chambermaids were almost meritorious."[7]

We begin to sense the realistic Yankee in Hackett when he took up trading in Utica, New York, a thriving upstate, frontier town west of Albany, reached from New York via the Hudson and Mohawk Rivers. In 1820 fortunes could be made by sharp, ambitious bargainers, and Hackett had good connections in New York, besides a Yankee's knack for a quick deal. Groceries, earthenware, tea, wines, and liquors were the main items of his business which supplied the extensive area from Utica northwest to Oswego, Sackett's Harbor, and the Ontario posts. In five years he turned a profit of $18,000. Even more valuable were the contacts he made with people and situations, experiences which later undoubtedly provided the rich background for his comedy delineations. The western New England Yankee from Vermont and western Massachusetts was commonly seen in this area during the early twenties when the migration to western New York and Ohio was extensively underway. How better could anyone meet Yankees than in the trading business, where one was sure to encounter all the traits of character distinguishing the New Englander from the natives of other sections, where the talk, the argument, the sheer bargaining must

[6] Joseph Ireland spells her name as one word, viz. Leesugg, and this form has been frequently followed. Hackett himself refers to the name as "Lee Sugg."
[7] In *Fifty Years of a Play-Goer's Journal*, Ireland is frequently excessively complimentary, captured as he was by the glamor of the stage. This is more than his customary effusion and indicates the extent of her charm. One son was born to the Hacketts, John Hackett. Mrs. Hackett died at Jamaica, Long Island, on December 5, 1845. Hackett later remarried and had a second son, James K. Hackett, who won star status during the early years of the present century.

have been daily business. Hackett was at the impressionable age, and this open, independent existence must have seemed far different from the conventional, well-ordered life of his New York Dutch background.

Was it ambition for greater profits or merely the desire to return to the excitement of city life that took the Hacketts back to New York City again in the spring of 1825. Whatever it was, this time he is not so lucky. Within a few months he was in a financial jam from which he escaped only by the intercession of Luman Reed, an elderly friend of long standing with whom Hackett had done business. Reed helped him liquidate his property and avoid bankruptcy with its disgrace and criminal penalties. In 1826 he looked out on the world again in the same financial status as when he had departed for Utica five years earlier.[8] It was at this point that Hackett decided to become an actor.

James Hackett made his first appearance on the professional stage at the Park Theatre on March 1, 1826. Acting was not entirely unknown to him. His wife had certainly introduced him to theatre circles, but before his marriage he had participated in amateur theatricals.[9] Durand would have us believe that he even told Yankee stories previous to his formal stage appearance. This is credible in view of Hackett's bright humor and social capabilities. It is entirely possible that an evening's party could have drawn forth a Utica adventure, a song, a story, and perhaps it was on one of these occasions that Luman Reed and many of the other New York businessmen who later attended Hackett's openings as a testimonial of their support for the young actor saw him perform. Nevertheless, despite their good wishes the inexperienced Hackett did not enjoy a successful debut.[10] Nine days later, however, his fortunes changed for the better when he played a well-received program of *Sylvester Daggerwood* with imitations of Mathews, Kean, Hilson, and Barnes, and told the "Story of Uncle Ben"—the same program he gave at his London appearance at Covent Garden. For his debut he played Justice Woodcock in *Love in A Village*,

---

[8] Durand ("Souvenirs of Hackett the Actor," *Galaxy*, XIV [October, 1872], 550 ff) has the best account of this.

[9] It is usually reported that he had first tried acting at the age of sixteen when he played under the stage name of "Young" in a Newark theatre.

[10] One of his biographers attributed his failure to "extreme nervousness." See Hackett, *Notes*, p. 336.

but we see that on March 10 he was already busy at imitations and storytelling—the Mathews' style of entertainment. It was in October of the same year that Hackett's mimicry attracted unusual attention as he played Dromio of Ephesus in a version of Shakespeare's *Comedy of Errors*. He imitated Barnes, the other Dromio, so precisely that every person who has written about Hackett has remarked on this singular performance.

It was Hackett's particular association with the Yankee characters, however, that began to attract attention. He repeated his "Uncle Ben" story in June, July,[11] and probably several times during the fall previous to his departure for Europe in early November. What stimulated the use of this material? Did it come directly from Mathews? He must have seen the English comedian in several performances during the latter's tour in 1823–1824, for he is ready to imitate him before audiences that still have a fresh memory of his eccentric style. If the notation on Hackett's manuscript of "Uncle Ben" is to be believed,[12] he met Mathews during his tour and told him the story of "Uncle Ben and the Squirrel Hunt," which the English actor used in *Trip to America*. Was "Uncle Ben" really Hackett's original property? Even if it did belong first to him he was undoubtedly encouraged in its use by Mathews' big success with it in London. We find Mathews so continuously peeking through the Hackett façade from this point forward that it is easy to conclude that the American comedian found his model there and proceeded to copy it. When Hackett goes to London it is a second, and lesser, Mathews that the critics see on the stage. He could not completely borrow the Mathews' form of entertainment in the *At Homes*, but he could do much the same thing with imitations, costumes, and stories in a similar format. This he proceeded to do in *Sylvester Daggerwood*. He went even further and borrowed such regular Mathews pieces as *Monsieur Morbleu* and *Monsieur Mallet*. Hackett's opportunist sense told him that if he wished to be successful as a comedian, he must work in the prevailing popular style, and in this there was none better than Mathews. As an "American" Mathews he could hold a singular position in comedy.

This was Hackett's background when he journeyed to England.

[11] George C. D. Odell, *Annals of the New York Stage*, III, 192.
[12] Enthoven Collection, Victoria and Albert Museum. " 'Uncle Ben' as related by me to Mr. Mathews in New York in 1822."

His pretension to the position as "leading American comic actor" had much of the puff about it. Nevertheless, in an area where few natives had tried their hand, he was left standing pretty much by himself, and he could indeed claim to be the best. His Yankee sense of humor, together with his business sense, which could well be the same thing, made it seem entirely logical.

3

Hackett himself prepared *Sylvester Daggerwood* for the Covent Garden performance. He borrowed and rearranged to his own purpose an old play in the English repertoire, *New Hay at the Old Market*, for many years known popularly as *Sylvester Daggerwood*. Though it had once been a legitimate play about a Dunstable actor going up to London, over the years it had acquired an acting tradition which permitted its performer to mimic other actors, to introduce any stage character, or to tell any stories the actor performing the piece might think entertaining to an audience. It was a format which could give Hackett a dramatic unity while he ran through a variety program, expanding, contracting, or shifting parts of it while the performance was in progress. This device also permitted costume changes to support different dialect characters in the accepted Mathews' style.

In Hackett's arrangement of the piece, Fustian, a young playwright, is waiting to see a London manager about his new play when Sylvester Daggerwood, who has been traveling as an actor in America,[13] arrives to see about a London engagement. We first hear him offstage in the Yankee character he has sketched while abroad, as he prepares the specimens he is to offer the manager. Then, on he comes, singing a Yankee tune in a nasal twang. The remainder of the piece is composed of Hackett's Yankee stories; his character of Hans Knickerbocker, the American Dutchman "in the costume of the Dutch Settlers in the western part of the State of New York, a pipe in his hand"; imitations of Edmund Kean and Charles Macready; and, as he apparently played it in London (no other characters are mentioned in the reviews), a return to the situation of Fustian and the Dunstable actor, with Fustian complaining that

---

[13] Was this a take-off on Mathews?

such stories the actor has told will not do for his tragedy. Later, when Hackett played the piece in America, he noted the time of representation as about fifty-five to sixty minutes. In his London engagement *The Wife's Strategem* opened the program, Hackett followed, and the evening was concluded with *The Hundred-Pound Note*.

Why was Hackett so bold as to think he could get up such a piece on his own with the expectation of pleasing a critical London audience? Did he really think it had the flavor and content of a Charles Mathews' *At Home*? Only his utter confidence, brought about by his success at home, and a sort of brash actor's courage could have led him to such a position, for certainly he must have been fully aware that Mathews always employed a professional writer to help him put his entertainments together and that much of what was presented in the artful *At Homes* was the result of hardheaded planning and careful sifting of available material. Yet we find Hackett requesting permission for performance from the Lord Chamberlain with a playscript of highly questionable form and value.[14] It is no wonder that one critic was induced to remark that "the performance had little or no resemblance to anything yet represented on any stage."[15] A less emotional reviewer excused Hackett's failure on the basis of "want of arrangement rather than talent," that without some narrative in the Mathews' manner in which to set the Yankee stories, the audience could not be expected to penetrate the eccentric, peculiar, highly foreign world they represented.[16] This may be Hackett's first foray in the theatre as a playwright, but it certainly is not the last; he was to continue to work at his own stage materials for a number of years.

But if Hackett could not be excused for the obscurity of his presentation, who could possibly have prepared the indigenous material for him? No one. That was the Yankee-theatre actor's problem. And it is part of the description of what this theatre was as an American *commedia dell'arte*, as an actor's theatre of imagination and invention. Hackett in preparing his own materials was proceed-

[14] Lord Chamberlain's Collection, No. 42883, British Museum. Hackett's name appears as author on the first page.
[15] *Morning Chronicle*, April 6, 1827.
[16] *The Examiner* (London), April 8, 1827.

ing in the only way he could. Only later when he had encouraged others to write materials for him could he fall back on the less hazardous, and also less potentially inventive, prepared script.

Hackett's master notebook in which he wrote his adaptation of *Sylvester Daggerwood* is a mine of information on the whole process of the Yankee actor at work on his own materials.[17] Besides the complete copy of the script, which includes materials Hackett did not use in London but may possibly have employed in playing the Dunstable actor elsewhere, the handwritten manuscript contains (1) some notes of a specific nature related to the play, (2) a list of stories, (3) and a brief but very explicit statement on Hackett's notion of the Yankee character.

The notes are of primary interest because they not only help date the manuscript, but they demonstrate the accordionlike structure of Hackett's piece and how he approached it in the acting, together with the editing for the London performance. The first two notes bear Hackett's initials.

[1] The whole of these sketches are seldom given in one night, but varied according to the humor of the audience and the actor at the time of representation.

[2] These sketches are as near, as I can commit them to paper, to what I give them on the stage. I frequently vary the *order* of some of the incidents from the difficulty of committing my own nonsense to memory, and consequently, are more embellished at one time than another, as my *humour* may dictate.

[3] Instead—here introduce Imitation of Kean in his first soliloquy in Richard—& Exit.

This last note is inserted before one of the sketches not performed in London and is signed T.R.C.G. & R/A. Was this Richard Arnold, Manager of Covent Garden Theatre? If so, together with the first entries, it offers evidence that this was the manuscript Hackett had in London with him. A fourth item included in the notebook, and further evidence in support of its early dating, is the 1826 cast of the sketch when it was performed in New York: Sylvester—Mr. Hackett; Fustian—Placide; Servant—Nexsen.

The list of stories is even more revealing of the potential of Hackett's stage activity. The entries are merely rough notes and

[17] Enthoven Collection, Victoria and Albert Museum.

stand uninterpolated. In the light of *Sylvester Daggerwood*, however, these titles, phrases, and quoted lines appear to be alternate story possibilities which Hackett did not think necessary to set down in words.

Frenchman Rec^t to kill flies
Methodist Priest & the Fiddle
Yankee & Dutchman dividing a hog
Honce and Towcob (sic) joining the meeting
The Stuttering gentleman who picked up scraps of paper
Abram Bishop, Visit to S. Carolina, Governor Rutlege
Mons Mallet & the Letter
Capt Benson & Van Neoyer
Kentuckian consent to marry his daughter Sal
   "Who had—a *black* bastard—but had had two
   white ones since"—
Dutchman & the two Yankee boys, or "Dat is sam
   strong powder"![18]

The list is most intriguing as one tries to imagine what Hackett would have done with them. "Mons. Mallet and the letter" later became, in an expanded form, one of his most successful sketches.

Hackett's notes on the Yankee character are unique. They provide the only description by a native actor of this regional type in this early period of invention and discovery. These rough notes are not particularly original, in ideas, but they give in a very precise statement the character points Hackett thought important to demonstrate on the stage.

The *Yankees* are
Enterprising and *hardy—cunning* in *bargains—back out* without *regard to honour—superstitious* and *bigoted—simple* in *dress* and *manners —mean* to degree in *expenditures—free* of *decep.—familiar* and *inquisitive*, very fond of telling *long* stories without any *point*, which just as they appear to approach is diverted by some new digression—when they finish, will laugh *themselves*, and never care whether the listener does or not—the only sure way of knowing when they are done is their throwing away a chip or stick, which they invariably keep whittling

---

[18] I have omitted three entries in this list because of the illegibility of the writing or confusion as to their meaning. They look like this:
   "I arra weak g on felt afore"; "Want my money now!"
   "So it seems to me"

while telling a story, and putting their *knife* in their waistcoat pocket, after sitting an hour on a wood-pile—

In view of Hackett's upstate New York background and his consequent touch with Yankees these notes are significant in the detail they offer of the new process of "going to life" for the character. To London audiences Hackett's Yankee might seem like a strange, unreal, half-imaginary person. Here is evidence, however, to support the closeness of observation Hackett thought necessary in reconstructing such a type for the stage. It is perhaps just this realistic touch that gets him into trouble with the London audience, for, unlike Mathews, he had not yet learned how to make art from life, how to separate the symbol from reality. Hackett had apparently done very little thinking about these things, and he approached the preparation of his materials without the experience and the know-how that had made Mathews' "caricatured reality" the toast of the London stage. The "American Mathews" had a very great deal to discover about the business of comedy performance.

Appended to the playscript is a supplement which contains a Mathews-like female impersonation, Uncle Ben's wife, Jonathan's Aunt Coziah Freelove. Hackett apparently never played this sketch. It is significant because it shows the extent of Hackett's borrowing from Mathews, who always included female impersonations in his comic annuals. It is also the only extant record of a Yankee actor considering such an impersonation.[19]

In the wide range of materials included in *Sylvester Daggerwood,* it is, of course, the Yankee stories which are of primary interest. In the slow nasal drawl of New England country speech, Hackett's Jonathan tells how he gets lost on a trip to New York. This reminds him of a story about Deacon Bigelow's mare. He then relates his adventures while trying to buy a gown for his sister Tabitha.

You see, when I was there in New York I tried to *hunt* up a *curious nice* gown for sister Tabitha, aginst the boys come *bundling* and sparking on it with her, and as I went looking into the shops for one—I snore! if the folks didn't keep following me and staring and giggling, and I turned right about upon one on 'em: and I guess, I gin him his own and a

---

[19] The lone possible exception is Yankee Hill in *Seth Slope, or Done for a Hundred.* The assumption of female dress is only a momentary masquerade, however, and no attempt is made to actually impersonate a female character.

leetle more too—says I "You had better go to home, I reckon!" and a trading looking feller come up, and ketch'd hold on thy green eel-skin, and asced me what I tied my hair with such a thing for. "Why," says I, "You darn'd fool, to make my hair grow to be sure"—but says I, "if you have taken sich a notion to it, I'll sell it to you, or any think else I got—now," says I, "if you want to speculate, jest go with me to my waggon. I got plenty of *wooden nutmegs*—tinware, *wooden* bowls— right good blue clay indigo, *horn* gun flints, and *mustard* seed. . . . Now, you *do* want to buy some, don't you? Oh, you don't, do you? Yes! You *do* don't you? La?"—"No," says he, "well then" says I, "be oft! for if you don't, I guess *I* will"—for I began to grown a lettle skeared among 'em.

After telling this story, Hackett shifted to another Yankee yarn about an adventure while fishing with brother Joe off New York during the last war, and how they were brought to be questioned by Commander Hardy for approaching too near the British squadron. Their fish and boat being seized, he sent his "daddy" on board to demand restitution.

So daddy, went, and squatted right down upon a bale of rope alongside the Commydore and cocked his eye and looked him right in the face, and took out his knife and whittled a chip—"Now an't you a tarnal pretty Sarpent, and a devil of a fellow for fish too?" So the Commydore looked at him as mad as blazes, and jumped up and says, "What do you want you scoundrel?" [When Daddy told him, the Commodore reminded him of the War, and indicated that the boat was a lawful prize.] "War! War!" says Daddy, "I got nothing to [do] with your wars—and I don't care a cent for all the wars in the world nor nothink about 'em and I guess if you don't want to go afore a justice of the peace, you'd better make it up, for my Uncle Ben is a Captain in the Militia, and has got a blazing fine company, all true Connecticut blue. . . . And now I tell you once for all if you don't do what's right Uncle Ben shall come along with me and will carry you and your ship, and all, right up before Squire Perkins in Stonningtown."

Later on in the playscript Uncle Ben of New Haven is introduced in person when Hackett tells the story of the Squirrel Hunt. This is the story Hackett claimed he had told Mathews, and the latter had used in his *Trip to America*. It is highly typical of the Yankee story in its characteristics of length, run-on quality, and lack of specific point. As a piece of entertainment, it is as curious to us today as it

was to the London audience of 1827, who listened to it with irritation and vocal reaction. Nothing could have been more typically
Yankee.

Never mind let *him* go, twas *Uncle Ben* I wants to tell *you* about—
Uncle Ben married into a *genteel* family, Uncle Ben *did*, a *shocking*
clever *proper* nice woman, as you wish to see—and knows *what's what*,
as well as any on em, though she wan't *college-larnt*, nor Uncle Ben
neither, but he was a dreadful smart man, "I gulp"—Poor critter! he's
dead now and buried in the church yard at New Haven, fourth turn
from the entrance on the right hand side as you go in, *marvel* tombstun
too—I guess he's better off now, 'case he always loved good *powerful*
preaching, & went to meeting, twice every Sunday, and said *grace* afore
he eat his *dumplings and molasses*—and he never swore, that is not
exactly swearing, I guess—once a cat bit him, and then he said "Darn
the beast how sharp her teeth are," and you know that warnt swearing
—and he never *lied*—why yes! darn him! he *did* though *twice* to *me*,
and I'll just tell you about it, he was most *plague nation* fond of gunning, so one day he comes to our house, and says *he*. "Jonathan"! well
says I, *what*—(you see I was named Jonathan, arter my mothers grandfather, that preached in the great stun meetinghouse in Harford, and
owned all the land awayover—) but where was I? O, yes! "so," says he
"Jonathan I'm going a gunning tomorrow, I guess! are you a mind to
go along?" "well" says I. "I should be *proper glad* to go I guess"—so
the next day he come with, I *vow!* one of the *darndest longest* guns I
ever seed—so out we started, and the darnd a bit of any thing did we
see, till jist about sun an hour high, when we was going through the
woods—Uncle Ben, who was *dreadful* sharpsighted critter, stopped as
sudden as a *streak of lightning*, and says he, "look there Jonathan!"
(You know I told my name was Jonathan) so I looked up into a tree,
and says I, "*Uncle Ben*! its a squirrel," "oh yes!" says he—so he put
up his 'tarnal long gun—"so" says I—"you need not go more than half-
way with *that* gun—the *gun* will reach the *other* half;" and then he
laughed, Uncle Ben did, when any thing *tickled* him—so up went his
gun (*Jonathan throughout imitating the manner of the gun with his
whip*) I knew he wouldn't miss *fire*—because he always shot with the
very best of Holland gun powder, he bought it in New Haven, and gin
four and six pence a pound for it, *Connecticut* currency—well, where
was I? O Yes! so he tuck dead sight on him, and just as he was going
to pull trigger if that 'tarnal devil of a squirrel, didn't jump round *to
the side the bough*—O Massy souls! how mad Uncle Ben was—now

says he "Jonathan! *dont that beat the rot and all natur?*" "so" says I "Uncle Ben, you stay there, we'll see if we cant be a *leettle too sleek* for him"— so *I* went round the other side and poked up *my* gun at him— (my gun was a pooty good gun—a *real, genooine, bunkum* gun, might fill it half full 'twouldn't burst). so I took sight at him, and the critter cocked his tail over his back, and jumped round the side, where Uncle Ben was—and *whang* went the long *gun*—killed him dead as a mitten —so we laughed, I, *tell* you—well, the plaguy critter, fell about *half* way down the tree, and catch'd among the scrags, and there he stuck. So Uncle Ben leaned on his gun, & *first* looked at *me,* and then at the Squirrel—oh, darn you! thinks I—I *know* what you *want*—but see if you'll make me an *offer*—so by and bye, says he—"Jonathan! thats a *real fat* one—a great deal of *grease* in him"—"o yes," says I, "Uncle Ben, but he an't *down,* & I reckon he *wont*"—so say he, "I'll tell you what, Jonathan!"—"well" says I—"*what?*" "I'll gin you *nine*pence if you'll go up *shake* him down." says I, "will you?" so I scrabbled up. I *snore* if I *didn't*—I *cotched* him, and *chucked* him down at Uncle Bens feet, "now" says I—"I'll trouble you for that *trifle,* I guess"—so says he "I'll gin it to you *next* time I *see* you"—If I want *mad,* then its no matter for I had *calculater* on it—So says I, "now that wont do—you promised *four pence ha' penny* last new years, & you never *paid* it to me—now" says I "it an't the money, but its the *principle* of the thing, I *look* at"—says I "if I didn't know your wife is a *miserable fat* woman, and makes good *pumpkin* pies, and *gives* me when I go to your house, I'd *whip* you like a dog—But she is ugly enough to stop a nigger burying—if I wouldn't I'm a *teapot*"—well now how long do you think it was afore he paid me—Darn me if the curse *ever* paid it and, I never *seed* him from that day to this—but not him! I hope he's gone to the *Devil* for *lying*—and I don't believe his *grace* ever went higher than the wall and though he never got *drunk* on a *parade* day ('case he had to *cut* that 'ere caper with his man, that they did afore the meeting-house) he used to get *blue* as a *rason* every *Saturday* night,—whenever he could get brandy for nothing—he'd fill a tumbler, and just *chip* her up and *swigg* her down, he wished his neck was as long as from *Nantucket* great Point to the coast of *Peru*—saying if his mammy had gin him sich milk, he never would have left off sucking under heaven, howsom-never, the Deacon lectured him every week, when he promised he never do so agin—one day the Deacon cotch'd drunk, two days running—so says the Deacon—"Well now Uncle Ben, this is *too* bad— how can you do so—I am sorry really" so says Uncle Ben to him—"are you so *sorry* Deacon?" says he "I am, really sorry"—"well then" says

Uncle Ben, "if you *are really sorry* Deacon—I forgive you." (*Exit Jonathan R. H. singing*)[20]

Was such a story as this really stage entertainment? The London audience voiced an emphatic "No!" The problem seemed to be not so much that of finding the material but of turning it into an art form audiences could understand and respond to positively. No matter how genuinely representative of America the Yankee might be, unless a stage form for clearly delineating him was developed, he would remain as obscure to others as the original object itself.

4

For Hackett's debut Covent Garden Theatre was better filled than "it had been for several weeks." It was an excited and curious audience, augmented by a larger free list than usual.[21] Playgoers had been told in the press and the playbills that Hackett's stories were original and that he had long been celebrated in the United States for his talents at mimicry. Enthusiasm ran high.

Hackett was greeted with a warm burst of applause as he walked out on the stage in the role of the Dunstable actor impersonating a Yankee.[22] They saw a middle-sized, well-proportioned person, with handsome legs, a capacious mouth, good articulation, a strong and flexible voice, and a pleasing countenance, rather broad and open. He was clothed in what was taken for the genuine Yankee dress: a black hat, blue coat, flowered waistcoat, and bluestriped trousers.[23] His hair was set in a pigtail and tied with a green eelskin, and he carried a cart whip under his arm.

Without ceremony or explanation Hackett advanced to the front of the stage and began his story about Jonathan in New York. For

[20] The original spelling, punctuation, and italics of the manuscript have been left unchanged except for the addition of quotation marks where they were occasionally omitted.

[21] The Covent Garden account book for 1827 shows a total free list of 435 for the evening of April 5, 1827. Since this is 100 to 150 more than the usual number, one wonders if this was part of Hackett's special agreement for the evening.

[22] The events of the evening were fully reported in the press. The description here is based on reviews from *The Times, The Morning Chronicle, The Morning Advertiser, The Globe and Traveller, The Morning Herald, Bell's Life in London, The Theatrical Observer, The Courier, The Atlas, The Sun, The Examiner,* and a few unidentified clippings in the Enthoven Collection.

[23] Note the likeness to the Uncle Sam dress even at this early date.

about a quarter of an hour the audience listened attentively. Then, entirely puzzled and confused by what Hackett was doing, a low muttering was heard, and shortly a warning hiss began. Apparently Hackett sensed the unrest and shifted quickly to another story which, after a brief respite as the audience listened, met the same fate as the first. Again he shifted, but with the same results, only this time the audience was not content with an experimental hiss but began the actor's doom chant of "Off, off"—to which Hackett promptly responded and left the stage.

But his evening had only begun. He shortly returned in his Dutch character of Hans Knickerbocker. The audience quieted for a bit, as it listened, but when the actor got to the election of that personage to "a seat in the Congress and drinking water with the President"[24] the audience again went into an uproar, hooting the "Off, off." Hackett complied, again in good humor as if he half-expected it. It was perfectly clear that the audience was going to have nothing to do with pointless stories, no matter how typical they might be. For his second return he appeared in the character of the Dunstable actor "in the ordinary out-at-elbows coat" for his mimicries of Kean and Macready. This was something the audience could understand, and the performer recovered a good deal of his lost ground. His delivery of a soliloquy from *Richard III* in the Kean manner was highly successful, and the crowd responded with "the warmest bursts of applause that can be imagined." A similar reception was given to his mimicry of Macready. After returning to his Dunstable actor for the closing moments of his play, Hackett retired from the stage amid vehement applause. He was not announced for the following evening.

The criticism of James Hackett's debut that appeared the next morning not only reported the events in full but tried to explain the American's errors of the evening which had provoked the bad audience response. No ill feeling toward America or Americans is in any way demonstrated. Except for a mild ribbing of the American republican spirit—"Why Mr. Hackett should die (all republican as he must be) without a struggle" (prompted by Hackett's unexpected departure from the stage)—and a good-humored mention of free

[24] According to the playscript, Hans Knickerbocker was elected to the New York State Legislature and had lunch with the governor. Did Hackett change the dialogue? Very probably.

trade, the reviews are as objective as any theatre notices of the time, and would have been valid at home, except for the English point of view which they clearly showed. Hackett could have no cause for complaint on that score. They complimented him highly where they could, but as representatives of their own audience, and thus sympathetic to its reaction, they spoke their views frankly and openly. One reviewer even went so far as to apologize for the behavior of the audience which he thought should have "at least heard him in silence, and given him an opportunity of showing what he was capable of."

Hackett was even complimented for his "stern republican nerves," his courage and good humor, which showed he was accustomed to the boards of a theatre. In spite of the disaster of the evening some thought his future was promising, and they looked forward to seeing him again in other material. The high opinion of his impersonations of Kean was almost unanimous—amazing, excellent, pure in conception, charming the house, best we have seen, perfect in voice, attitude and every point—with only an occasional opinion that it was on the brink of caricature or that it was on the coarse side. And his duplication of Macready, though not rated as highly, was well complimented.

Critical reaction to the Yankee stories—the American part of the evening—was quite a different matter. In view of the audience behavior Hackett could hardly have expected otherwise. The reviewers thought them tedious, excessively lengthy, miserably contrived, wretchedly introduced, dull, highly obscure and puzzling, clumsily done, defective, unintelligible, rambling as conversation, valueless as entertainment, pointless to an extent perfectly extraordinary. "Imagine an unknown actor," wrote one reviewer, "in an uncouth disguise, without ceremony or explanation, advancing to the front of the stage, and entertaining an audience with a cock-and-bull story in relation to persons and peculiarities of which nine out of ten of the spectators had not a single previous conception." The critics were as honestly baffled by Hackett's Yankee stories as was the audience. When they tried to explain their confusion they made their highly unfavorable comparisons of the American comedian to Mathews. In this they were unfair, through their failure to acknowledge the great gulf that separated beginning-actor Hackett from the highly experienced and seasoned professional comedian Mathews, now in the mature years of a colorful and successful career. Hackett may have been a native American with an advantage in firsthand knowledge of the character type both were interpreting, but a very great difference distinguished the two actors in their capacity to handle such a character on the stage. No matter how unfavorable the comparison, one can suppose that Hackett might have been flattered by the linking of his name with that of the English comedian. At the very least it was certainly good business, and the Yankee in Hackett could well appreciate that.

The comparison is highly revealing of Hackett's state of development as a creative actor. What might have delighted New York audiences, and might even have been so highly admirable in its fidelity to the real thing "that any person who had seen such a personage could not fail to recognize an old acquaintance," as it was claimed, was doomed outside America to obscurity—without skill and experience in the performer to arrange and present it artfully. Mathews enjoyed one advantage in the comparison by having been the first to present the character, thus leaving on the audience his own sharply drawn image of what Yankee life was like, and with this Hackett was forced to contend. But the ineptness of the American actor's preparation of the material and its presentation only helped to emphasize the impression of accuracy and the high entertainment value of Mathews' acting of the type. His delineation might have been nothing more than a broad caricature, they argued, and Hackett might indeed have been responsible for instructing the English comedian. But aside from the difference in content of what they showed of the character on the stage, Mathews was superior because his presentation was superior, because he so arranged this "dramatically valueless stuff" that it could be communicated readily to an audience and be highly regarded as the best of stage entertainment. Amusement was the function of such comedy and not the presentation of an obscure reality. "What is wit and entertainment in one country may not be so in another," they argued, "particularly when extracted from customs and habits."

Taken altogether, the reviewers concluded, Hackett's debut could hardly be accounted successful. In spite of the vociferous applause at the impersonations of Kean and Macready, the audience had been disappointed in its chief purpose in attending an evening's performance by Hackett—to see an American actor interpret Amer-

ican characters. Perhaps the audience had been unfair in not giving
him an opportunity to be fully heard. But Hackett also had an obli-
gation to the audience in the preparation of his materials. That obli-
gation he had obviously failed to fulfill. As far as the English
attitude toward America was concerned, the evening's performance
also revealed one important thing which two reviewers were careful
to point out: Mathews had been extremely tolerant and harmless in
his mild laughter at American peculiarities. "If there was truth in
Mr. H's American sketches, which 'out Herod' all Mr. Mathews said
or did, the forbearance of the English comedian is truly astonishing
and he can hereafter no longer be attacked on the grounds of his
ingratitude."[25] The English were to have the last say even on the
subject of the Yankee.

[25] Anonymous clipping, Enthoven Collection, Victoria and Albert Museum.

chapter 6

Hackett Learns the Trade: 1828 - 1832

AMES HACKETT was twenty-seven when he returned from London in the summer of 1827 and took the plunge into the rough waters of career building in low comedy. During the next five years he slowly built a reputation in New York, Philadelphia, and Boston; tried his hand at managing the Chatham Street Opera House and the Bowery Theatre; extended his range of native character portrayals to include a French émigré, the Catskill Dutchman Rip Van Winkle, and the Kentuckian Nimrod Wildfire; undertook a national tour to Charleston and New Orleans; and eventually wound up with the label of "American national comedian" and a highly laudatory "profile" in the *New York Mirror*. His progress as a stage performer took him to London in 1832, where again a body of criticism gives us the Hackett image with some clarity and objectivity.

Of greater importance at this stage of his career was the range of Hackett's creativity, his capacity as an innovator, as he attacked, without precedent, the difficult problem of building from original native materials a performance repertoire. From 1827 to 1832 he introduced to American audiences eight new pieces, five of which featured the Yankee character. Of course he had Mathews' work as a model, along with Woodworth's and Dunlap's, but his methods are quite different from the others and, for the most part, unrelated to them. It is the actor we watch as he uses every means to obtain material to suit his talents—pilfering, encouraging others to write for him, offering prize awards for new plays, writing himself.

Hackett is the example of the nineteenth-century actor in search of an original comedy line he can call his own, in search of an individual style of performance that will set him off from other comedians. Without professional writers to call upon, with a scarcely defined stage character to develop, Hackett was truly alone as he moved in the new direction.

Over a year elapsed before Hackett brought out his first piece. In the interval he told his Jonathan and Uncle Ben stories, sometimes separately, sometimes in the context of *Sylvester Daggerwood*. He continued his imitations of Kean as Richard III and Othello, imitated Macready as Virginius, and played *The Comedy of Errors* as before, getting "the chief effect by absolute copying" of his fellow Dromio. He tried his talents as Sir Pertinax Mac Sycophant in *The Man of the World*, made a curious excursion into Shakespearean tragedy by playing Iago, and attempted Falstaff in *Henry IV, Part I* for the first time.[1] Shakespeare's comedy-character creation was later to become one of the mainstays in Hackett's repertoire, but at this point it was just one of many experiments in the search for playable pieces to give him some variety in his Park Theatre appearances. In another direction he worked at the development of a French émigré by playing *Monsieur Tonson*, which Mathews had performed most successfully during his American tour.

On December 3, 1828, Hackett introduced to Park Theatre audiences his first fully developed Yankee character. This performance officially launched what has been designated in this study as "Yankee theatre"—a body of plays featuring the Yankee character, developed and performed by specialist comedians in the type.

2

John Bull at Home, or Jonathan in England, as Hackett's "new" Yankee piece was titled, was an adaptation of George Colman's *Who Wants a Guinea?*, with the low-comedy role of Yorkshireman Solomon Gundy, a minor character in the original play, altered and expanded into the principal role of Yankee Solomon Swap. Colman premiered his play in 1805, and though it had met with a poor reception—"a tissue of plagiarisms" from Colman's own work, without "the slightest interest excited for an instant"[2]—it had, through

---

[1] Odell, *Annals*, III, 320–321.
[2] For comment on early presentation of Colman's original see Jeremy Bagster-

occasional playings, come to be considered a part of the standard repertoire of English comedy. Charles Mathews had tried it in London in the 1820's, but not without the disappointed criticism of Samuel Coleridge, who reproved the comedian for wasting his time on a character which contained "not one element of genuine comedy, no, nor even of fun or drollery."[3] Apparently Hackett saw unusual acting possibilities in a redevelopment of Solomon as a Yankee. His hunch soon proved itself, for the play won immediate success and long remained in Hackett's repertoire as well as that of all the Yankee comedians who followed. What induced Hackett to offer the play at this time is not known, but it may well be more than coincidence to find it at the Park simultaneously with William Dunlap's *Trip to Niagara* (with Mr. Chapman in the role of Yankee Doolittle) at the Bowery Theatre, where it had made a strong hit. Managerial competition, as keen then as now, demanded a reply in kind. Two Yankee plays were certainly better than one, for each could give the other courage in showing the American-made product in a theatre dominated by English drama.

Colman's piece[4]—certainly one of his weakest—is a situation contrivance in which a lecherous Irishman tries to seduce an innocent, beautiful orphan girl but is foiled at the last moment by a generous do-gooder, her bitter and cynical father, and her young fiancé. The creaking plot is helped along by a group of country types   a Yorkshireman, a gentle old man, a cantankerous housekeeper, and the character that Hackett adapted, Solomon Gundy. Gundy is a cockney Malaprop, ratcatcher, and *valet de chambre*, who takes a trip to France to study the heads of the nation and returns "a very monkey that had seen the world," with a smattering of French phrases which he garbles throughout the play. As we look at Colman's work today, we puzzle at its busy life on the stage. We can accept it only when we recognize it as a vehicle for a gallery of comic-stage types. What satire it may have contained for the audience of its day, beyond the unsympathetic image of an Irishman and the familiar one of the Yorkshire farmer, is hard to discern. Hackett

Collins, *George Colman the Younger*, pp. 319–320, and Richard B. Peake, *Memoirs of the Colman Family*, II, 413.

[3] Mathews, *Memoirs*, II, 257.

[4] This play has been published several times. An interesting edition because of the preface is that published by John Cumberand (*n.d.*, c. 1828).

probably saw it as a kind of Mathews-like device which could show off the Yankee to good advantage because of the other types surrounding him. The American type would do even better than the Yorkshireman because the contrast could be much greater.

Hackett's version, from our view, is a stronger acting piece than the original. His "mutilation," as it was later dubbed in London, shortened the play to half its original length by eliminating the loquacious Heartley, by reducing in importance the rather unbelievable Torrent, and by cutting Hogmere to a bit part. The comedy elements were strengthened by raising Solomon "Gundy" Swap to a major role. And to give him even more focus, Hackett retained and developed the minor character of Andrew Bang, another Yorkshireman. The dramatic action remains intact, and the comic characters are sharply etched against it. From the moment that Swap enters in Act II, he dominates the proceedings until the final curtain. Solomon Gundy's French joke in the original is thin and wearisome, but the Swap dialogue, simple and naive though it may be, is much fresher and more various throughout. Not only does the New Hampshire Yankee, who was hi-jacked to England by the British Navy, have a role directly involved in the plot; he also has opportunities to spin a yarn, make a joke, and exhibit such Yankee wit as his quip to Hogmere: "Why, consarn you, your soul is leetler than the leetle end of nothing whittled down to a pin." Or the exchange with Henry, who asks, "Were you ever at sea before?" "O, yes!" says Swap, "I used to sloop fruit and lumber down to New York." "What do you mean by fruit and lumber?" queries Henry, and Swap replies, "Why, punkins and broom-handles." A few minutes later Swap exhibits his primary Yankee trait—cleverness in driving a hard bargain, and this time it is against his English counterpart—Yorkshireman Andrew Bang.

SWAP. Well, come, I'll trade watches with you, unsight, unseen.
AND. Noa! Will ye, tho?
SWAP. Yes; but mine's a first-rate watch, double patent pinchback. Now, I'll gin my watch—(aside) it haint' got no insides—for yours, if you'll gin me that guinea boat.
AND. I be to gi' you *my* watch and a guinea for yourn—doane!
SWAP. (Gives watch and takes guinea.—AND. going.—Calls him back.) Here, where's your watch?

AND. I ain't got no watch. I be Yorkshire. (Exit, R., chuckling.)
SWAP. (Alone) Well, I rec'on that Bank don't know more than the law
allows. (SWAP laughs.)

Although *John Bull at Home, or Jonathan in England* undoubtedly entertained to some extent through its intrigues and
complications, its primary comedy lay in the comic drolleries of
Solomon Swap. Such a vehicle gave Hackett every opportunity to
display his talents in the American character, and the performance
could be adjusted with insertions as the comedian saw fit.

Did Hackett make the adaptation himself? There are several reasons to believe that he did. The first performance was advertised as
"altered and adapted . . . by a gentleman of this city"; and a news
story notes that Swap had been "engrafted on the original comedy
with a good deal of skill and humor by one of the wits of this city."[5]
Was Hackett both the "gentleman" and "the wit"? One of the official prompt copies of the play,[6] the one prepared by W. E. Anderson, prompter at the Charleston Theatre, bears the entry: "Altered
and compressed into 3 acts by Mr. Hackett." Hackett's signature
also appears on this copy. Since the adaptation consisted of editing
Colman's dialogue primarily by cutting lines, and then inserting
appropriate speeches for Solomon Swap, Hackett could easily have
made the alterations himself. His primary job would have been the
insertion of Yankee materials he already probably had in quantity.
It is possible that someone suggested the possibilities in the play to
Hackett, but certainly he was astute enough to have perceived these
himself.

When Hackett played it for Mrs. Hackett's benefit performance
on December 3, 1828, and repeated it again on December 13 and
again on the 23rd for the benefit of his sister-in-law (Mrs. Sharpe),
he seems to have discovered the vehicle he had long been looking
for, so completely successful was it with audiences. The *New York
Post* reported that he "so convulsed his hearers with fits of laughter,
that it was with difficulty his best points could be heard." The reviewer also thought the reception of this "admirable" comedy "conclusive evidence of the improved taste of a New-York audience."[7]

[5] *New York Post*, November 28, 1828.
[6] Enthoven Collection, Victoria and Albert Museum.
[7] *New York Post*, December 5, 1828.

Hackett kept Solomon Swap in his stage bag until he abandoned the character when George Hill and the other Yankee actors superseded him in the role. In 1836 he sued Hill for "stealing" his play, but the action, for obvious reasons, was withdrawn: Hackett had committed his own piracy of Colman's work several years earlier.

3

With Solomon Swap to add substance to his growing repertoire of comedy roles, a year passed before Hackett found another new play to show Park Theatre audiences. From May 20 to August 5, 1829, he managed a summer season at the Chatham Street Opera House, which he promptly renamed the American Opera House in keeping with his stubborn view that native works had a place on the stage. Here he played Swap several times. In December he returned to the Park Theatre, and on the tenth of that month, at his own benefit, he played his first performance of *The Times, or Life in New York*. This play, billed as a comedy in three acts and "founded on our manners and peculiarities," if not the first, is certainly among the earliest to locate the action in the streets of New York, and it stands as a preface to Anna Cora Mowatt's *Fashion*, Mose the Fireman plays, and the later Harrigan and Hart city comedies of the 1870's. Among its various staging opportunities was a chance to show "Views of the Battery and of Wall Street," as Dunlap had done in his *Trip to Niagara*.[8] Again the authorship is attributed to a mysterious "gentleman of the city," though Rees[9] asserts that John Ingham, who later wrote a play called *The Usurper*, may possibly have written it. But whoever it was who originally put it together, Hackett certainly, as he had before, worked directly with the script, particularly in developing the central character of Industrious Doolittle.

A complete version of *The Times, or Life in New York* is not extant. All that remains is an actor's "side" for Doolittle, perhaps the one that Hackett himself used in preparing his role for performance.[10] Brief though this is, when filled out with cast descriptions from playbills and the reviewer's description in the *New York*

[8] See the discussion of this Dunlap piece in Chapter 9.
[9] James Rees, *The Dramatic Authors of America*, p. 93.
[10] Enthoven Collection, Victoria and Albert Museum.

Harbour and Shipping in View.

Scene Last;
COURT OF JUSTICE.
The piece concludes with the identification of Rips' person.

After which, the favourite new Comedy of
THE TIMES:
OR,
LIFE IN NEW-YORK.

Mr. TRAFFIC, [A wealthy Merchant, plain and unostentatious in his manners and
  habits—Guardian to his deceased brother's daughter Caroline,]   Mr. CHAPMAN
RICHARD DASHWOULD, [Traffic's Step-Son, ruined by his mother's false ideas
  of Polite Education,]   -   -   -   -   -   Mr. RICHINGS
PERCIVAL, [An English Gentleman, long resident in America, partner in a Com-
  mercial House,]   -   -   -   -   -   Mr. BARRY
CHA'S BARTON, [A Professional Gentleman, and friend to Percival,]   Mr. T. PLACIDE
INDUSTRIOUS DOOLITTLE, [A Busy, Talkative Native of one of the Eastern States
  —Speculator in every thing—Auctioneer, Bank and Insurance Director, and Stump
  Candidate for Assembly, with a sneaking notion for Caroline, or more " specially"
  her large inheritance in Rice and Cotton Plantations,]   -   Mr. HACKETT
SIR CRŒSUS MUSHROOM, [Making the Tour of America, with the intention of Pub-
  lishing a Book of Travels—a great despiser of every thing Republican, as too plebi-
  an for his taste,]   -   -   -   -   -   -   Mr. SIMPSON
MONSIEUR RAGOUT, [A grand Valet de Chambre, imported by Sir Crœsus,]
        Mr. PLACIDE
SLY HAZARD, [President of an Insurance Company,]   -   Mr. POVEY
Mr. POMPEY, [A dandy Negro Waiter, leader of the Broadway fashions,]   Mr. BLAKELEY
Mrs. DASHWOULD TRAFFIC, [Wife of Traffic, and Step-Mother of Amelia, very
  ambitious of Fashionable Life,]   -   -   -   Mrs. WHEATLEY
Miss CAROLINE TRAFFIC, [A rich Carolinian Heiress,]   -   Mrs. HACKETT
Miss AMELIA TRAFFIC, [Traffic's Daughter,]   -   -   Mrs. SHARFE
Mrs. JENKINS,   -   -   -   -   -   -   Mrs. DURIE

During the Comedy
VIEWS OF THE BATTERY
AND OF
WALL STREET.

Park Theatre playbill (c. 1830) for *The Times:
or, Life in New York* with James Hackett as Industrious Doolittle.

Mirror, much of the spirit of the piece can be reconstructed. The
Mirror gives the outline:

[It] consists of a dozen or so of scenes thrown cleverly though loosely
together, exhibiting the manners and habits of the worthy inhabitants
of the city, and the birds of passage that flock to it and through it from
every quarter of the globe, and sketching, pleasantly enough, a few of
their follies and peculiarities. . . . There is a pretended English baronet
on his travels, a Frenchman, two Broadway dandies (a black and a

white), a plain merchant and his fashionable wife, a talking speculat-
ing Yankee, and a brace of young ladies and gentlemen. Some of the
jokes are old, though without being stale, but as they are adroitly introduced and well-told, they answer just as well as new ones, and there is
considerable bustle and knowledge of stage effect displayed throughout.
Altogether it appears as if it were the careless off-hand production of an
exceedingly clever writer.[11]

From this we can again note that Hackett is provided with a gallery
of types within which he can contrast his own particular wares.
This time he can set off his scheming Yankee against a wealthy New
York merchant, an English merchant, an English traveler who hates
America, a Negro dandy, and a French valet. With an eye cocked
for all the local satire he could get out of the piece, Hackett quite
possibly intended the English traveler to represent Captain Basil
Hall, whose travel volumes were published in the spring of 1830.
Hall's highly inflammatory views were already New York gossip
and Hackett would have seen the advantages of exploiting this situation. Here is the pale image of what was to become a fully developed character in Hackett's later comedy, *Lion of the West*—
Mrs. Wollope, a direct travesty on Frances Trollope. The main interest in *The Times* is, of course, Industrious Doolittle, who, according to the *Mirror*, contrary to what his name imports, "did
enough to keep the audience in a merry mood from the beginning
to end."

Doolittle differs sharply from Solomon Swap. He is announced in
the playbills as a "busy, talkative native of one of the eastern states
—speculator in everything—auctioneer, bank and insurance director, and stump candidate for assembly." He is something of a
country boy moved to the city, and some of the material used in
Sylvester Daggerwood can be detected in the stories and lines that
make up the Doolittle character. As a New York speculator in all
sorts of enterprises, he confides in the English merchant various
schemes for making money, honestly if at all possible. The important thing is to make it. "Oh, for a war in Europe! Good Gracious
what a go there'd be for naval stores." Then he kids the Englishman
on the poor market for indigo in New York. "Oh that makes him
rather blue don't it; be a shade better soon." He also talks about

[11] *Mirror*, VII (December 19, 1829), 190.

speculation in feathers, tries to sell Mr. Traffic some stock shares, and tells a Yankee story about tricking a greedy insurance broker. Doolittle carries a pocketful of loose papers, of which one outlines a plan for "Heads of an Association to be called the anti steamboat-bell ringing society to discourage the noisy practice of ringing bells and blowing bugles on board steamboats before starting." When the Negro porter from the City Hotel comes by with the traveling bags of Sir Croesus Mushroom, Doolittle has a chance to hear his complaints about life in America as they talk about Boston, the Brooklyn Navy Yard, the size of the North River, and the state of the theatre. A few minutes later Doolittle entertains the ladies with a dance, for which he calls the figures himself, and when he gets badly confused and they cannot follow him, he dances wildly alone. Later he announces his plans for running for the New York State Legislature: "Three dollars a day, and asked to champagne dinner by some lobby member who has got an axe to grind. I'll make a speech in the Park tomorrow. Politics and cider." He finally leaves for Pearl Street for his first job as auctioneer. Sir Croesus Mushroom is left behind with the opinion that all Yankees are savages. Doolittle is shown throughout the piece as a speculator-pretender, a bragging Yankee who tells grossly exaggerated stories in a hearty and friendly way.

Was it satirical of American life? Probably mildly so. Hackett, from his days in New York before he failed and turned to the stage for a living, had a first hand knowledge of what speculation and business were like in that free-for-all world. Had he deliberately overdrawn Doolittle to show the absurdity of concluding that Americans could be simplified into one image, as English travelers were beginning to portray them? The cartoon of the unhappy English traveler could have been borrowed from William Dunlap or from Charles Mathews. The Negro dandy and the French valet were probably familiar types in the city, and Caroline, heiress to a large inheritance in rice and cotton plantations, could probably be readily identified. Again this play gave Hackett an opportunity to impersonate a Yankee—more of a general American here than anything resembling a New Englander. Another hand had written it for him, but Hackett undoubtedly had closely supervised the development of the principal character.

When Hackett performed it at the Park Theatre, he met with fair success. Mrs. Hackett played Caroline and his sister-in-law, Mrs. Sharpe, acted Amelia Traffic. The events of the first night went unrecorded in the columns of the *New York Post* because another American play and American actor had pre-empted the space— Edwin Forrest in his première performance of *Metamora*, which was played shortly after *The Times* opened.

4

Hackett's star had definitely begun to rise. In January, 1830, he played at the Bowery Theatre for the first time, but in April he was back at the Park, where Mrs. Hackett acted frequently as a regular member of the company. This time the comedian, with three pieces to show Park audiences, was prepared as he had never been before. The first of these, *Down East, or the Village Gazette*, he performed first on April 17, 1830. Five days later he followed it with *Rip Van Winkle*. This play does not concern us here except as it supports the view of Hackett as an innovator in native American stage materials. In the role of the Catskill Dutchman, a type much closer to Hackett's background than the Yankee, he displayed a new facet of his comic capabilities. From this date forward *Rip Van Winkle* became a principal character delineation in Hackett's repertoire and long survived many of his other plays. In the third piece, H. J. Finn's *The Indian Wife, or The Falls of Montmorency*, the busy comedian played Sergeant Peletiah Peabody for the first time on May 27, 1830. No fragment has survived to tell us about Sergeant Peabody except that he was a Green Mountain boy, a Vermonter. Since Hackett played it only a few times, its value is slight in the overview of his work. Henry Finn, who will be given more extensive treatment later in connection with George Hill, was a gifted light-humorist. It is quite possible that Hackett encountered real difficulties playing a Vermonter. His Yankees, said his critics later when there was some basis of comparison with George Hill, were generalized Americans and not New England local types at all. The special Yankees would have to wait for Hill's more refined and subtle approach.

Down East, or The Militia Muster, as it was later called, is of definite concern to us because Hackett played it for nearly a quarter of a century after its 1830 opening. He played it so frequently and so individually that Major Joe Bunker became as closely identified with him as Rip Van Winkle, Colonel Nimrod Wildfire, or Falstaff. No sketch amused American audiences more, yet we will note its dismal failure in London when Hackett played it there in 1832. There is a broad gap between Noah Ludlow's comment, as he watched it from a theatre manager's point of view with one eye on the box office—"I never enjoyed any performance of the comic kind more"—and that terse, conclusive epitaph on the cover of the En- thoven manuscript—"Damned at Drury Lane Theatre, Nov. 1832." As we look back at this acting sketch today, the London dictum seems entirely warranted, but we are as much outsiders as London- ers were in 1832, and what Hackett reported about American life can be as illusive to us as it must have been to them.

Jokes and stories about the militia had long been current in the States. Mathews had picked them up and worked them into a song in his *Trip to America*. Where did Hackett get the idea? Was it from hearing of Mathews' success with the material, or was this one of the items he had recounted to Mathews, as he claimed indi- rectly in London when the point was raised about his borrowing from the English comedian? And who put the sketch together? All the evidence points to Hackett's again composing his own material for the stage. There is more than a hint in the brief news item in the *New York Evening Post* for April 22, 1830, which advertised the first performance of *Rip Van Winkle* to be followed by the third of *Down East*: "One of the pieces is said to be from the pen of the comedian himself, and the other has received considerable altera- tions and improvements at his hand." Since we know that Hackett played a revised version of John Kerr's adaptation of *Rip Van Winkle*,[12] the original piece mentioned in the advertisement must be *Down East*. How original it was is a matter of question in the light of Hackett's previous borrowings, but he undoubtedly shaped whatever material he found to his own style of comedy. It would not be reading too much into the play to see Joe Bunker as the com- mon image of the flounderings and confusions of democratic society, as an image of what democracy meant in everyday practice. The sketch might be good low comedy, in a general way, but in an age when satire was expected, it could poke gentle fun at the common institution of militia mustering and a militia that, inept as it was at

[12] Quinn, *A History of the American Theatre, From the Beginning to the Civil War*, pp. 325 ff.

the formalities of military ceremony, had declared and maintained the sovereignty of a country trying hard to succeed at the Great Experiment. Joe Bunker, barkeeper for Colonel Hodgkins, was a simple and meaningful symbol of the American disregard of vested authority, and of the view that one man was just as good as another. It is no surprise that London damned it; how could it possibly comprehend such an intuitive overtone.

The version that Hackett used for the first performance of *Down East* has not survived. Two later versions—"The Skeleton" and the Beazley rewrite for the London performance[13]—are extant, and these, together with a summary in the *Mirror*, give a good idea of what Hackett did with the material. The *Mirror* described the piece as a farce of ten or twelve scenes "thrown loosely together" as a framework for Hackett's Yankee character.[14] Apparently the piece could be altered to suit the occasion, for the advertisement of the second performance noted that it would be "comprised" for that evening, and a few days later at the Chestnut Theatre in Philadelphia Hackett played it with "the entire new Yankee story of 'How to Sell a Fox Skin'."[15] Durang characterized it as a facsimile of a Maine militia trainer on a field day, "full of old military saws and conceits," in which Joe Bunker was a self-complacent rustic and his foil, Hateful Perkins, a stolid Puritan.

The Beazley version, apparently specially prepared for the London audience, is a fifteen-minute sketch with a plot. Colonel Hodgkin insists that his ward Emily marry his son, despite her love for Melville, whom she met while in England, and to ensure it he locks her in her room. In the meantime the Englishman arrives incognito. The Colonel and Joe Bunker think he is a spy, and they lock him up while Joe goes for the militia. Florence, the maid, helps the lovers escape and get married while Joe is drilling the militia for the assault. When they return and the marriage is revealed, the Colonel's plot is thwarted. It is not likely that Hackett played this version on his return to the States but continued with what he had previously developed. Some of the major speeches in the Beazley

[13] "The Skeleton" is in the Enthoven Collection. The "Beazley rewrite" is in the Lord Chamberlain's Collection, No. 42924.

[14] *Mirror*, VII (May 1, 1830), 339.

[15] Reese James, *Old Drury of Philadelphia*, p. 541.

version are so typical that they may well have come from the early version.[16]

MAJOR JOE Now you see, gentlemen. As these spies have no suspicion that we know them, we'll pretend to parade. Perhaps they may look out of the window and see our discipline. Then after training, as tho' nothing were the matter, at a signal we'll surround the house, rush in at the door and secure our prisoners. That's a "ruse de Guerre." I shall be a Major General for this. Attention! Gentlemen will please to leave off playing and fall in and take their places. Them that like bean poles will come to this ere side, and them that like Cocks of Meadows hay, fall to that there, so as to make a kind of a sort of an even slant like. Them that an't got no guns get in behind the lower eend. Now we'll just call over your names to see the missing. Answear quick and lat Captain out here, and the leftenant in there among the bushes. See if their Major can't lick 'em all hollow in forming a company. Gentlemen! Please answear to your names as I calls 'em.

     (The Soldiers answer "Here" when called.) Hateful Perkins. I say, Hateful, why don't you say "Here" to that rotten ugly name of yourn?

HATEFUL My name is Hateful W. Perkins after my grandmother.

JOE Well, tch, Hateful W. Perkins.

HATEFUL Hullea!

JOE Now we'll just give a touch to show that we havn't forgot the Mannul, and then off to that ere part. Company, Tention, the whole! Gentlemen, why don't you hold up your heads like corn. Don't hang 'em down like taters. Right Dress! Now, gentlemen, don't form a straight line so tarnal crooked. You're as twisted as a rams horn. There's no excuse for getting out of a straight line now. The last muster day you kept moving along with the shade cause the sun was so almighty hot. Don't begin to crack at both ends again. Dress! Dress, I tell you. If you don't dress, I'll undress to once. You'd better not go to rise my darnder much higher by

---

[16] The punctuation and some of the spelling have been edited here to avoid confusion for the reader. The manuscript copy work is typical of the period: frequent use of capital letters on nouns, and the use of the dash for the period.

carrying on so, or I'll take my old sword and charge bayonet right shut into some of your gizzards.

HATEFUL   Look here now, Major Joe. You are gitting to be a leetle too superflewous! And arter trainings over you'll be mighty apt to ketch a licking or to stand treat.

JOE   No talking. Taint military. Tention, the whole! Shoulder hullock! Cock Hullock! Take aim! Ram down cartridge!

HATEFUL   Pugh! Don't everybody know that fire comes next to take aim? You don't know as much as a half-grown gosling. Read the Mannul at once!

JOE   Come! Let's have at them! Hand over! Now then, Tention the whole! Half cock hullock! Shet pan!

NICK   I say Major Joe!

JOE   What tehn?

NICK   I an't got no pan to shet!

JOE   Pretty good that! Handle cartridge! Draw ramrod! Return ramrod! Shoulder hullock! The right shoulder. Wrong. Bring the hullock up to the left shoulder. That's right. Tention the whole! Ground hullock! There, Hateful, why the plague don't you bey orders, and ground hullock.

HATEFUL   'Cause you think I'm going to put my brand new umbrella in the mud? I'll see your nose cheesed first.

JOE   Well, we'll soon be over now. So take up your guns. Now spread yourselves into platoons. Tention the whole! Eyes right!

HATEFUL   I say, Major Joe. How's this man going to eyes right?

JOE   Wats the matter of him?

HATEFUL   Why see how he squints.

The other extant version is titled "The Skeleton of the Ludicrous Scene of the Militia Training." It consists of only the muster scene without other plot details. Such is its arrangement, it could possibly be the major scene in the original 1830 version, and is here extracted for individual use outside the context of the other scenes. The cast listings and the property list are illuminating details. In addition, the use of the word "Skeleton" in the title may indicate that the sketch could be expanded as occasion required.[17]

Dramatis Personae

Joe Bunker . . . . . . The Yankee Major
Hateful Parkins . . . . An Independent Disorderly

[17] Modern punctuation has been inserted to avoid confusion.

Nick Weaver . . . . His feet chalked "R" and "L"
Twelve militiamen; the Drummer; the Fifer

Equipment and properties: 8 muskets, each lightly loaded; 5 cartouch boxes; 1 pistol; 1 blunderbuss; 6 bayonets; 1 old gun without lock, a padlock fastened in its place; a cigar for Nick Weaver; 1 old umbrella, very ragged when opened, and tied around so as to conceal its defects.

Scene

A lawn. A country inn is set L.H.U.E., with the sign: "Trooper on Horseback" and the word "Entertainment" printed beneath. A company of Militia are discovered in disorder. Some are seated on the ground playing cards on top of a hat; others are throwing up coppers. Their guns are resting against the house or lying on the ground by the sides of their owners. As the curtain rises, Hateful Parkins and Nick Weaver come down the stage.

HATEFUL. I say, Nick. What's the reason of our being all warned out in sitch a thundering hurry? Do you believe the story of the British having landed? I don't.

NICK. Nor I, nother. I say, Hateful, it's only some nonsense of that fool, Major Joe, cause its war time. Some one seen a red cow in the bushes and telled him it was a red *coat.* If the British had landed, we'd have found it out long ago.

HATEFUL. Well, next time I'm warned out in sitch a pucker, I won't come.

JOE. (Outside R. and C.) Whow, you Sarpent!

HATEFUL. There's Major Joe trying to get on his old mare, and she won't stand it. She's got the most sense of the two. Then he's gin up and is coming this way. No, he's fell down. His sword's got between his legs and tripped him up. Ha, Ha, Ha! Oh, here he comes again! Let's gin him room, eh? What a swarth! (Nick and Hateful go up and mix with the other men.)

JOE. (Enter RI-C) Come, Fall in! (The Militia form in single file across the stage and on a line with 1st wing R and I. Parkins about center and Nick on the extreme left.)

JOE. Charge bagnet right into some of your gizzards.

HATEFUL. I'll tell you what, Major Joe. If you act so superflous, arter traings over, you'll get a licking.

JOE. What?

HATEFUL. O have to stand treat!

JOE. Put him in the smoke house.

HATEFUL. Take you and the Colonel both to do it.

JOE.   You shan't talk so.

HATEFUL.   Well, I will!

JOE.   I say you shant!

HATEFUL.   Well, I say, I'm d——d, if I don't!

JOE.   Well, it's no matter! I call the roll. (Calls roll.)

JOE.   Hateful Parkins. (No answer twice) I say, Hateful, why don't you answer to that rotten ugly name of yours?

HATEFUL.   Cause it ant my name.

JOE.   What is then?

HATEFUL.   My name is Hateful W. Parkins, after my Grandmother.

JOE.   Well, then, Hateful W. Parkings!

HATEFUL.   (Bawling in Joe's ear) Hulloa!

JOE.   Make ready! Take aim! Ram down the cartridge!

HATEFUL.   That's wrong! Every fool knows "Fire!" comes arter "take aim!"

JOE.   *I* say *it* don't. If you aint lodened and some on em ant got no guns!

HATEFUL.   Yes, you ant got as much larning about rank and file as a half grown goslin. I say, sodiers, I motion and second it, the Major's a d——d fool! If you don't know the exterctice, why don't you get the Manual and read it.

MILITIA.   Yes, Major. Read it! Read it!

            (Nick takes book out of his pocket and seems to read.)

JOE.   I'll bet a gret apple there ant a volum of the exercise to be had in the hull country.

HATEFUL.   And lose it too. Why there, Nick Weaver got one reading now.

JOE.   (Reading) Shet pan!

NICK.   I say, Major Joe!

JOE.   Waht is it?

NICK.   How am I going to shet pan, got none to shet.

JOE.   Return ramrod!

            (Hateful takes a ramrod from a man L.H. and carries it over to another on the R.H.)

JOE.   Parkins, where are you going?

HATEFUL.   Why obeying orders! You said we must all return ramrods, and I see him borrow it when we fell in.

JOE.   Parkins, you shant obey orders so.

HATEFUL.   I will, I tell you!

JOE.   I say you shant!

HATEFUL.   Well, I'm d——d, if I don't!

JOE.   Ground fullock! Parkins, why don't you obey orders now and ground fullock?

HATEFUL.   Think I'm going to put my brand new umbrella in the mud? I'll see your nose cheesed first!

JOE.   Well you must!

HATEFUL.   Well, I won't.

JOE.   I say you shall!

HATEFUL.   Well, I say, I'm d——d, if I do!

JOE.   A new leaf. Charge bagnet!

MEN.   Wrong, Major.

HATEFUL.   Ha, Ha, Ha! How are the men to charge bagnet when their guns are on the ground?

JOE.   Don't care. It's so in the book.

HATEFUL.   I know better, It can't be so. Let's look.

JOE.   There! There! (Gives Hateful the book.)

HATEFUL.   Why you've turned over two leaves too once. (Returns book to Joe.)

JOE.   (After firing salute.) I return you thanks, Soldiers, for your military conduct and regular firing.

HATEFUL.   (Who has a pistol and now fires it. Lights gradually lowered. Rain and thunder ready.) Stop, Major Joe! (Thunder and rain.) Looks like a rain!

JOE.   Dismiss!

    (The company scatters and runs off R. and L. wings.)

JOE.   Eyes right!

HATEFUL.   I say, Major, how is this man going to eyes right? (Brings forward a man who has a hat slouched over his face.)

JOE.   Why the blame critter squints awful.

    (As they afterwards march around and up the stage, Parkins, in the rear as he wheels up I, opens his umbrella towards the audience showing its tattered state.)

        Exeunt Omnes in haste and disorder.
        Curtain falls.

How old a man was Major Joe Bunker? Solomon Swap was a country boy; Industrious Doolittle could have been in his thirties. Was Joe Bunker Hackett's "old" Yankee? It looks very much like it. There is nothing in either extant version to indicate age. But the general tone implies it, and such a contrast with the other Yankee characters would have appealed to Hackett's theatrical sense. And now that he was playing *Rip Van Winkle*, an ancient Yankee would be readily useable in a repertoire.

5

So successful was Hackett with his American plays that scarcely a week after *Down East* opened he advertised his first Prize Play Contest in the interest of building his repertoire. Edwin Forrest had acquired his Indian drama of *Metamora* in this way, and Hackett undoubtedly thought he could turn up new pieces and get some free publicity of a prestige sort in the bargain. So he offered two hundred and fifty dollars for a three-act comedy and stipulated that one of the characters had to be "a native" adaptable to Hackett's "powers and style of acting."[18] How much like a patron of American letters Hackett sounds in his advertisement: "The Subscriber desirous of affording some pecuniary inducement for more frequent attempts at dramatising the manners and peculiarities of our country and the numerous subjects and incidents connected with its history, hereby offers . . ." His announcement also declared his specific interest in "manners and peculiarities" because eccentricities provided his best acting materials.

There was nothing exceptional in Hackett's offer. In a day when playwriting as a paid profession simply did not exist in America, it was the only logical method of procuring actable plays. Moreover, because the winning play would become Hackett's property, he could do with it as he pleased, even to having it rewritten by another hackwriter if it did not at first succeed. If such plays were carefully developed and jealously guarded to prevent pirating by other actors, they could be kept alive in a repertoire for the major part of an actor's career, winning fame and fortune for their actor-owners.

Hackett's contest turned up not only one play but two: *Lion of the West, or A Trip to Washington* and *The Moderns, or a Trip to the Springs*. The first play won the prize. The actor must have given consolation money to the author of the second, however, for he advertised its first performance as "the new prize comedy" when it was premiered a week before *Lion of the West*. The latter play, with its principal character of Colonel Nimrod Wildfire—Davy Crockett

---

[18] *New York Evening Post*, April 24, 1830.

in disguise—was twice rewritten, and its third version, Bayle Bernard's *The Kentuckian*, became one of Hackett's principal plays for the remainder of his career. It is *The Moderns*, however, that interests us here, because it is a Yankee-theatre play.

Hackett first acted Melodious Migrate, a Yankee school and singing master, on April 18, 1831. Again the author hides under the anonymous label "by a Gentleman of New York." The author of *Lion of the West* had tried to do likewise, but gossip and report soon led to a newspaper announcement that James Kirke Paulding, Washington Irving's brother-in-law, had written the piece, primarily in the interest of encouraging native themes and characters and to get away from "those hateful English types" on the stage. But no such disclosure was made about the author of *The Moderns*. Anonymous writing was fashionable during this period, particularly among the young men of fashion about the city who turned their hand to literary pieces for the amusement it offered. Some of the mild satire in *The Moderns* on the opera of the day would indicate that the play's author was familiar with the prevailing musical styles and clichés.

All that remains of *The Moderns* is a fragment, an incomplete actor's "side" for the principal character of Melodious Migrate.[19] Since this was Hackett's Yankee, we have a fair idea of what the play intended, although what the plot may have been is difficult to imagine. This play was not successful, and it is entirely possible that again it was a series of sketches, with opportunities for Hackett to tell stories and insert special pieces of business, perhaps no more than an outline that would be given body when the principal character was acted.

Melodious Migrate describes himself as a singing master over four schools "chock full of obstropolous" girls. He begins with a story.

"You see we were singing Holden, page seventeen, and were going it full blast, the four parts, like a four horse team o'er a bran new turnpike—when I consated the tenor was a leetle mite too weak and opened myself like a tree toad in wet weather 'full-chisel'—Well I had hardly got over a bar or so when a blasted dog who had got into the room set up such an almighty howl imitating that all the gals and boys busted

19 Enthoven Collection, Victoria and Albert Museum.

out laughing, and then fell to throwing peas as thick as a fiddler's musty!"

When it is suggested he should be well paid to put up with such he says, "Sometimes I get four bushels o rye in the grain—sometimes two weeks' board or a barl of cider for a quarter—some will send a punkin pye as large as a wash tub and crust as thick as a nigger's foot:—other some will send a gallon or two of apple sauce sour enough to make a pig squeal." New York band music next occupies his attention and he praises a Negro band as the best. Then he turns to Italian opera and Rossini in particular.

"I never heerd such almighty guaveration before! If you call that singing! Why they make a clean straight streak of it from low G to high C. Sometimes when the fiddlers are all scratching away like an Eclipse right on eend, the whole kit and biling on em would set up a long whine-running on a rheumatic scale as they call'd it that it put me in mind of Uncle Frank's three year old bull along the road in springtime!"

The other says, "Chromatic scale you mean." "Well, maybe; but it was scaly enough for anybody who likes fish!" When asked if he had composed an opera, he says, "Do you think it's right to make a man sing while another is sticking a long knife in his gizzard. . . . Mercy on the *I*talians. Yes, I'd cut all their cherrupin throats!"

In the second act he recalls he "got read out of meeting in Connecticut for swearing." When he again takes up the subject of New York, he says:

"As for York, they know as much about music as a Jackass knows about an Anthem. When I was there, they were in a desperate all sufficient way about Signorinas and such kind of Italian stuff and nonsense! Why I heerd a woman sing with a trumpet, and soon they both went it, just like Beacon Bigelow's saw-mill in freshet time—clip, clip, clip! and though I couldn't understand a word she said, yet I thought the devil was to pay somewhere!"

In Act Three we see Melodious Migrate in the classroom. As he enters all is confusion. "Hem," he says, and the boys fly to their seats as he walks to the stand with great dignity. The scene continues as we watch him trying to control a roomful of rowdy students.

Hackett's new Yankee comes from Connecticut, speaks a New England country dialect, and rejects the pretensions of city fashions. Poking fun at the "*I*-talian" influence on opera, something of a Mathews touch, undoubtedly exemplified a popular point of view, for the practice of singing opera in foreign languages was apparently as much criticized then as now and pretense to "Culture" was open to ridicule. *The Moderns* was the final Yankee-theatre play Hackett introduced to American audiences before he made his second trip to London in 1832.

6

What was James Hackett's contribution to the American theatre up to this point? Aside from his capability in arousing laughter, had he given anything of significance to the stage, His chief American competitor, Edwin Forrest, had fostered an Indian drama and would shortly add Robert Montgomery Bird's Roman play, *The Gladiator*, to his repertoire. These roles were not the usual parts in Forrest's repertoire, however, for he moved solidly into competition with the English tragedians in the standard roles of Shakespeare and Sheridan Knowles. Hackett might have pursued a parallel path in English comedy, by acting the Sheridan and Colman comedies that still graced the Drury Lane stage, or by trying his hand at the new ones by Placide, Poole, and Buckstone. He had already experimented with a few characters from Shakespeare, but without much success. Later he would try seriously again, but only Falstaff would survive his attempts. There is certainty, however, about one thing. Without other competition to threaten his position Hackett could become the almost exclusive patron and innovator of native American stage comedy.

Did this take courage? Many thought it did, because it meant not only traveling an unknown, unpredictable route, but it also thrust whoever tried it into forced battle with the English repertoire and English actors and their style of acting. There must have been something of the maverick in Hackett that interested him in this action. On the other hand such a move was also good business. Joe Cowell was later to label Hackett a "dramatic merchant," and other biographers would continue to call him an opportunist. Yet is it precisely his talent that led him to take the independent route. Someone had to break track; Hackett elected to do it. With the *Mirror* behind him, a support which meant specific encouragement from literary figures and other gentlemen about New York whom Hackett highly respected and probably wished to be associated with, the path was easier. But the theatre with its box office was hard fact with no fancy about it; it was no place for a man without wits and a certain hardness. The comedian in Hackett was warm and open to audiences in the theatre, but there may have been something cooler and detached about his manner off the stage that did not encourage the warmth of personal response and anecdote which was inspired by Charles Mathews, Tyrone Power, and other principal comedians of the day.

The value of the dramatic fare James Hackett introduced to the stage during this early period is certainly debatable, but to scoff at it is also to scoff at the Park Theatre audience and the *Mirror* supporters, and literally to fail to see the plays in the context of their day. Though Hackett had no literary talent that could help him construct a stageworthy play, he did have an eye for comedic movement and he knew his own limitations as a performer. His observation was keenly developed and he could hear and see the characters he would play himself. But in the absence of playwrights with whom he could work as intimately as did Charles Mathews with James Smith, Hackett was forced to depend on hackwriters, contributing friends, or his own capacities. And more than that, finding a writer who could perceive even the general American character, much less the Yankee type, and bring it out in a stage comedy asked almost the impossible. Those literary talents who might have been capable of doing such were far too busy with other, more esteemed literary activity and could not afford to waste time and energy on something for the stage from which there was neither money nor reputation to be earned. It is indeed remarkable that Hackett was able to develop any playable stage pieces at all.

Today Hackett's comedies seem crude and naive. At this great distance we are inclined to view them only as situation pieces, largely dependent on their eccentric activities for amusement. This neglects an important procedure with comedy: the necessity of placing it against the times for which it is written. Comedy becomes dated very quickly, and satire, as a more subtle aspect of comedy, evaporates when the world being satirized becomes obscured by time. Unless the play is of a literary sort, or the characters are freshly perceived, the comedy in such work soon disappears. The

Yankee pieces Hackett developed usually featured only one character, the Yankee Hackett was to play himself, and the other roles were primarily supporting instruments. In addition, the dialogue provided, except for the Yankee, was again of secondary consideration. The speeches that appear in the playscripts for the Yankee character, as in no other play form, it must be remembered, were not literary compositions but lines to be spoken by a live comedian with all his special style of delivery and capacities as an active stage personality. Such theatre ideas defy recording on paper. They can exist only in the theatre. Our literary record, then, is a poor report of what happened on Hackett's stage.

Hackett's Yankee characters were satirical of American life. The last strong impetus in comedy had been felt with Sheridan and Goldsmith in the 1770's, and all comedy since that day had copied the style but had gradually grown thinner and thinner, no longer satisfying the new times. James Hackett was on the threshold of a period in new comedy, comedy that would try to define what was funny in the period's own manners and behavior. Hackett, more particularly, was trying to reflect American society, which differed sharply from the European in its political patterns and in its social organization, especially in its huge lower-to-middle class that had the cultural appearance of a classless society. What was funny about the manners and people in this society? Hackett, through various characters—Solomon Swap, Industrious Doolittle, Major Joe Bunker, Sergeant Peabody, and Melodious Migrate—tried to show what he thought it was. He caught much of the flavor of American life—its country types, its city speculators, its military democrats, and its exuberant frontier adventurers. Because the old satirical comedy was passing and the new was still only roughly defined, other Yankee actors would turn more to story-situation plays, and with this direction Yankee theatre would decline. But James Hackett, because of his tie to Charles Mathews and the old spirit of comedy, was a satirist, mild and crude though his comedy may have been. He ventured to record on the stage what was incongruous in American life, and he failed of total success because his talent was not great enough to overcome the difficulties that confronted him. What he did achieve was encouragement of a whole race of impersonators of Yankee character to compete with him, competitors who, within a few years, practically eliminated him from the field he had laid out and tilled.

chapter 7

Hackett's Second London Tour, 1832 - 1833

THE POSITION of native American actors in the theatre of the 1830's is nowhere brought more sharply into focus than in James Hackett's second London appearance in the fall of 1832. In studying his capabilities as a performer in the Yankee-type character, we can see also the background against which he played: Anglo-American political and cultural relations, the state of development of the American stage in contrast to that of the English stage, and the significance of an American actor in London. The travel reports of Frances Trollope and others had greatly intensified English interest in America, and Hackett found Englishmen in 1832 far more curious than in 1827 about the national character of their cousins across the Atlantic. The newspaper reviewers who came to judge Hackett's Yankees asked much more basic questions than they had before: What is a Yankee? Is Hackett's delineation the real thing? They knew they could easily categorize him as an actor, but the other points were much more controversial. Because of the many newspapers reporting affairs of the theatre in England, our view of Hackett's acting—his techniques and style—is illuminated in London as it could not possibly have been at home. Instead of the small handful of sketchy comments in American journals such as the *New York Evening Post* and the *Mirror*, some two dozen accounts of the opening night alone are available, and these were followed by many more during the next months as Hackett showed his other characters—Monsieur Tonson, Rip Van Winkle, and Nimrod Wildfire. Of course we see here the images through London eyes, but

English critics were removed from the Yankee character and situa-ation, as are we today, and their pronouncements, despite whatever prejudice may have crept into them, are still more objective and less overtly sympathetic than an American view could possibly have been. Hackett in London was a novelty, for he was the first to dare aspire to the heights of the English stage and all that success there meant.

As a young American actor Hackett's position in 1832 was highly exceptional. In the six years he had been on the stage he had earned a reputation as first American comedian, a position which ranked him with tragedian Edwin Forrest. During the year and a half after Hackett added *The Moderns* and *Lion of the West* to his repertoire, he had played highly successful engagements in New York, Phila-delphia, and Boston; brought out a second version of *Lion*, this time by American playwright John Augustus Stone; and undertaken the rigors of a national tour which took him to Charleston and New Or-leans. In June of 1832 the *Mirror* published a lithograph and an extravagant front-page profile that lauded his pioneer efforts in be-half of American drama and labeled him the patriarch of comedy.[1] When London saw him at his Drury Lane opening on November 17, it could not push him lightly aside as it had done in 1827, for he was a comedian of established reputation. It was an American repu-tation, however, and this, to Englishmen, was of dubious value.

Theatre life in London during the early 1830's was a vigorous, highly competitive business.[2] The principal actors vied for top posi-tions by performing various characters in the common repertoire. It was not unusual to find two leading actors playing the same role in rival theatres either simultaneously or consecutively, or one star following another at the same theatre in a similar line. Jealousies were often aired openly in the press, sometimes with editorial prej-udice clearly indicated, and occasionally they reached the status of street combat. The critics were all-powerful and their criticism often extremely personal. Unlike today's theatre reviews, which devote the largest part of the space to play analysis, the actor and his style

[1] *Mirror*, IX (June 2, 1832), 377. The content of this chapter is based on an article by the author, "Yankee in England: James Henry Hackett and the Debut of American Comedy," *Quarterly Journal of Speech*, 45 (December, 1959), 381–390.

[2] Charles Macready's *Diaries* provide one of the most illuminating backgrounds for picturing the actor in London during the 1830's.

were given lengthy descriptive treatment. Critics frequently associated themselves closely with actors, and sometimes they acted as
private agents for them in procuring playscripts, making production
arrangements, or writing puffs. Daily changes of theatre bills induced daily critical comment, with many newspapers devoting extensive space to such reporting.

The life of the star actor was individual and creative. He "directed" himself in his roles and worked constantly at perfecting
them. Charles Macready's procedure before performance consisted
of rereading the play to be acted, rehearsing certain parts of it by
himself, and working for refinements. Sometimes he sought tips
from professional critics, but he often depended on a close friend as
a barometer. If the stock actors around him were of poor quality, he
had to carry the full weight of the play himself, with his own acting
not infrequently suffering because of their inadequacies. Macready
made a judgment on his playing—an entry in his diary—every time
he performed, setting down details about distractions or noting improvements or regressions. Like other actors he drank wine when
playing strenuous roles, for both energy and clarity of mind. He ate
dinner after performance, with an early tea beforehand. Each day
he played his clothes were laid out by his dresser from his own special wardrobe, although the theatre provided certain dresses for the
stock actors.

With most of this Hackett was familiar, either firsthand or by
report. He certainly knew, from his previous visit, about the censorship arrangements. Only the patent houses enjoyed the privilege of
performing plays, but they were required, in return for their protection against competition, to obtain licenses for all new scripts
from the Lord Chamberlain's Examiner, who could censor them in
whole or in part.

2

For his debut Hackett chose his adaptation of *Who Wants a Guinea?*
(Jonathan in England) and *Down East, or The Militia Muster,* his
two most successful Yankee pieces, and with this choice his troubles
began. Alfred Bunn, Drury Lane's manager, later blamed the American comedian for the decision, with the comment that the alteration
of Colman's play reflected "less taste than talent," but there is no
question that as manager he not only consulted with Hackett but

probably also encouraged him in the choice.[3] Bunn was too independent a manager, too much the avid businessman, to have haphazardly left such an important decision to an actor. Drury Lane business had been suffering badly during the previous weeks and needed the most careful attention. Besides, from his American experience Hackett had positive proof that these plays could draw business. So businessman Bunn undoubtedly came to terms with businessman Hackett, and Bunn took the first steps toward performance by setting up the company that was to act Hackett's pieces, and by applying to the Examiner of Plays for a license.

Now the fun began! George Colman, the Examiner of Plays, a much venerated playwright of the Sheridan-Goldsmith school of classical English comedy, had been providing entertaining plays for the English stage for half a century. As far as the London stage was concerned, Colman was considered John Bull himself. He was now asked to grant permission for performing a "mutilation" of his own play. And by a Yankee! Bunn realized the thin ground he was treading, for he approached Colman "in terms correspondent with those of the intimacy they were upon, merely inquiring if a license were necessary" for the alterations which he politely and respectfully delineated to author Colman as "rubbish." Colman's reply was as curt as it was prompt, and it clearly indicated his offended dignity. When Bunn opened the letter, so he innocently maintains, he experienced "considerable consternation" because of "the frigid monosyllable" with which the wit began:[4]

Brompton Square
14th November, 1832

Sir,

In respect to the alterations made by *Mr. Hackett*—a most appropriate name on the present occasion!—were the established play of any living dramatist, except myself, so mutilated, I should express to the Lord Chamberlain, the grossness and unfairness of the manager who encouraged such a proceeding;—but as the character of *Solomon Gundy* was originally a part of my own writing, I shall request His Grace to licence 'the rubbish,' as you call it, which you have sent me.

I am, Sir,
Your obedient servant
George Colman

[3] For Bunn's version of the affair see his autobiography, *The Stage*, I, 81–82.
[4] Bunn reproduces the letter. See also Peake, *Memoirs of the Colman Family*, II, 406–407.

The letter was clearly a cold reprimand of the Drury Lane manager, and a specific indication that, though Bunn might protest his innocence, Colman believed him as culpable in the matter as "mutilator" Hackett. The English playwright had not written any comedies for nearly a decade, but he was not about to be cast as the fool in a new one of Bunn's making without protest. Despite the outrageous affront, Colman did grant the license,[5] and plans for the opening moved forward.

Not all was clear sailing yet. Rumbling began in another quarter. The acting sides, or "lengths" as they were sometimes called, had been distributed to the actors who were to perform the two comedies with Hackett as star. It soon appeared that if the American comedian was to have his opening, it would have to be with the fullest cooperation and the kindest graces of the several actors who were to take part. What the other members of the company felt we do not know, but on November 16, the day before the opening, William Dowton, who was cast to play Torrent, showed himself to be as much irritated and affronted as Colman had been. In language not unlike that of the colorful, vigorous, audacious country gentlemen he so often took off in his comedy characters, he addressed himself to Manager Bunn:[6]

T.R.D.L.

16 Nov. 1832

My Dear Bunn,

D—— all Yankee editions of *Who Wants a Guinea*? Mr. Hackett seems a civil man to me, and I wish to oblige him if I can; so I am studying three lengths of his alterations; he is the only actor by-the-by, that designedly cuts out all his jokes—perhaps it's the American fashion. Now after all this d——d nonsense, do give me an order for tonight.

Yours truly,

W. Dowton

Dowton's irritation was no laughing matter. He was an actor of first-

---

[5] Lord Chamberlain's Collection, British Museum, No. 42919. This MS is a "side" for the role of Solomon Swap. Hackett undoubtedly assumed that the play was acceptable and only the alterations would be needed for approval. No authorship is credited. The title on the MS: "The character of Solomon Swap altered from the original Solomon Gundy, in Who Wants a Guinea?" Allardyce Nicoll does not include this in his playlist, *A History of the Early Nineteenth Century Drama, 1800–1850*, Vol. II.

[6] Bunn, *The Stage*, I, 81.

class reputation in the classical school of comedy, and in his forty years on the London stage, he had won high praise for his Sir Anthony Absolute, Sir Peter Teazle, Dr. Cantwell, Mr. Hardcastle, and Old Dornton.[7] Many thought him not only the best Malvolio but also, without question, the best Falstaff of his day. Leigh Hunt described him as a comic genius; Hazlitt praised him as "a genuine and excellent comedian"; and playgoers considered him the most finished actor in his line then on the stage. On the Monday preceding Hackett's opening the *Times* praised Dowton as "one of the most sterling actors of the day."[8] The transaction with Colman was a paper affair, but the inimitable Dowton would have to be dealt with in a very live fashion after the curtain went up. No matter how much warmth the English actor might profess for the American visitor, Hackett was still a potential rival as a comedian.

Whatever the usually mild-mannered Hackett thought about all this is not recorded. In view of his gentlemanly behavior during the opening performance, we can probably assume that he was fully aware of the rumpus he had stirred up and the difficulty he might have in quelling it. The situation was undoubtedly made even clearer when the two comedians came face to face in the rehearsal that preceded the opening. It would have been difficult indeed for Dowton to suppress his distaste for the entire affair, but he also had to reckon with a determined Hackett, who was not merely a pale stage representation of a Yankee but the genuine, stubborn, and clever "article" itself.

Opening night arrived. For several preceding nights Drury Lane audiences had been entertained with a succession of brilliant performances: Edmund Kean in *Hamlet* (Monday); Macready, Dowton, and Cooper in *School for Scandal* (Tuesday); Macready, Dowton, and Power in *Every Man in His Humour* (Thursday); and on the evening before Hackett's debut, Kean in *A New Way to Pay Old Debts*. And now it was the American's turn. Unlike his 1827 appearance, this time Hackett was to have a full evening to himself.

Ever since the Hallams had brought their company of actors to America in the 1750's, British players had crossed westward to the wildness and frontier civilization that was America. But the American-born actor was a rarity indeed, and now one was actually

[7] *Dictionary of National Biography*, XV, 408.
[8] *The Times*, November 12, 1832.

going to exhibit himself on Drury Lane stage. Washington Irving and James Fenimore Cooper might have won acceptance as men of letters, but the stage was quite a different matter. One could be howled down and hissed off in a matter of minutes. But for Hackett the gamble was worth it. If he were even moderately successful, his reputation in New York and other stateside cities would be greatly enhanced, and with it his pocketbook. Hackett had learned a great deal about those unaesthetic matters during his years as a goods merchant, and he viewed the London engagement with the practical eye of the character he was about to perform—shrewd bargainer Solomon Swap, "merchant in broom handles and other notions."

What happened that evening of November 17 must be put together from the play criticisms of the next few days.[9] When Hackett made his entrance on the stage in his long-tailed coat, bright vest, striped trousers, and red wig, he was greeted by one of the best houses of the season. Before the evening was over the courageous American had heard it run the full range of response from loud laughter and applause to hissing. *Jonathan in England* had been well cast; Bunn knew his job in that respect. The entertainment was promising, and the performance began quietly. But soon confusion began to reign. The irritated Dowton dropped some lines. The prompter undoubtedly gave support in his usual manner, but Dowton's line failure increased and he began to say whatever came into his head. Tyrone Power, who was cast as Sir Larry, also missed lines, as did some of the others, and the play became confused and erratic. As the situation worsened, so did Dowton's improvisations. With his resourceful imagination, and probably his growing anger at the injustice done him, Dowton's witticisms became more and more vulgar and indecent, "so gross and disgusting," reported one reviewer, "that no modest woman could listen to them without feelings of shame." In the midst of this predicament Hackett continued as calmly as he could, with a Yankee's determination to win the battle. Oath followed oath, so the report goes, "interspersed with

[9] The description of the performance and the criticism of Hackett's acting which follows is a composite of the following sources: *Journal of Belles Lettres, Figaro in London, The Age, The Athenaeum, The New Monthly Magazine, The Drama, The Examiner, The Times, The Morning Chronicle, True Sun, The Sun, The Courier, The Globe, The Morning Advertiser, The Morning Herald, The Morning Post.*

witless ribaldry," until Dowton had shocked and irritated every "respectable person in the house." The audience, which had been growing more and more active in its protest, finally took a vigorous hand in the affair and hissed its indignation and reproof at Dowton for his bad taste. This action must have had its effect, for the play finally ended to applause.

The performance of *The Militia Muster* concluded the evening.[10] Though Hackett had had a new version prepared, the reviews give the impression that only the muster scene was actually played. And that was enough! American theatregoers thought it was one of Hackett's funniest pieces, but the London audience reacted oppositely. They listened attentively for a few minutes, then began to show their disapproval. Again, as in 1827, Hackett heard from the house the galling cries of "Off! Off!" In the words of one of the critics, "A vigorous hiss closed the melancholy exhibition, and the debutant looked as foolish as under the circumstances might be expected. Drury Lane is clearly going to the dogs, as fast as bad management can carry it."[11] *The Militia Muster*, the totally original Yankee piece on the bill, was a total failure. Decision as to who had won the battle of the entire evening would have to wait for the critics and time.

3

When the reviews appeared during the ensuing days, the American fared much better than could be expected. He was defended, praised, and vigorously damned, with the weight of the scales largely on the last. *Figaro in London* lived up to its reputation of name calling and dyspeptic diatribe by crying down Hackett's treatment of *Who Wants a Guinea?* as a disgraceful mutilation of one of the best standard comedies in the English repertoire and labeling Hackett an American mountebank. Not having the talent to act a good part, asserted the critic, Hackett attempted to thrust himself upon the public in a bad one, the consequence of which was a monstrous failure. Likewise, the *Times* thought the "extravagant caricature"

[10] Nicoll (*History of the Early Nineteenth-Century Drama, 1800–1850*, Vol. II) records a Lord Chamberlain's entry for November 19, 1832. See L.C.C. No. 42924. The manuscript copy is dated 1833 but this is an error. The authorship is credited to S. Beazley.

[11] *Figaro in London*, November 24, 1832. This is the most blatant of the criticisms.

of Solomon Swap a damnable substitute for "amusing" Solomon
Gundy. Not only was Swap's slang incomprehensible, but, when
comprehended, "appeared to us to boast of no quality beyond sheer
vulgarity." Equally irate, but from another point of view, were the
critics for *The Athenaeum* and *The Journal of Belles Lettres*. The
first directed an attack on Colman with the quip that *Who Wants a
Guinea?* was written by the present licenser when he was "licen-
tious, or rather when his only license was that poetical one which he
now refuses to others." He then seriously castigated Dowton for his
offenses of the evening. "Mr. Dowton, when he will learn his part,"
he argued, "is a great acquisition to any theatre; but when he not
only forgets his part, but forgets himself in the bargain, the very
excellence of his acting increases the magnitude of his offence."
The second critic, without mentioning Dowton by name, was
equally incensed over Hackett's maltreatment. The reviewer
threatened to name names if something were not done about such
behavior in the future. To add insult to Hackett's injury, the
Times blandly praised Dowton and the other Drury Lane regulars,
scarcely mentioning the imperfection in the lines.

The diatribe against the American continued with serious ques-
tioning of the authenticity of Hackett's Yankee. One reviewer
thought the portrait so exaggerated that it bordered on that of the
West Indian Negro. Another thought it as far removed from reality
as the stage views of English ploughboys and peasantry in red
jackets, drab breeches, and white ribbed stockings with blue ribands
were from their real counterparts. And he goes on to assert that such
amusing beings as Solomon Swap were very rare in America, and
that Hackett caricatured his fellow countrymen more outrageously
than Mathews. While maintaining that it was hard to resist the
comicalities of Hackett, he declared that the half-idiotic expression
assumed by the actor was no more characteristic of a New Englander than the sing-song drawling tone was expressive of his
idiom. While he could recommend Hackett for a hearty laugh, he
cautioned against taking Swap seriously as the representative of the
"kind-hearted, shrewd, industrious, and somewhat reserved peasant
of Vermont and Massachusetts."[12] Another reviewer took exactly
the opposite view, by asserting that Hackett's celebrated delineation

[12] *Courier*, November 24, 1832.

Frances Trollope's *Domestic Manners of the Americans*

1. Ancient and Modern Republics.

Frances Trollope's *Domestic Manners
of the Americans*

2. Box at the Theatre (c. 1830).

3. View of the Bay of New York from the Battery in 1830.

4. Park Theatre and part of Park Row in New York in 1831.

5. Frances Trollope as drawn by Miss L. Adams.

6. Fanny Kemble as Juliet (c. 1830's).

7. George Pope Morris, editor of the *New York Mirror*.

8. Thomas Wignell as Jonathan in Royall Tyler's *The Contrast*,
an engraving by William Dunlap.

9. Charles Mathews in 1818.

10. Charles Mathews in 1833.

11. Charles Mathews as Agamemnon
in *Trip to America*.

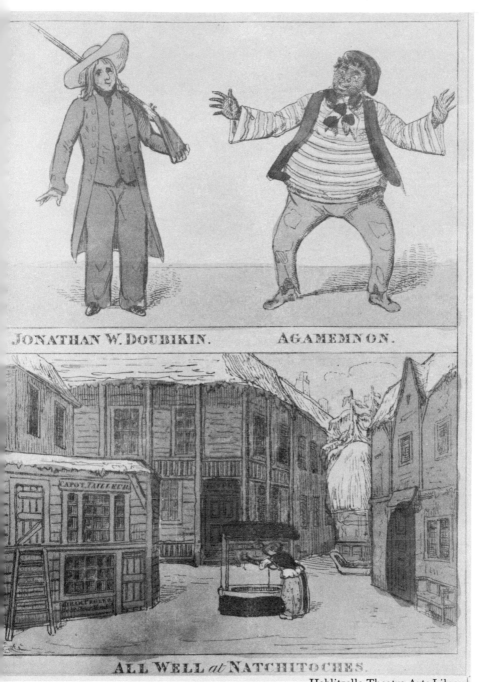

JONATHAN W. DOUBIKIN.   AGAMEMNON.

ALL WELL *at* NATCHITOCHES.

12. Charles Mathews as Jonathan W. Doubikin and Agamemnon, and the stage setting for the sketch of "All Well at Natchitoches" in *Trip to America*.

Colonel Hiram Peglar.   Monsieur Capot.   Agamemnon.

Pub. by Hodgson

Hoblitzelle Theatre Arts Library

13 Charles Mathews as Colonel Hiram Peglar, Monsieur Capot...

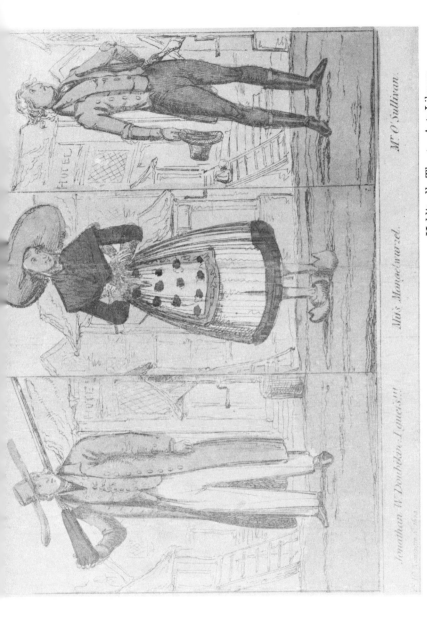

Jonathan W. Doubikin. I guess!!!　　　　Miss Mangelwurzel.　　　　Mr. O'Sullivan.

Hoblitzelle Theatre Arts Library

14. Charles Mathews as Jonathan Doubikin, Miss Mangelwurzel, and Mr. O'Sullivan in *Trip to America*.

The MATHEW · ORAMA · in 1824 ··
Pretty considerable d'improvement on Till Bits from America being th'mist of Natchitoches.

Hoblitzelle Theatre Arts Library

15. Charles Mathews in the roar, lower lanuder larger In T

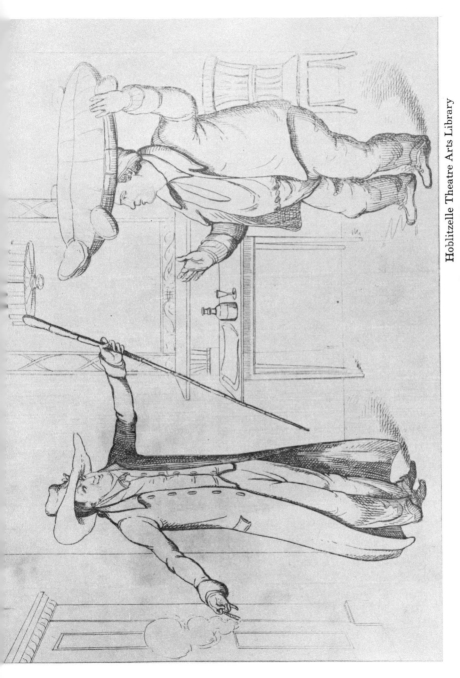

16. Charles Mathews as Jonathan, with the character of Agamemnon in Richard B. Peake's *Jonathan Doubikins*.

17. James Henry Hackett in 1832.

19. Catherine (Leesugg) Hackett, first wife of James H. Hackett.

18. Mrs. Sharpe, sister-in-law of James H. Hackett.

Mr Hackett as Solomon Swap.

"How will you swap watches, unsight unseen?"

20. James H. Hackett as Solomon Swap in *Jonathan in England*, his adaptation of George Colman's *Who Wants a Guinea?*

back, stranger! or I'll plug you like a watermillion!"

Mr. Hackett as "Nimrod Wildfire."

From the original painting by A. Andrews in the possession of Thomas E. McKee Esq.

21. James H. Hackett in his backwoods character of
Nimrod Wildfire in *Lion of the West*.

HACKETT AS FALSTAFF,

22. A caricature of James H. Hackett in his famous characterization of Shakespeare's Falstaff.

23. George Handel Hill in 1834.

24. George Hill as Jedidiah Homebred in J. S. Jones' *The Green Mountain Bo*

25. George Hill as Nathan Tucker in W. Bayle Bernard's *Wife for a Day*.

MR HILL.
(The admired American Comedian)
as "MAJOR WHEELER" in the Farce of "NEW NOTIONS".

26. George Hill as Major Enoch Wheeler in W. Bayle Bernard's *New Notions*

George Hill as Hiram Dodge in W. Bayle Bernard's *The Yankee Pedlar*.

28. George Hill in a familiar Yankee pose: whittling a stick.

29. Danforth Marble (c. 1840).

31. Dan Marble as Jacob Jewsharp in J. P. Addams'

30. Dan Marble as Sampson Hardhead in

32. Joshua Silsbee (c. 1851) as Jonathan Ploughboy in
Samuel Woodworth's *The Forest Rose*.

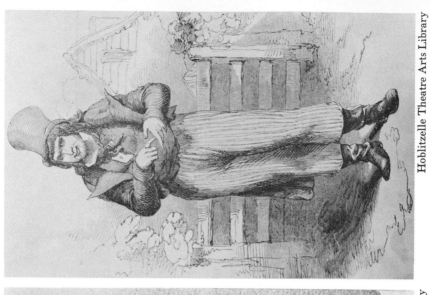

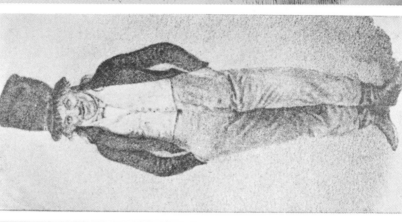

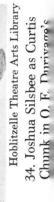

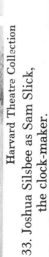

Harvard Theatre Collection
33. Joshua Silsbee as Sam Slick, the clock-maker.

Hoblitzelle Theatre Arts Library
34. Joshua Silsbee as Curtis Chunk in O. E. Durivage's

Hoblitzelle Theatre Arts Library
35. Joshua Silsbee, the American Corn. lin

38. Charles K. Fox, the first Gumption Cute in *Uncle Tom's Cabin.*

37. Charles Burke (c. 1855).

36. Joshua Silsbee in a character.

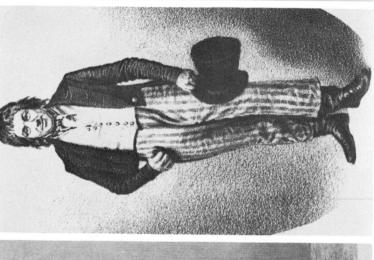

41. William F. Gates as Peter Spyk.

40. George Locke
in a Yankee character.

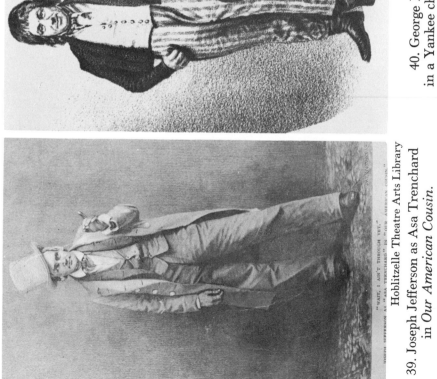

39. Joseph Jefferson as Asa Trenchard
in *Our American Cousin.*

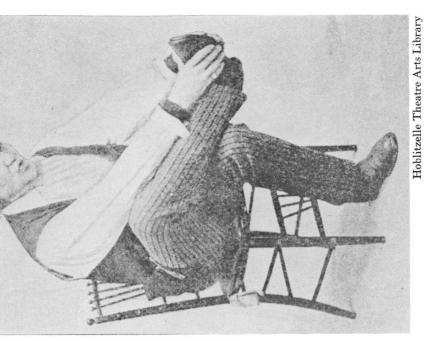

SOLON SHINGLE.

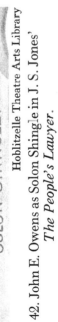

43. James A. Herne as Nat Berry in his own play
Shore Acres.

42. John E. Owens as Solon Shingle in J. S. Jones'
The People's Lawyer.

44. John Augustus Stone, author of
The Knight of the Golden Fleece.

45. David Humphreys, author
The Yankey in England.

46. Samuel Woodworth, author of
The Forest Rose.

47. Joseph M. Field, author of
Family Ties.

Harvard Theatre Collection

48. Cornelius A. Logan, author of *Yankee Land*.

New York Public Library Theatre Collection

49. Joseph Stevens Jones, author of
The Green Mountain Boy.

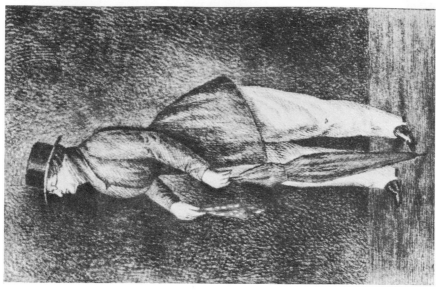

51. Henry J. Finn, author of

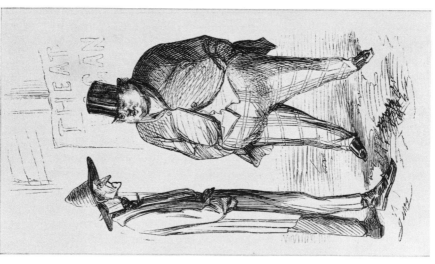

50. Cornelius A. Logan in a character.

of the American character utterly failed because it was not a conscious imitation but the real thing itself. He argued that the American comedian had not sifted out the characteristic points and given a concentrated picture, but had made a "random, indiscriminating assumption of the character in mass."[13] "Mr. Hackett says to himself, 'Now I will be a Yankee,' and accordingly he brings the monster in proper person before us, and in that short space of time one can gain as little knowledge from him as from so many hours of residence in America, or less." A good imitator, the reviewer wrote, should not merely consult his own experience of character but also inquire into the ignorance of the audience in order to devise a comprehensible delineation. A more favorable point of view assumed that since the American press had declared the correctness of Hackett's Yankee, the audience could assume that it was seeing the real thing—familiar, civil, obliging, simple, cunning, with imperturbable good humor, insatiable curiosity, and a spirit of inquiry which asks for all sorts of information. Some reviewers argued over what should have been done, with one declaring that Hackett was too much heralded in advance; another that the choice of appearing in Yankee characters was an unfortunate decision; a third that he seriously doubted the popularity of ridicule of Americans; a fourth that it was far from judicious to turn Gundy into Swap.

The Militia Muster was attacked by both those for and those against its principal actor. Reviewers saw in it an original American piece that, despite the borrowing from Mathews' sketch, would have to be judged completely on its own merits. The kindest comment thought it poorly arranged for the stage, and, because of the similarity of phrases to those in the first piece, dull and tiresome. *Figaro*, as expected, called it a "trashy opiate," as "equally glaring and tiresome" as *Who Wants a Guinea?* Other reviewers agreed, one asserting that it was so stupid that no talent, however great, could have saved it. Another thought Major Bunker and his muster must come from Louisiana or Kentucky. A third thought it identical with Solomon Swap. The most interesting comment, though it was labeled "twaddle" by another critic, came from the reviewer of the *Times*, who thought it not only a "stupid farce" but "a gross piece of impertinence" and a serious reflection on the American charac-

[13] *True Sun*, November 19, 1832.

ter. The critic of *The Age* disagreed with its giant friend and, with tongue-in-cheek, took the opposite view that it was "an insult to the British character, by endeavoring to point out to us 'the rugged rascals,' in the shape of soldiers, that say they beat the English 'regulars' in divers military rencontres. Honest John, thy head is now and then thick as a mill-stone."

When the reviewers turned directly to Hackett's acting, they were not as blunt and outspoken as they had been about the plays. Most were cautious in their comments, evincing a wait-and-see attitude. He was not openly controversial, as Edwin Forrest would be, nor was he regarded indifferently. Those who took a more negative position saw him as an overcharged caricaturist, more mimic than actor, with a lack of variety in his manner. In their view the American was easily transcended by Mathews, and he should not expect much favorable response from the London public. On the other hand his confidence and "high opinion of his powers and of the treat he was giving his audience" were noted. One reviewer argued that Hackett's personation of a "genuine" Jonathan was "life itself," and that his "constant watchfulness of eye, his gait, and his mingled cunning and boorishness," were very cleverly portrayed. This reviewer also thought there was much dry, quaint humor about him and that he was an inimitable "teller" of American stories. Another labeled him an actor of "considerable humour" and "considerable ease." This reviewer attested Hackett's truthfulness in the Yankee character by recalling firsthand experiences with Yankees on a visit to the States several years previously. A third was much delighted with Hackett's personations and thought that he "hit" off the peculiarities of the Americans "very happily." He urged further that Hackett be signed for a regular engagement. Some thought his acting was free and easy, and that he had much fun about him when stage business excited him to action. Even the *Times* grudgingly admitted that he possessed a certain portion of low humor, and would probably be seen to advantage in broad comedy or farce. The most favorable comments accorded him ability, ease of manner and breadth of humor.

In the overview, however, the real significance of Hackett's rejection did not lie in what the critics and the public thought specifically of his choice of materials or his acting. The hardest and perhaps the most honest criticism was the unstated but implied recognition of the difference between levels in theatre and cultural activity in England and America. Because this was the first attempt by an American to place himself in contrast with English actors on London's stage, no comparative criticism was possible though a great deal was implied. One critic preferred to make the point, and then make light of it, by asserting that the balance of account for good acting, "sold and delivered" between the two countries was very much against the Americans. But "seeing how slender is our present stock of raw material, we don't care how soon they take measures for paying off." Though the difference was not overtly stated, many sided with Alfred Bunn's point of view expressed later when London had seen Edwin Forrest, Yankee Hill, Mr. Barrett, Mrs. Sharpe, and T. D. Rice. Bunn thought that Americans could not, or would not,

draw the line of distinction between the advanced degree of taste and refinement at which this country has naturally arrived, and the struggle which their own (like other countries in their infancy) is making to possess taste or refinement at all. We have had to go through the same fight ourselves when we were emerging from barbarism into civilization, and our children should learn from our example, that it is impossible to become perfect at once.[14]

Bunn's view was argued honestly and sincerely, and though he might have underestimated the American's humble view of himself, his was still the best statement of the case. The American's desire for recognition in stage matters was to continue for the rest of the century and was to have serious consequences in the Forrest-Macready controversy.

The Hackett-Dowton story was not without its ironies. When the "most finished comedian of his times" paid a starring visit to the States four years later, his Park Theatre engagement was a financial failure.[15] No matter how much the critics might respect him, the popular audience could not accept his highly refined talents and abilities, and they turned easily to the broader drolleries of Hackett. The final ironic postscript was recorded at Dowton's last perform-

[14] Bunn, *The Stage*, II, 34–35.
[15] Odell, *Annals*, IV, 64 ff.

ance in America, when both comedians, on the eve of the disappointed Dowton's departure for England, appeared at the New York National Theatre's benefit for William Hamblin after the burning of the Bowery Theatre. *I Henry IV*, with the best cast that New York could muster, was the major piece of the evening. It was to be followed by dancer Celeste and two afterpieces. Who performed Dowton's famous role of Falstaff? American comedian James Hackett! And Dowton played the second afterpiece.[16]

The unusual history of Hackett's adaptation of *Who Wants a Guinea?* and *The Militia Muster* could hardly have been anticipated on the basis of their London receptions. Hackett subsequently played Solomon Swap over five hundred times, and it was "borrowed" by other Yankee actors for probably an equal number of performances. With the possible exception of Samuel Woodworth's *The Forest Rose*, it was probably the most widely played theatre piece in America before 1850. Major Joe Bunker in *The Militia Muster* achieved almost as much popularity, and he remained in Hackett's repertoire for a quarter of a century. The similarity of the two roles, which the English reviewers had pointed out, apparently made little difference to American audiences. A *Mirror* critic probably spoke for audiences in the States when he wrote: "We saw Jonathan Swap for the fiftieth time, more or less, and laughed with the same relish as when we first witnessed his [Hackett's] amusing parody of New Englanders and their manners."[17]

The thumbs-down verdict of the London play reviewers discouraged Hackett from attempting a Yankee character in London again, though he played there in 1836 and again in 1839. But his tour was not without its compensations. Before Hackett left London in the summer of 1833, he had won moderate praise with *Rip Van Winkle* and a third version of *Lion of the West*.[18] These performances gave reviewers a much firmer basis on which to refine their views of his capabilities as a low comedian. He had also paved the

[16] *Ibid.*, 140–141.

[17] *Mirror*, XIII (November 19, 1835), 91.

[18] For an account of the play in London see an article by the author, "Biography of a Lost Play," *Theatre Annual*, 1954. Hackett also played one more performance of *Who Wants a Guinea?* on November 23, 1832, in combination with *Monsieur Tonson*, another play in his regular repertoire.

way to Drury Lane Theatre for other Americans. During the next few years London saw all of the new crop of native-born comedians and tragedians, a trans-Atlantic move eastward that truly began the establishment of an indigenous American theatre in accomplishment as well as in name.

chapter 8

Hackett Expands the Repertoire

AMES HACKETT returned home from the London tour to face a high wave of excitement over what he had done. The welcome he found at the Park, and in Boston and Philadelphia, where he played between the frequent New York engagements, even he had not anticipated. So potent were the Drury Lane, Covent Garden, and Haymarket theatre labels now attached to his name that playgoers simply forgot, even if they had known, that he had met catastrophe with the Yankee character. Those who did think of it tended to write it off as British retaliation for past embarrassments and not as a failure of the actor's capabilities or the materials he had used. To take the Yankee directly into the stronghold of the ancient enemy was courting misunderstanding and worse, and such courage was recommendation enough for a hero's medal. So Hackett prospered vigorously at the box office and found a reputation he had not enjoyed before.

Nevertheless, though temporarily forgotten, the London failure was to leave its mark on the comedian. Within three years, except for Solomon Swap and Major Joe Bunker, he would give up playing the Yankee character and turn to the broader area of dialect comedy. The London judgment was merely the first indication of what was to follow, for Hackett simply could not play "genuine" Yankees. He had thrust himself directly into competition with the indomitable Mathews, whose images of the Yankee were still fresh in the audience mind. The extensive talent of the older, far more experienced comedian had won out in the battle where the material used was in the category of general American description rather than in the specifics of New Englanders. Where Hackett's American images could not be readily compared—Rip Van Winkle and Nimrod Wildfire—he came much closer to acceptance. Mathews had set no pattern for these natives, and they were as fresh and unexpected to London theatregoers as they had been to his audiences at home. To do battle with *The Militia Muster* was to copy poorly from Mathews and to repeat his "Uncle Ben" misfortune of 1827; to transpose Solomon Gundy into Solomon Swap, though for the better, was again to borrow but in an unsanctioned way. When Hackett was able to move with originality, he did not have the unique capacities of a top comedian that would allow him to survive. Durang's evaluation, as he compares him to other stars of the day, may be the most accurate epitaph: "One of the weakest of the great ones."

The major threat to Hackett, however, was not the critical judgment of the London play reviewers. This was paper dictum which the box office did not necessarily reflect. The really dangerous challenge was on the home front in the person of George H. Hill. While Hackett was in London busily preparing for his opening, Simpson and Price invited Hill to play a Yankee at the Park. The damage to Hackett from this engagement is revealed in what follows during the next three years as we watch Hill push the older comedian aside and usurp the position of first Yankee actor. The London dictum and Hill's sudden rise occurred simultaneously, and together they declared Hackett's decline in Yankee theatre. The innovator from Jamaica had given much to the development and nurturing of the stage Yankee, but no sooner had it been fully declared than a performer of greater talent in the role took his place. Hackett would try hard to hold his own, but with Hill on the scene, and then Dan Marble and Joshua Silsbee, he would gradually abandon the competition. In the long run Hackett was not to suffer greatly from it, because, unlike the others, he could play a wide range of character-dialect roles which would continue to sustain him in a long stage career until his death in 1871. In the overview of Hackett's work on the stage the Yankee character was a passing inspiration for him. He made the most of its possibilities as long as the audience favored him, and then, when more capable actors appeared, left it for those roles to which he had an individual and unrivaled claim.

2

When Hackett debarked in New York, Hill's challenge was as yet scarcely noticeable. He plunged immediately into the business of first comedian, and within a year tried out five Yankee plays, three of which were new. On September 18, 1833, he played Mathews' original piece, *Jonathan Doubikins*; on March 17, 1834, in Boston he tried *Paul Pry from Down East*; on April 16 he showed Park audiences *The Wag of Maine* for the first time; on May 10 he performed *Major Jack Downing, or the Retired Politician*; and on October 1, thirteen months after he began playing again in New York, he introduced *Job Fox, or the Yankee Valet*. These new pieces were the novelties to fill out his standard repertoire of Rip, Wildfire, Swap, Tonson, Mallet, and Joe Bunker. Always an opportunist and a businessman, his intention was obviously to reap as much profit from the Yankee as he could before others discovered its lucrative possibilities. So constantly are we made aware of this, not only from the theatre gossip of the time but as we watch him work out situations, that we are prone to push aside his craftsmanship as an actor and call up Joe Cowell's image of "dramatic merchant." But in a highly competitive theatre where actors had no agents to do business for them as they do today, and a star system in which only the fittest survived, usually at the mercy of a few important theatre managers, Hackett had no illusions about where he stood. There was real money in the native dialect type of theatre he had found, and he set about the business of exploiting it with Yankee astuteness and enterprise.

A good example of his keen business sense is illustrated in his choice of *Jonathan Doubikins* for his first Yankee role at the Park. At first view this takes on the appearance of another direct borrowing from Charles Mathews, since this play is, of course, the *Jonathan in England* that Peake wrote for the English comedian to follow *Trip to America* in 1824. As already noted, Mathews tried it but a few times, and then withdrew it because of its highly offensive satire on the American attitude toward slavery.[1] This did not deter

---

[1] See Chapter 4 for a detailed treatment of this play. Mathews acted it on

Hackett, who undoubtedly saw a real opportunity. With some judicious arranging, the play could easily be turned about to become instead of an attack on Americans, something of a mild satire on the English themselves, while providing a story framework for still another sort of Yankee. Did Hackett arrange with Peake for the use of the play, or did he also "borrow" this one outright as he had done with Colman's comedy? We do not know.

What the Park audience saw was quite different from Mathews' version.[2] The biting satire on Jonathan's treatment of Agamemnon was entirely eliminated, as was Blanche, the free English Negro who encourages the slave to rebellion. With the songs cut, all that remained was a straight situation comedy. But as an opening piece for an actor-traveler who had just returned from England, *Jonathan Doubikins* was more than adequate. Instead of an English actor like Mathews playing a Yankee just arrived in England and determined on noting all quick impressions for his travel report to Americans, we have the authentic American repeating the same lines and going through the same business. Thus the play is turned back upon itself. Instead of a hard satire on Americans, Hackett was probably able to turn it into an amusing look at the English themselves, with clever and slick Yankee Jonathan emerging as a superior wit among his more prosaic and inept, even stupid, cousins. Comedy ideas fade quickly as time submerges their application, but to assume that Hackett was interested only in the external story possibilities of the play is to underestimate his awareness of the fun he could have at the expense of the English. No actor could have been clobbered more completely than Hackett had been in London, and now here was a chance to return some of the "misunderstanding." There is a note of irony in all this as Hackett again entertained his home audiences with comedy they understood and enthusiastically appreciated. Was Hackett having something of a last laugh at the English in turning *Jonathan Doubikins* about? Other Yankee actors to follow Hackett were to

---

September 7, 1827. This may have been his last performance in the character. Had Hackett's visit encouraged its use at this late date?

[2] Hackett's promptbook for the new version is included in the Hackett papers of the Enthoven Collection, Victoria and Albert Museum. This version is dated May, 1838, and was prepared by J. C. Ferrer of the National Theatre, New York. The first page presents a property list.

play the role, but it could not have had the same overtones of meaning that Hackett could have given it.

What induced the businessman-comedian to try *Paul Pry* in Yankee dialect, first at Boston's Tremont and then a week later at the Park (March 26, 1834), is much more obscure. A single performance of the play is recorded, with Hackett as Paul, at the Chestnut Street Theatre in Philadelphia three years earlier (March 28, 1831), but there is no indication that the actor played him as a Yankee. In the 1834 version, Paul Pry has definitely become a "down-Easter," or at least Hackett's version of one. The manuscript of the original play indicates that Paul is a middle-aged character type, with an umbrella, who assists the workings of an involved plot. No dialect is indicated although on the English stage, where most prominent comedians played him at one time or another, he was probably acted with a county accent. Did Hackett see in this play the same possibility that he saw in *Who Wants a Guinea?*, the chance to coat the character with Yankeeisms and thus make something fresh and original for his American audience? Since he played the role only a few times, it probably did not add much to his gallery of Yankee personalities.

Of much more interest is *The Wag of Maine*. Though again Hackett found it playable for only a few performances, it is an important Yankee theatre piece because, in its rewritten versions, it became a mainstay in Dan Marble's repertoire under the title of *Yankee Land*. No authorship is credited on Hackett's manuscript;[3] but since the Marble version is unquestionably the work of Cornelius A. Logan, and he is credited elsewhere,[4] it can be assumed that this actor–stage-manager–writer[5] provided Hackett with the first draft. Did they meet when Logan was acting in Philadelphia, or in Albany, where he was working as an actor in 1832? Could the play have been submitted for Hackett's prize contest that turned up *Lion of the West*? Again we do not know. There is evidence that Logan had a firsthand acquaintance with the stage type because he had tried acting the Yankee himself. Durang tells us he performed Joel Jedjog in *Green Mountaineer* fairly successfully at the Arch

[3] Enthoven Collection, Victoria and Albert Museum.

[4] Robert F. Roden, *Later American Plays*, p. 77; also James Rees, *Dramatic Authors of America.* p. 98.

[5] See Chapter 13 for additional reference to Logan's work in Yankee theatre.

Street Theatre in the fall of 1833, and on one other occasion had tried Zekiel Longshaw in *Nighthawk*. In trying to find a repertoire of Yankee plays Hackett had borrowed from English plays, had sought them from occasional writers at home, and had even written some of his own material. What is different about Logan's appearance on the scene is that he is a native-born actor-writer, in one view the first of what might be called Yankee-theatre playwrights. His work is purely journeyman, for his use is that of plot provider to sustain the Yankee impersonations of specific actors with whose style and approach he is already familiar. He is not at all a writer in the literary sense, but only in the primitive-stage sense. Any criticism of his work must therefore be judged completely in the light of what Hackett, and, later on, Dan Marble were able to make of it before audiences.

Logan was anything but a Yankee.[6] He was born near Baltimore on May 4, 1806, the son of an Irish-American farmer who was killed by British troops while working in the fields during the fall of 1814. We find Logan for a brief time studying for the priesthood at St. Mary's College, then working in a shipping house, and finally traveling to Europe as a sailor. He took a job as Assistant Manager of the *Baltimore Morning Chronicle*, and shortly thereafter started a penny newspaper with William Leggett, then a drama critic in Philadelphia. With the trade of printer and the ambitions of clergyman as background, Logan drifted into the theatre in 1825, first in Philadelphia, then at the Bowery Theatre in New York where he played Smith in *The Road to Ruin*, Claudio in *Much Ado About Nothing*, and Trip in *School for Scandal*. Assured of a living as an actor, Logan moved on to management in Albany and then later to the Ohio River towns, where he spent the remainder of his life "working the rivers," with the family at home in Cincinnati. As an actor Logan later attained some celebrity, especially in the West, where he was generally accepted as a successful comedian. The roles of Peter Teazle and Peter Simpson were so firmly attached to him that he was called Peter in private life by many who supposed

[6] Logan is frequently mentioned in nineteenth-century theatre accounts. See the autobiographical works of his daughter, Olive Logan, *Apropos of Women and Theatres* and *The Mimic World and Public Exhibitions;* Phelps, *Players of a Century*, p. 156; Sol Smith, *Theatrical Management in the West and South for Thirty Years*, pp. 186, 216, 228; Ludlow, *Dramatic Life*, pp. 583, 706; Rees, *Dramatic Authors*, p. 98; Brown, *History*, p. 222; D.A.B., XI, 357.

it was his real name. A close friendship sprang up between Sol Smith and Logan, and the intimate letters on theatrical matters which passed between them fully reveal the character of both men. When he wrote *The Wag of Maine*, however, Logan was in his late twenties, with the fashioning of a career still ahead of him.

This first version of *Yankee Land* is crude and undeveloped, though all the essential elements of the later play are intact. Mischievous Joe, the Yankee character, is a foundling and a country rustic who lives with his guardian, Mr. Rowell, on the river Kennebec, State of Maine. In a series of involvements he helps to expose the scoundrelly Rowell, the steward of Sir Charles Anson, after Rowell blackmails Lieutenant Marshall into giving him his daughter, who loves another, in exchange for keeping secret Marshall's supposed murder of Sir Charles Anson. Sir Charles suddenly appears at Kennebec. Surprised by this employer whom he thought dead, Rowell attempts to murder him, but Mischievous Joe melodramatically intervenes. Rowell is apprehended and Marshall is absolved. The latter finds his long-lost wife in Mrs. Westray; Lavinia marries her lover; and Joe turns out to be the long-lost son of Sir Charles. Impossible and unlikely though it may be as a plot, in later versions it will be widely played as a framework for the comic Mischievous Joe, or his later name, Lot Sap Sago.

How different this piece is from the others that Hackett has brought to the stage. No satire or fun poking at Yankee oddities is apparent here. *The Wag of Maine* is a situation comedy-melodrama, with a sketchily drawn Yankee and two or three other miscellaneous comic types to set him against. Its success would depend entirely on how amusing Hackett could make Mischievous Joe in the playing. Was Hackett looking for a country-boy type in order to compete with *Green Mountain Boy*, which George Hill had introduced so successfully the previous year at the Park? There is much in the play that suggests this. Jonathan Doubikins was probably a youthful Yankee, but he is not the full-blown, bear-hunting rustic we find in Joe. Always on the lookout for possible new directions in which he could move with the character, Hackett may have seen unusual possibilities in the awkward love scene with Lavinia or noted Joe's ambling, open qualities which relate him more closely to Nimrod Wildfire than to Solomon Swap. Was Joe really a Yankee? The closest Logan had touched New England life was in his work at

Albany, where, like Hackett at Utica, he had undoubtedly talked with many of this country species. But he does not really know them firsthand. In the playing of the piece Hackett probably inserted his own Yankee stories as he saw fit, and with the basic fund of lore he had already developed around the character type, he undoubtedly could use *The Wag of Maine* to fair advantage. Rees reports that the New York papers pronounced this the best American comedy that had been written up to that time. Hackett's use of the play, however, scarcely supports such a bold assertion, for he played it but a few times and then set it aside. Again, was the competition with *Green Mountain Boy* too noticeable? If *The Wag of Maine* had been specifically useful to Hackett, Logan could not have recovered it and turned it over to Dan Marble as he did a few years later.

Hackett's move away from the Mathews-like satirical approach with the stage Yankee is a definite turning point in his work with the character. Hill's amazing success with the story-type play must have been at least partially responsible for it. Satire, no matter how mild, was giving way to the popular, lower-level audience demand for novel entertainment. As playgoers rushed to see the new melodramas of the day, they also must have expected only the simplest sort of humor from comedy. But Hackett had not given up entirely. Less than a month after he played Mischievous Joe for the first time at the Park, he made a last effort at satire on May 10, 1834, with *Major Jack Downing, or the Retired Politician*.

No script or fragment survives to tell us about this piece. Yet there is no doubt about its source. Seba Smith had introduced the character the previous year in *The Life and Writings of Major Jack Downing of Downingville*, and the Major had become a highly popular literary concoction. He is a sort of Yankee Davy Crockett, not dissimilar from the backwoodsman-politician Hackett already had featured in *Lion of the West*. The new Yankee piece is undoubtedly drawn from the letters about Jack's life in the state legislature in Portland, Maine, and his office seeking in Washington. Hackett had already told similar tales of political life through Sylvester Daggerwood and Josh Doolittle, and now a sketch was shaped from Smith's amusing rustic biography. Was it actually intended to be a companion piece to *Lion of the West*—a New England rustic politician to contrast with the Tennessee or Kentucky backwoods democrat? The cast of characters has the New England flavor: Ser-

Seba Smith's *The Life and Writings of Major Jack Downing*
Major Jack Downing.

geant Joel, Uncle Josh, Aunt Rachel, Prudence Bigelow, and, of
course, the Major. And the satirical overtones are obvious as we
follow the naive and clever Major in Portland and Washington.

Again Hackett has competition, only this time it is he who com-
petes. On April 24, W. F. Gates had first played the Major at the
Bowery Theatre in a piece titled *Life in New York, or The Major's
Come*.[7] This was a sort of extravaganza with scenes for T. D. Rice,
who had only recently made a sensation with his Negro character
of Jim Crow. Hackett, however, had nothing to fear from Gates,
whom the *Mirror* reported as a promising but by no means firstrate
comedian. The presence of such a sketch at the Bowery, neverthe-

[7] Odell, *Annals*, III, 685.

AMERICAN
THEATRE.....BOWERY.

LAST WEEK !!!

OWING TO THE UNPARALLELLED SUCCESS OF

LIFE IN NEW-YORK,
And the great anxiety, nightly manifested, to witness

MAJOR JACK DOWNING,
That piece will be repeated every Evening until the arrival of Mr. Forrest.

The Manager is happy to announce, that an engagement has been effected with

Mr. Rice, the Celebrated Jim Crow,
To appear in the above piece for a few nights, for whom several NEW SCENES have been Expressly Written.

On Wednesday Evening, May 21st, 1834,
Will be performed a New Local Entertainment, called

Life in New-York,
Or, the Major's Come
EMBRACING THE VARIOUS PROMINENT FEATURES IN ITS PURSUITS & AMUSEMENTS
Which continues to be received with the most enthusiastic cheers.
SCENERY by DUKE WHITE.............MUSIC by ST. LUKE.
The whole got up under the direction of MR. ANDERSON.

Frank Dashaway,	warranted sound, and free from Vice,	Mr. G. Jones
George Wheatfield,	a green one at home, but ripe when transplanted,	Flynn
Old Evergreen,	an evergreen,	Gale
Ezekiah Eddy,	a careful Guardian, spirituously spirited,	Farren
Old Dashaway,	Too fond of his son to make a good father,	McClure
MAJOR JACK DOWNING,	well known in the city, but better understood at Washington,	Mr. GATES
Jack Nasty,	a knowing one for a novice,	Taylor
Harry Holdstakes,	a loafer, better known than trusted,	Conner
Tom Mason,	an exception to the general rule,	Stevenson
JIM CROW,		MR. RICE
Dandy Crooks,	Too well known to need description,	Hanson
OSLUMBER,	a night mare,	ANDERSON
Ned Nobody,	a hard character, struggling for importance,	Collins
Captain Rowbell,	making a haul out of the Yankees,	Wheatley
Jem,	Loafers occasionally employed as	Lewis
Sam,	Government Stone Cutters,	Addis
Spouting Owlit,	a stage struck here, good colour for Othello,	Sowerby
Caesar Scrapeclean,	a low nigger of high birth,	Blackley
Tailer,	Mr. Flim	Cate Oakstick,	Mr. Bloson
Frenchman,		Mr. Jean Crapeau
Lucy Wirlove,	a sentimental young Lady, but not backward in her pursuit of a good husband,	Mrs. Flynn
Rose Evergreen,	More spirit than sentiment	Herring
Mrs. Dashaway,	a Lady of Liberal expenditure	Stevenson
Miss Volatile,	Rather flighty	Gale
MRS. TROLLOPE,	and Family Group, by a well bred Lady of Foreign distraction, and her appendages	
Master of Ceremonies,	La Ponji	Miss Johnson
Antonio,		Irish

With many others, well known but too numerous to be mentioned,

LIFE IN THE COUNTRY,
Chorus—"Lo, brightly the Morning." City Temptations and Youthful impulse. Three Cheers for Life in
New-York. An old fashioned Rail Road. Chorus—"Away to the City, gay delight."
HUDSON STEAM BOAT LANDING.
Chorus—"Coach, Coach." Major Jack Downing's Marsh. Arrival of a Private Character of Public Notoriety
Prejudice.
TATTERSALLS.
Chorus—"Who'll buy a Mare to Run or Trot." A City Outfit,
BROADWAY.
A Green One among the Girls. Appointment. The Quickest Method of Getting Rich,
MISS VOLATILE'S.
Lucy in a new character. Duet—"With my Hat cocked aside."
BALL ROOM, in all its Brilliance.......Mr. St. Luke has kindly volunteered to take the management of
the floor on this occasion.
PAS de DEUX, BY MR. ST. LUKE AND MISS JOHNSON.
The Major and Mrs. Trollope. Family Groups. Unhappy Blunder. Chorus—"Oh what a lubly nigger wench.

Bowery Theatre playbill (May 21, 1834) for *Life in
New-York, or, the Major's Come* with W. F. Gates as
Major Jack Downing.

less, indicates the growing popularity of the Yankee play and the fact that Hackett no longer had the field to himself, particularly with Seba Smith's fanciful invention. Scarcely a year later George Hill would also be playing the Major, with only a slight variation of the Bowery's title: *Life in New York, or Lion of the East.* How good was Hackett's play? The comedian soon abandoned Jack to other Yankee impersonators, and we can only assume that it was not of the best.

The last Yankee play that James Hackett introduced to American audiences was *Job Fox, the Yankee Valet,* which he first played on October 1, 1834, at the Park Theatre, scarcely eight years after he had first begun telling his Yankee story of Uncle Ben. What a wide gap there is between the two. Uncle Ben was absolute confusion and perplexity to London audiences in 1827. What effect *Job Fox* would have made had Hackett played it at the English Opera House on August 1–3, 1836, as he was scheduled to do on his third trip to the English capital, we cannot know. For some unexplained reason his engagement was cancelled, and he never acted the piece there, despite permission granted by the Lord Chamberlain. Had he played it, we can surmise that no such perplexity would have been present as on the first occasion, for *Job Fox* is a situation farce, simple in design, and drawn in the style of a J. A. Buckstone or Placide comedy. The authorship is attributed to W. Bayle Bernard, an American-born hack playwright for the English stage, who was useful later to George Hill.[8] Hackett probably negotiated the script during the 1832–1833 London visit, and held it during the year after his return until he needed a box-office stimulant. He found the right moment when he was engaged at the Park Theatre for twelve nights at the opening of the 1834–1835 season. The play found immediate audience favor and Hackett added it to his permanent repertoire.

This time, Yankee Job Fox from Weatherford, Connecticut, is again in England, a Yankee "help" or servant in the English country house of Mr. Testy, a retired merchant, a penurious guardian, and a crochety husband.[9] Job catches Testy's wife in a liaison with Lord Pedigree, and Testy himself in shady deals with his ward's fortune. Job proceeds to play one party against another, as they buy his serv-

---

[8] See Chapter 11.

[9] Two manuscript versions of this play are available, one in the Lord Chamberlain's Collection, No. 42937, and one in the Enthoven Collection.

ices, and the climax of the piece finds Testy, at Job's urging, on the roof of his garden house peeking through a hole in hopes of catching Mrs. Testy with Pedigree. Mrs. Testy arrives, Pedigree embraces her, and Testy falls off the roof in his anxiety to catch the lovers, only to discover that Mrs. Testy is Job Fox in disguise. Testy is forced to apologize to his wife and to let his ward marry her intended or suffer exposure as a fraud. Mrs. Testy loses her uppity house guests when Job smokes them out of the house by covering the chimney pots. Thus we see caught in his own trap a dishonest guardian and jealous husband who would trap his wife in a liaison. It is all intrigue, disguise, and farcial situation.

Why did Hackett choose to act it? For the first time in his eight years of playing the Yankee character he had found a dependable farce written expressly for him by a professional playwright. The piece was routine, but it was precisely because of its familiar style and context that it had good audience possibilities. Moreover, it could be used as an afterpiece to Rip or Wildfire or Falstaff. Its only vaguely satirical point lay in placing the Yankee in an English environment where he could look smarter and more clever than his English cousins. There is something personally revealing about Hackett in his decision to play *Job Fox* for his third London appearance. Did he think it harmless, nonprovocative stuff for an English audience? It would have taken an actor of the most stubborn determination to face London with a satirical piece after what had happened earlier. When his engagement was inexplicably cancelled,[10] he returned immediately to New York. But whom had he left behind him to completely charm London audiences in the character with which he had worked so hard? George Hill! Did he fear comparison with him in the eyes of the critics? Hackett had clearly lost the contest to a genuine, born-and-bred New Englander.

3

By 1836 James Hackett's work with Yankee theatre was largely completed. He would continue to play *Jonathan Doubikins, Job Fox,* and *Jonathan in England* for two or three seasons, but then even these were dropped, and except for an occasional revival of Solomon Swap, he no longer played the Yankee. His range of dialect char-

---

[10] R. B. Peake requested permission to act *Job Fox* on July 28 and it was granted on August 1. Hackett's mysterious departure is unexplained.

acters was now large enough to give an ample repertoire of character types in which he would not have to compete with other actors. Besides the French and Irish types, and Falstaff in both *I Henry IV* and *Merry Wives of Windsor*, he stood alone with Catskill Dutchman Rip and backwoodsman Nimrod Wildfire. His portrayal of those characters was not to be seriously challenged until Joseph Jefferson, who would also begin his career playing Yankees, introduced his version of Rip in the 1860's, and Frank Mayo staged a new Davy Crockett play a few years later. In his long career of nearly half a century on the stage, Hackett was the mainstay of American comedy.

James Hackett also knew how to fight stubbornly to win and retain his place as a star. He had not been able to convince London of his merits, but he was certainly able to hold a top spot at home. That he forced Dowton into a secondary position on the occasion of their simultaneous New York appearance when that actor visited America in the fall of 1836 should not be forgotten. And two years previously he had successfully won the battle with the aging Charles Mathews when that veteran actor made a second tour of the States in the 1834–1835 season. The two comedians were thrown into sharp comparison at the Park Theatre. Hackett played *Jonathan in England*, *Job Fox*, and *Jonathan Doubikins* in a series of performances from September 27 to October 11, and Mathews acted *The Comic Annual for 1835* and *Monsieur Tonson* from October 13 to October 16. Hackett was back again on October 17 with *Job Fox, Sylvester Daggerwood, The Militia Muster*, and *Monsieur Morbleu*, a program calculated to show even a wider range than his English rival. On the eighteenth Mathews again repeated *Monsieur Tonson*, and on the twenty-seventh he played *Trip to America* for the first time in the States.[11] The sequence of performances had shown that, with American audiences at least, Hackett was now able to hold his own with England's best.[12]

The ten-year period of his association with Yankee theatre was a rich one for James Hackett. Since his first crude falterings with *Sylvester Daggerwood* in 1826,[13] he had climbed rapidly to a posi-

---

[11]*Mirror*, XII (November 22, 1834), 167.

[12] Hackett played twelve nights in this group, with each night averaging $500. His benefits attracted $809 and $1030. See Odell, *Annals*, IV, 6 for details.

[13] In a playing of *Sylvester Daggerwood* in Mobile, Alabama, in January,

tion of prominence in stage matters in an entirely new line. His borrowings from Mathews had been obvious, but after his first lesson at Covent Garden in what that meant, he turned to more original channels. His adaptation of *Who Wants a Guinea?* began the experimentation that led him not only to a wider range of Yankee characters but to other dialect roles as well. At first he had written materials for himself, but he soon encouraged others to write for him. American playwrights such as Dunlap and Bird were certainly available, but Hackett's problem was in the development of sketches and plays which could intimately suit his own peculiar talents. The actor was more important than the material. And as he worked with the problem, he found talents in Paulding, Stone, Logan, and Bernard. When Hackett thought he had enough to show, he took the Yankee character and his capability in acting it to London for a second close scrutiny. He failed, but in his failure he laid the groundwork for the success of other American actors. During this intensive period of development he had tried to carry on the tradition of satire which Mathews had fostered, but he gave way toward the end to situation comedies which audiences seemed to like better. As a mild satirist, however, he had worked with a style of comedy which Anna Cora Mowatt would later bring to success in *Fashion*.

The over-all result of James Hackett's work was the establishment of a line of comedy which could be acted by only native actors. He clearly pointed the way with his innovations in script development and his fearlessness in letting the London critics look at it. He so successfully popularized the Yankee on the stage that he directly encouraged other young American actors to take up his line and compete with him. One of these was George Handel Hill. James Hackett was the innovator and experimenter in the Yankee line, but George Hill was its flowering genius.

1838. Noah Ludlow (*Dramatic Life*, p. 495) notes that Hackett in this, and imitations of Kean, Hilson, and Barnes, was "astonishingly clever." In *The Militia Training* "he convulsed the theatre with laughter."

part 3 Flowering and Climax

chapter 9

Yankee Hill: From Storyteller
to Stock Actor to Star

EORGE HANDEL HILL was indisputably the most perceptive
and authentic impersonator of the Yankee character on the American stage. With him a native New Englander for the first time
comes face to face with his stage image. Hill's background and
training were very different from Hackett's. The comedian from
Jamaica stepped onto the Park stage in his first performance as a
star performer, but Hill had to undergo an apprenticeship of several
years as a stock actor before he could play the characters of his own
choosing. And to follow his developments from storyteller to star is
to follow the whole process of stock-company training in America
in the nineteenth century.

Once Hill had achieved stardom, however, his position as the best
of the Yankee actors was never seriously challenged. In 1836 he
was accorded such an unusually favorable critical reception in London that he returned there again in 1838–1839 and played not only
in the capital city but in Edinburgh, Dublin, and Paris as well.
During the forties his career is marked by a series of ups and downs,
including a departure from the theatre for a brief time in an attempt to find a new career, but he soon returned to the stage to act
a character part that eventually provided the main link between
the early stage type and the close-to-life "new" Yankees of the
1860's. Since his death in 1849 all subsequent reviewers of the
Yankee on the stage have assigned "Yankee" Hill, as he was gen-

erally known throughout his lifetime, the position of top impersonator.

A study of Hill's early years is highly illuminating of the problems and concerns facing the new American actor of this period.
His reputation was earned slowly over seven years during which he
was on the move from New York to Rochester, Albany, Philadelphia,
Charleston, again to Philadelphia, and finally Boston, before Simpson and Price gave him an experimental engagement at the Park.
Later on, this rich experience in training from the daily pressures
of the stock company, with its continuous changes of bill and constant demands on the full energies of the actor, was the cushion of
his success, for it led him away from the fatal errors Hackett had
made. Though also plagued with the difficulty of finding adequate
acting pieces, Hill never imagined himself a playwright, as did
Hackett, but encouraged others to write flexible pieces for him, developing his scripts in collaboration with writers and forging new
scripts in the process of stage experience. He is not the inventor and
innovator as is Hackett, yet his steady professional attack made
success more certain. And because he was a native New Englander,
in these early days of intensive comparison of what was seen on the
stage with the "real thing," he could bring perceptive insight and
understanding to his portraits of country rustics familiar to him
since childhood. When Jedediah Homebred or Major Wheeler
walked out on the stage of the Park or the Walnut, it was first Hill
the New Englander and the close observer of New Englanders, then
Hill the mimic, that gave them life and credulity, that convulsed an
audience with a sly wink or cold stare. Hill possessed the perfect
temperament for the projection of this colorful and eccentric regional type.

James Hackett, surprisingly enough, never indulged himself in
an autobiography. His long career on the stage and his pretensions
to writing certainly should have encouraged him to do so. Not so
with George Hill. Though some details are inaccurate in part, he
has provided us with a personal record of his stage activities in one
of the first autobiographies by a native-born American actor. *Scenes
from the Life of an Actor*, edited by his wife, Cordelia Hill,[1] after

---

[1] Hill died intestate. In the judicial review of his estate (Genesee County
Court records, Batavia, New York) we learn that his wife, Cordelia Hill, collected his manuscripts, and with the help of her son rewrote them in part and

his death, gives us a most intimate and revealing view of the early American on the stage. The account is often piecemeal, the style is sentimental and overly personal, and there is nothing of the intellectual perception, the eccentric imagination, the keen observation, and perceptive wit which characterizes Charles Mathews' remarkable journals. As a record of ambitions, hopes, errors, and enthusiasms of a Yankee comedian, however, it furnishes the best firsthand information available, though it stops short of what he might have provided. Three years before Mrs. Hill's editing of the comedian's papers, W. K. Northall had published a biography based on some papers she had sold him from Hill's estate. Together these two volumes give us an extensive image of Hill's work. Both include not only the famous "Lecture on New England," which Hill used many times in platform appearances, but also anecdotes and incidents that were probably also stage material. Hill had set them down, perhaps in the early forties, with the full intention of publishing them, but he put it off when some of his views were changed by the appearance of such a work from "the pen of a master."[2]

Despite the limitations, however, in his potpourri of the odds and ends of an actor's life, with its "facts" which must constantly be held against other sources and reviewed against other critical opinion, we can follow "Little" Hill through most of his career on the stage. In trying to present the most favorable and positive report on himself he omitted much that would have been of value in judging

---

arranged them for sale. "The manuscripts left by him were such that no person but one particularly acquainted with Mr. Hill could make anything of them. . . . I had to compose parts so as to make it readable." She sold a large part of them for $125.00 but kept others. These papers were published a few months after Hill's death. W. K. Northall, as a practicing journalist, undoubtedly saw the business advantage of getting a book about Hill's life into print as soon as possible, and he probably bought the papers directly from the actor's wife. In 1850 he turned out a biography, *Life and Recollections of an Actor*. Three years later Mrs. Hill arranged the original papers she had kept back and published her own volume under the title: *Scenes from the Life of an Actor*. Both volumes include anecdotes and stories. Both are used in this study and will be subsequently referred to as *Life* or *Scenes*.

[2] Did he mean Seba Smith, or even the early work of James Russell Lowell? Hill could also have referred to Sol Smith's *Theatrical Apprenticeship* (Philadelphia: Carey and Hart, 1847. The 1854 edition, published by T. B. Peterson, notes Carey and Hart entered the title "according to Act of Congress" in 1845.) Who Hill referred to is not clear because the date of his note is indefinite (*Scenes*, p. 68).

him, and too often his narrative is confused with theatre gossip. Nevertheless, the main outline is clearly delineated. Hill is no literary craftsman, but he is a storyteller. With the magnetic aura of his stage personality, his adventures might have stood out vividly had he fully spoken them. Had he followed his first impulse to tell his life in the form he used for stories on the stage, something he had already partly done in his "Lecture on New England,"[3] he would have provided an invaluable document on himself, the theatre, and the "real-life" Yankee of the period.

2

George Hill was born in Abraham Lincoln's year on October 8, 1809, on Water Street in Boston. His grandfather, Frederick Hill, was a highly respected lawyer in Rutland, Vermont, but Hill's father, Ureli C. Hill, one of five children, broke sharply with family tradition and turned to the highly unstable profession of music for a career, at one time serving as organist at the Brattle Street Church in Boston. Here is the strain of Yankee independence that later led Hill to the stage, and his brother to a career in music which included an important role in the founding of the New York Philharmonic Symphony Orchestra.[4] George Hill's mother was Nancy Hull of Hartford, Connecticut. While George was still an infant his parents separated, and his mother moved to Raynham, a few miles south of Boston, where George went to school before he attended Bristol Academy in Taunton. One wonders how much this lack of a male parent, identical with James Hackett's situation, had to do with George Hill's later decision to make acting a career. Such a profession was not in the New England tradition, and it could have been conceived only in an environment where the boy had utter freedom of decision. That he left home for New York when he was scarcely fourteen or fifteen would indicate that the family hold over him was not strong.

If childhood activities ever mark the man, they certainly were influential in the life of George Hill, for he was tremendously in-

---

[3] He performed a series of stories under the title "Lectures on New Englanders" at the Brooklyn Museum on January 28 and March 24, 1842, and again at the New York Museum in May-June, 1842.

[4] Ureli Hill became its first president in 1842. See James Huneker, *The Philharmonic Society of New York*, p. 3.

fluenced by a performing Negro ventriloquist, singer, and legerde-
main artist by the name of Potter who visited Taunton. The traveling performer had so caught his imagination that Hill proceeded to
imitate him for his friends on a homemade stage constructed of
blankets and patchwork quilts. He also acted parts of *Richard III*,
impersonated country bumpkins, and repeated stories of huskings
and quiltings. Hearing about such famous actors as Cooper also
excited young Hill's imagination, and when the family moved from
his uncle's parsonage back to Boston he probably attended his first
theatre. Hill does not tell us he actually saw Charles Mathews on
the stage in Boston, though it was possible, for Mathews visited that
city in 1823. We do know that he heard and read a good deal about
him. Within a few months Hill was in New York. With time to
study and prepare comic songs, he resolved on his own initiative to
stage an entertainment in the Mathews manner.[5] Whether he gave
any performances as a professional entertainer before 1826 is not
recorded, but one can conjecture that, like Hackett, he entertained
his circle of friends with his singing and storytelling. In the meantime he found employment as a jeweler's apprentice in a shop near
the Chatham Street Theatre. Like many young men who lived in
the city, Hill was immediately drawn to the bright and enchanting
life of the stage. He shortly became associated with the company at
the Chatham and made his first appearance as a supernumerary in
Pizarro.[6] At this theatre he first saw Alec Simpson play Jonathan in
The Forest Rose, sometime after it opened on October 7, 1825. He
was greatly excited by Simpson's Yankee and he resolved to pursue
this comedy line. Within a very short time we find Hill on a Brooklyn stage as a variety performer.

The first notices of these performances are revealed in advertisements for the Military Garden and Denyse's Hotel, New Utrecht.
At the former, on August 3, 1826, a Mr. Handel is billed to sing the
songs, "Big Booby, the song of the Public Robber in New York, or
the Man that Ran away with the New City Hall," and "The Hunters of Kentucky." George Odell assumes that this was George Hill,
since his biography mentions Brooklyn performances, and sets 1826
as the date.[7] Hill would have been scarcely seventeen at that time.

---

[5] *Scenes*, p. 55.
[6] In comparison with other dating this probably took place in 1825.
[7] Odell, *Annals*, III, 230.

Again on September 22 at Denyse's Hotel, on the same program
with a silhouette cutter, Hill sang two of his favorite songs, "The
Hunters of Kentucky" and "Barney, Leave the Girls Alone."[8] A
stage career is now definitely underway. In December he gave performances at the Court Room of the Apprentice's Library and the
P & S Ways Hotel at Newton, and in January, 1827, at Mrs. Ches-
ter's Exchange Coffee House and again at Denyse's Hotel.[9] Was
this something of a vaudeville circuit? Whatever it was, Hill's scope
and experience as an entertainer must have been broadened. Only
a brief period now intervened before he found regular employment
as low comedian in a stock company engaged for western New York.

Again a Yankee actor, as in the case of Hackett, comes in contact
with New York State and its rapidly expanding regional culture,
helped by Yankee émigrés. The period of this association was a
most impressionable one for Hill. His experiences in Rochester, Le-
Roy, and other towns west to Buffalo, provided part of the background for the stories that so delighted his audiences a few years
later. Such titles as "Jonathan's Visit to Buffalo, Seneca Village,
etc." and "Jethro R. Dutton's Journey to the Genesee Country" are
definitely drawn from these firsthand contacts, though they do not
exist in body to tell us what was specifically recounted. Hill's western venture also shows us the stock actor on the frontier as we follow him with the company that certainly must have been among
the first to play in western New York after the Canal opened in
1825. On this 1827 tour Hill tells of playing in halls and barns,
sometimes to numerous audiences composed of every class of persons. If the performances were well attended, the company could
pay its bills and depart in respectability; but if the takings were slim,
the actors stole out of town under cover of darkness. It was a vaga-
bonding life. Small towns were unaccustomed to the vagaries of
actors and they often treated them as undesirable drifters. Hill
passed nearly a year in this kind of life, picking up jokes, making
acquaintances, and "beginning to look a little more like a man."

Either the company encountered difficulties, leaving Hill
stranded, or he was temporarily fed up with the life of a traveling
actor, because he appears in 1828 to have found employment in a
business venture in the booming canal town of Rochester. Was it

[8] *Ibid.*, p. 296.
[9] The specific dates are December 21, 1827; January 1, 8, 9, 1828.

here that he first began practicing the trade of paper hanger which Henry Stone mentions?[10] Hill does not tell us about this work. Paper hanging in our view today seems to be a far cry from the acting profession, but in those days of handmade wallpaper designs such a craft might have appealed to Hill. Furthermore, if he were a stranded actor who needed employment he might have turned to paper hanging as the best work he could find. Whatever his employment may have been, it appears to have taken him to LeRoy, a few miles west of Rochester, for here he met and shortly married Cordelia Thompson, despite the protest of her family against his status as an itinerant actor. Hill was later to buy property and establish a home for his wife and family of eight children in this typical western New York village, so reminiscent of New England. Hill's lengthy recounting of his elopement is a Yankee story, possibly one he used on the stage, in which the facts are buried in the sentimental anecdote.

Never far from the theatre, Hill next turns up in Albany, where he again appeared on the stage in an evening of comic songs and Yankee stories at the Albany Museum.[11] So successful was he that Henry Stone encouraged Managers Duffy and Forrest to offer him a place in the regular acting company of the Albany Theatre. At the age of twenty Hill now settled down to the hard work of learning the craft of acting. In August and September, 1830, he was again in New York at his old haunts of the Military Garden and the New York Museum.[12] Whether he still held on to his Albany employment we do not know, but he continued his stage work in New York in 1831, with performances in March and several in June at the New York Museum, and in July at Chatham Garden.[13] His fortunes were steadily improving. In September he found a steady job with the Arch Street Theatre Company, also under the Duffy and Forrest management, and here, as part of the general work of a native stock comedian, he told Yankee stories from time to time.[14] Hill's career as an actor was now definitely underway.

[10] Henry D. Stone, *Personal Recollections of the Drama*, p. 192. Phelps (*Players of a Century*, p. 127) also notes this.

[11] Stone, *Recollections*, pp. 225–227.

[12] Odell, *Annals*, III, 480.

[13] *Ibid.*, pp. 533, 536, 584, 590.

[14] Durang, *History of the Philadelphia Stage*, Series III, Chapter 15.

3

During the brief period before his discharge from the Arch Street
Theatre Hill played his first Yankee role in a fully developed play
—Jonathan Doolittle in William Dunlap's *Trip to Niagara*. In Dunlap, the management had the most prolific native playwright. In
the course of fifty plays since he had first begun to write for the
stage in 1786, his general American types had been taking on more
and more specific form. *Trip to Niagara* is among his most amusing
pieces and certainly merits much greater attention than it has usually received. Nominally it was a travelogue which took the viewer
up the Hudson River and across the Erie Canal to Niagara Falls.
The stage incidents were played before the Eidophusicon or Moving
Diarama of the Hudson River. In New York, Mr. Jones, the scene
painter at the Park, had been highly lauded for his effects, and in
Philadelphia Mr. Leslie, a native of Albany who had been a mari-
ner, and Mr. Coyle performed the same service for the Arch Street
Theatre. Durang thought the Philadelphia staging was accurately
and beautifully done, with Leslie's ships and sea water very naturally and truly treated.

Dunlap wrote more than a gadget piece however. He attempted a
mild satire of Charles Mathews in his grumbling, prejudiced, fault-
finding English-traveler Wentworth. As the plot goes, John Bull,
an Englishman (the role played by Hill), discovers that Amelia, a
one-time sweetheart, is in America with her brother Wentworth.
He gains her consent to marriage on the condition that he convert
Wentworth to a better attitude on America. All three start on a
trip to Albany and Niagara. As a means of approaching Wentworth,
John Bull takes the guise of two characters, Yankee Jonathan Doolittle and an *émigré* Frenchman, Monsieur Tonson. He is assisted by
Leatherstocking, an American pioneer. By the time they reach Ni-
agara, John Bull in his disguises has been so successful that Went-
worth not only is converted to the merits of American life but
stoutly defends it. In addition to the English and French types,
Yankee Jonathan stands in relief against Dennis Dougherty, an
Irishman who holds the same view of America as Wentworth,[15] Job
Jerryson, a Negro waiter, and Nancy, Amelia's English maid.

In this stage contrivance Hill's three roles certainly gave him an

[15] Was Dunlap satirizing Basil Hall?

actor's romp, especially the Yankee with his dialect, stories, and clever dealing. In his preface to the published version of the play Dunlap argues that his Yankee is an Englishman and he (Dunlap) is not to blame for any mistakes in idiom. Was this a dodge to cover up his lack of authentic knowledge of New Englanders? At any rate, New Yorker Dunlap does not give his Jonathan a home, although he mentions the Connecticut River; still he does allow him characteristic dialect which Hill undoubtedly corrected and amplified. Doolittle exhibits the general traits of exaggeration, cleverness, and smart talk. He refers to making nutmegs out of planing, to Uncle Ben, to peddling tin and iron wares. And he tells a Yankee story about shooting ducks on the Connecticut River. The gullible Irishman Dennis is taken in by Jonathan's tall tales about a whip. "It's to whip Niggers. They drive the black creeturs into the tobacco patches, and keep 'em working in the hot sun, 'till their wool blazes again." And at another point he ribs him about Indians: "They have another dish they like meazingly. Barbacued papoos. Papoos is the name they give the young Indians." In his gross exaggerations Dunlap seems to be poking fun at the equally gross generalizations English travelers were spreading about American life, and particularly Mathews in *Trip to America* and *Jonathan Doubikins*. It is sly humor almost lost to our eye.

The playing of John Bull-Doolittle may have had something to do with the events which follow. Charles Durang thought Hill "sustained the Yankee part with great cleverness." Durang was certainly in a position to know because he was then employed at the Arch Street Theatre "to attend to any alterations or new and sudden arrangements." Durang relates Hill's subsequent movements. On October 17 Hill played the part of the Tramp in Edwin Forrest's production of *Metamora* at the Arch. At the end of December and early January he told Yankee stories nightly as part of the regular program, stories which included "The Fox Skin" and a Yankee recitation in the *Water Witch*. On one evening Hill took the liberty of borrowing Hackett's famous sketch of *Down East* with its Yankee, Major Joe Bunker, and he found he could entertain an audience with it as well as Hackett. On February 27, 1832, Hill appeared as Hikia Hatchway, a Yankee sailor in *The Green Mountain Boy, or The Capture of Ticonderoga*. At this point Durang gives us a touching picture of a young actor's plight as he tells of Hill's personal

difficulties during several months of his wife's illness and the death
of his baby daughter. Durang also defends the comedian on his discharge from the company because he would not "go on" as a cour-
tier, a walk-on super in the throne scene in *The Exile*. "He was not
wrong in this refusal," argues Durang, "and they [the managers]
were wrong in ordering him."[16] After Hill had told stories, played
Yankee characters, and acted other pieces of light comedy in which
he was cast, how could he revert to the negligible position of a super?
It was a most disadvantageous moment to be fired, but the actor apparently took his discharge with the independence of a genuine
professional who had to guard his own position and whatever reputation he had. The managers were to make restitution for this action
within a few months.

In the interim Hill was successful in finding an opening as a low
comedian with Faulkner's company in Charleston, North Carolina,
and there he went for the winter months.[17] Though he was limited
in what he was allowed to play by casting arrangements, these seasons of stock acting must have proved of the highest value to the
young actor. As he moved through the various activities of a day in
the life of a stock company—the brief morning rehearsals of the
daily changes of bill, the new and erratic directions required by
visiting stars, the perception and quick memorization of new roles,
the plain hack work of turning a miscasting into something that
would appear credible, the vigorous frequent performances with
preparations only half made before audiences who insisted on being
entertained—all this must have seasoned Hill in the craft of acting.
Occasionally he could tell his Yankee stories or indulge in the singing he loved so much. Most of his work was of the routine sort,
however, that molds the professional and gives him audience command and stage authority. While Hill reveled in the applause of the
audience, he was aware that they could just as quickly destroy him
with their hisses, or worse, their indifference. How to hold an audience and sustain its interest was the constant problem confronting
him, which he was gradually learning to master.[18]

[16] Durang, *History*, Series III, Chapter 27.

[17] *Scenes*, pp. 81–87.

[18] While playing at Charleston, Hill became involved in a political controversy over South Carolina nullification. He appeared at two suppers, one on each
side of the nullification question. For those in favor of it he sang a revamped
"Bundle of Nails." He arranged it for the other party to favor their cause. Next

In September, 1832, he was back in the good graces of the Arch Street management. From this point his rise to major status was very rapid. A hit in a Yankee story encouraged Duffy and Forrest to invite him to act a Yankee play. Hackett's four appearances in Philadelphia the previous year had left a strong audience demand for native stage character, and the management thought Hill might fill the gap. The comedian chose *The Forest Rose*. So successful was he as Jonathan Ploughboy that he was given the status of a featured actor,[19] and as news of his talents spread, Hill's star began to rise. Mr. Pelby, manager of the Boston Theatre, proposed an engagement,[20] and Hill departed immediately for Boston. Not only did he think the Yankee character would be better understood in New England than in Philadelphia or the South, but he also hoped to obtain from the Boston judges an endorsement of the correctness of his delineations, since he had "formed his style upon the originals" he had met when he lived there. He was also aware that all actors had to pass with favor the ordeal of Boston criticism if they were to succeed on the stage. It was during the Boston venture that Hill met playwright Joseph S. Jones, with whom he was to work closely for a number of years in the development of his repertoire. The Boston appearance was only one step away from the Park. Mr. Pelby gave Hill a letter to Simpson, and Hill went to New York. All of this had happened within a few short weeks.

The timing of Hill's application for a Park engagement could not possibly have been more opportune. His successes in Philadelphia and Boston had coincided in a most fortunate way with the movements of James Hackett, who was now in Europe. Moreover, Simpson faced the important visit of Charles and Fanny Kemble

---

day the papers carried both songs and Hill was on the spot. Here is his advice for other actors: "I yield not the right for myself to think and vote. That I am in a profession, which has for its purpose the amusement of the million, is no reason why I should lose the rights and privileges of citizenship. Whigs and democrats will laugh at us if we are comedians and cry with us if we are tragedians. In times of excitement, if the actor becomes too much of a noisy politician, he will make as many enemies as friends; and, if he tries to play Jack on both sides, he loses something of his dignity of character; and, perhaps, the stronger party at the hustings may be the weaker at the theatre."

[19] *Scenes*, p. 77.

[20] This is dated 1833 in *Scenes*, pp. 79–80. It is clear from its relationship to the New York appearance which follows, however, that either Hill or his editors made an error in the dating.

with only the usual afterpiece programing. The Kembles were an expensive financial arrangement even for the Park, but properly managed, and especially with Edwin Forrest following their engagement, the Park had the best box-office potential of many years. Shortly after he arrived in America in September, Kemble had seen Hackett perform his line[21] of American characters. He must have been impressed enough with what he saw to later encourage Simpson to fill the afterpiece spot with American comedy if an actor could be found to supply it. Hill was on hand, and Simpson took action. Perhaps Kemble also thought that by joining native American comedy to his own bill, he would definitely increase audience interest in his own ventures.

Hill's success at the Park is unique. Beginning modestly on November 14 with a Yankee story, "The Yankee in Trouble, or Zephaniah in the Pantry," he returned three days later in Hackett's acting piece, *Solomon Swap*,[22] which Simpson had suggested. On the twenty-fourth he played his first full evening of Yankee entertainment with *Solomon Swap* and *The Forest Rose*. Two nights later he was back again for the afterpiece to Fanny Kemble's *Isabella*. On December 3, he followed Edwin Forrest in *Metamora* in a completely American program of star actors as well as plays. And on the next evening he enjoyed his first Park benefit by playing a première performance of *The Inquisitive Yankee* and telling Yankee stories. The extent of his success is revealed in the Park Theatre's financial statement, which shows that Hill's benefit, though only modest on the first occasion, jumped quickly on two later evenings to approach Forrest's nightly average,[23] a remarkable position for any actor, especially a native comedian.

George Hill's engagement at the Park determined his status as a major star. To have reached the pinnacle of the nation's best theatre at the youthful age of twenty-three was indeed remarkable. His character line of a Yankee country boy had much to do with it, but at the root lay his inherent talent for mimicry and the disciplines in low comedy he had learned in his stock experience. From this point forward "Little" Hill's success was never in question. Whether in New York, Charleston, or New Orleans, he was greeted with equally

[21] Frances Anne Butler, *Journal*, I, 89.
[22] Odell, *Annals*, III, 611.
[23] Joseph Ireland, *Records*, II, 52–53.

enthusiastic praise. Like Hackett, he was later recognized by the *Mirror* in an engraving and profile study as a distinguished American talent. Hill's achievement met its most critical test, however, when he journeyed to London, for there he won his title as "the best American comedian."

chapter 10

Hill's Search for Individuality:
Building the Repertoire

OR AN OBJECTIVE DESCRIPTION of George Hill's style in acting the Yankee character we must wait for the critical opinion of the London reviewers after his opening at Drury Lane in November, 1836. The quantity of the London criticism of Hill on that occasion is so large and the opinions so diverse that we are able to view his image on the stage with great clarity and precision. We can see his development before that date, however, in another way. The style of an actor is greatly influenced by the nature and special qualities of the materials he acts. Hence, the repertoire which Hill developed during the three years following his Park Theatre success can tell us much about him. Unlike Hackett, Hill undertook, before he tested the authority of the London critics, the rugged and seasoning experience of accumulating a body of actable characters that would prepare him, as nothing else could, for the challenge of performing at Drury Lane.

The Park success had been substantial, but once the surprise at the enthusiasm of the opening had passed, Hill was immediately alerted to the absolute necessity of either finding a repertoire of new plays of his own or perishing in the mire of monotony and boredom with repeated fare. The first pieces he acted, *The Forest Rose* and *Solomon Swap*, had been borrowed, and only the Yankee stories were of his own making. These he continued to tell with all their characteristic buffoonery in dialect and situation. All that remains for our view today are titles, from which we must conjecture the contents. "Jethro R. Dutton's Journey to the Genesee Country" and "Zephaniah in the Pantry, or the Yankee in Trouble"[1] have already been mentioned. Others are "Amos in the Stage Coach, or the Yankee in the Lard Tub"; "Wild Animals"; "The Bunker Hill Back, or the La Fayette Dinner at Faneuil Hall"; "Solomon in the Pantry, or Custard Pudding No Seat for a Man." Hill not infrequently added the first soliloquy from *Richard III* in imitation of a Yankee spouter at a school examination in New Hampshire.[2]

In this oldest of Yankee stage techniques, which Mathews and Hackett had developed before him, Hill was an expert. He worked at a repertoire that could provide full evenings of solo entertainments. Joined to this were the songs, already mentioned in connection with the New York state tour, which the Yankee comedian made part of his variety performances. "Springfield Mountain," a sentimental ballad, became a popular favorite on the impetus given it by Hill's frequent performances; and as his fame spread, his name occasionally appeared on the cover of published songs—"As sung by Yankee Hill." During a single appearance at Bangor, Maine, Hill included five songs on a program of stories and olio numbers. One wonders what were the lyrics to such amusing titles as "Chit Chat for the Ladies," "The Country Bumpkin," "A Man of Business," "Down a Green Valley," and "A Hit at the Fashions." They seem to suggest satirical comment which raises them above the usual sentimental ballad to something like the Mathews' patter song. Since none of these are extant, there is no way of determining their nature and use.

It was to the playscripts, however, that Hill devoted his primary attention. On the occasion of his first Park benefit he played his first original Yankee piece—*The Inquisitive Yankee, or a Peep in All Corners.*[3] Nothing remains of this sketch but its list of characters, headed by Yankee Joel Peep. Hill did not retain it in his repertoire for long, nor did it receive much attention from those who saw it. But Hill's second new piece, *The Green Mountain Boy*, which the

---

[1] An alternate title is *Zephaniah at the Tea Party, or The Yankee in Trouble.* See James, *Old Drury of Philadelphia*, p. 545.

[2] Odell, *Annals*, III, 620. Later he would add other titles: "Hiram's Courting Scrape with Nancy Slocum and Sal Barter," "The Misfortune with the Pumpkin Pye," "Three Chances for a Wife and a Visit to Zeb Hawkins," "The Soap Tub and the Ugly Aunt."

[3] Odell, *Annals*, III, 613. He acted it again at the Park on December 5 and

'CORN COBS,'
A POPULAR
COMIC SONG & CHORUS
AS SUNG
BY MESS.RS HILL & BROWER.
WITH RAPTUROUS APPLAUSE
ARRANGED FOR THE PIANO FORTE.   50.cts.
Published by ENDICOTT, 359 Broadway, NEW YORK.

The cover of a music sheet for one of George Hill's famous songs. The character on the left of the drawing is thought to be George Hill.

comedian first showed to a Philadelphia audience on March 19, 1833,[4] became part of his permanent collection of plays. It is important because it specifically illustrates for us how Hill developed his acting material.

2

The Green Mountain Boy was the work of Joseph Jones.[5] He was not only the same age as Hill, and, like the actor, on the threshold of a theatre career, but he was also a kindred New England spirit from Boston and thus highly informed on Yankees. From their first meeting, Hill, the actor, and Jones, the playwright, apparently got on well together, forming an association which lasted throughout Hill's lifetime and was to provide several plays for the comedian's repertoire. Jones came from good New England stock without the blessings of riches or position. His father was a sea captain who died when young Jones was scarcely ten.[6] Some success in amateur theatricals encouraged him to try the professional stage as an actor, and this he did in Providence, Rhode Island, when he was eighteen.[7] Shortly thereafter he joined the acting company at the Tremont Theatre, Boston, and continued there for many years as actor, playwright, and, during the seasons 1839–1841, as manager.[8] Not content with the theatre as a career, he turned to medicine, and in 1843 he was granted a degree from the Harvard Medical School.[9] Though he practiced this profession regularly thereafter, he continued his work in the theatre until his death on December 29, 1877. The plays of Dr. Jones, variously estimated to number from sixty to one hundred and fifty, include almost every type of stage piece from farce and melodrama to spectacle.

March 13, 1833. In Philadelphia he performed it several times during 1833–4 (James, *Old Drury*, p. 572), but then appears to have dropped it from his repertoire.

[4] James, *Old Drury*, p. 545.

[5] Jones gave the play to Hill when they met in Boston during the fall of 1832. When Hill opened it in Philadelphia, it carried the same title as an anonymous but entirely different piece he had performed at the Arch the previous year. Could Jones have had anything to do with the earlier work?

[6] *Dictionary of American Biography*, X, 193.

[7] A brief biography of Jones is included in *Metamora and Other Plays*, ed. by Eugene R. Page, p. 145.

[8] William W. Clapp, *A Record of the Boston Stage*, p. 362.

[9] Rees, *Dramatic Authors*, p. 93.

The first version of *The Green Mountain Boy* as played by Yankee
Hill was never published, except for a fragment included in the
actor's autobiography. When this is held against the 1860 printed
version, though the latter undoubtedly contains changes and alterations introduced by other actors after Hill's death, we can get a
fair idea of the original. The plot adheres strictly to the traditional
pattern of the early Yankee plays. Patriarch, social-snob Mr. Tompkins resolves to offer his daughter, Ellen, to a supposedly rich English peer, Lord Montague, despite her professed love for her cousin,
Edward Merton of the U.S. Navy. Merton arrives in the nick of
time and plans to elope with Ellen, but is stopped by his friend
Sandfield. In the denouement Lord Montague, alias Wilkins, is
proved not only an impostor but the scoundrel who forced Sandfield
to a prison term in his stead. All ends happily when Merton finds
a wife in Ellen and a long-lost father in Sandfield.

The plot is obviously trite, but it brings on stage not only a Yankee
but Joe Shakespeare, a poetry spouter; Miss Squeamish, an elderly
comic spinster; Lucy, a maid; and Bill Brown, a Negro servant. In
a spirited interchange of dialogue with Bill, Yankee Jedediah Homebred's attitude toward the Negro and the free Negro's toward the
Yankee are clearly stated. Jed is trying to provoke Bill.

JED. Halloo. Say you, when did you wash your face last? Can't tell,
can you?
BILL. Who's you sarsen dere, you know?
JED. Are you a nigger? I never seen a real one, but I guess you be.
Ar'nt ye—you?
BILL. Who's you call "nigger"?
JED. Well, I only ask'd you. Why he's mad as a hen a'ready. Did your
mother have any more on you?
BILL. Dere child, you better keep quiet, and min what you say to me,
you little bushwacker. If you am saucy, I'll spile your profile. You
mind dat now.[10]

Audiences were apparently not only quite ready to accept such open
banter but also found it amusing. Despite the crudity, did they admire the free Negro's bold independence? How did it differ from
Peake's open abuse of the Negro in *Jonathan in England*? Was there

[10] *Scenes*, p. 169. The punctuation is modernized here.

something brazenly hypocritical in the American condemnation of the English for attitudes they permitted themselves at home?

It is Jedediah, however, who provides the main humor of the piece and gives it a distinctively original flavor. This nineteen-year-old country boy is a shrewd, clever bargainer. In typical meandering detail he tells where he lives.

I was raised on the north side of the Green Mountains, half a mile t'other side of Wider Simms' House, in the town of Danbury. Her house was on t'other side of the road, just after you pass'd the Johnson Meadows. A leetle further on there's a little yaller house. Well, our house wan't more than a stun's throw from this yaller one. Ours was red.[11]

He is a pure country type, simple, unaffected. His talk is of the farm—of huskings, of logrollings, of hauling wood, of rail splitting, of trips to the mill, of farm animals. At one point he reveals what he thinks of education.

There's my grammar [he says as he shows a] list of hard words schoolmarm writ out of a dictionary. They tell me that nothin' will get a feller ahead in these parts like larnin'. It's my notion, if I could let out here a month or so, just to see fashion a leetle, I could go into the city, slick as grease.

Like other Yankees before him, Jedediah is all fierce independence. He recognizes no superior. "Wait on him!" says Jedediah to Joe Shakespeare. "You can wait on him, if you like; but I shant. I never was brought up to wait on anybody but myself."[12] That this is Jones' first Yankee play is revealed in plot parallels to early Yankee comedies in such scenes as Jed's "sparking" scene with Lucy, and the "Hail Columbia" that carries him off the stage with a dance after he has won a bargained kiss. And once again we see in this play the contrast between rustic simplicity and false pretensions. Jones' character, as played by Hill, was directly from the country they both knew and understood. What might have been borrowed in plot was balanced by the original contribution in the close-to-life Jedediah rooted in the New England soil.

The Green Mountain Boy was apparently in an advanced state of

---

[11] *Scenes*, p. 177.
[12] J. S. Jones, *The Green Mountain Boy*, p. 22.

development when Jones first showed the play to Hill, though the latter probably added lines and speeches in his own characteristic style. In their subsequent work together Jones and Hill collaborated closely on situation and characters. Like Mathews, who had reported his observations on American life to Smith during his trip to this country in 1823, Hill wrote regularly to Jones when he went to England. His letters, no more than brief accounts of what he was doing, indicate the close professional relationship of the playwright and the actor.

Specific evidence of their work together is revealed in Hill's descriptions of a visit they made to Taunton and Raynham in the summer of 1835. He tells us he was accompanied "by a playwright," and that playwright is undoubtedly Jones. Nominally the purpose of the visit was to hunt up old relatives and friends, but Hill was clearly in search of original material for new plays.[13] They toured the neighborhood in a carriage, filling their notebooks with characters, stories, and situations. Out of this trip, says Hill, grew part of *Speculations*, the play Bayle Bernard later developed for him, and Abner Tanner in Jones' *Yankee in Tripoli*. Hill records a characteristic conversation with his uncle.

"Well, Uncle, you would not advise me to give up my trade?" said Hill.
"No, if you make money by it. I suppose if there's a demand there must be a supply. I think if I was you I should work at it a spell longer. What do you play?"
"Yankees are my favorite characters."
"Yankees?"
"Yes; country boys."
"And do the people in the cities pay a hundred dollars a night only to see in the theatre what they can see in our village for nothing?"
"They do. Before I played Yankees, I worked for ten dollars a week."
"The dogs, you did! Well then, George, speak well of the Yankees— always speak well of the bridge that carries you safe over."
"I shall," said Hill.

How close the characters Hill drew on the stage were to real New Englanders will be evaluated when his acting is discussed later. At this point it is certainly clear that the travel with Jones to the source

13 *Scenes*, pp. 86–101.

of the down-East character was a genuine attempt to find and somehow capture in play form the authentic everyday life of the Yankee.
At least in theory, if not always in practice, Hill "went to life" for
the reality of his stage material. In this early period such an attempt
to bring realism to the stage, as Hill apparently tried to do, was
indeed remarkable.

3

If Yankee Hill was able to clothe Jedediah Homebred in *The Green
Mountain Boy* with genuine reality and bring him to popular audience favor, he failed when he tried a few weeks later at the Park
Theatre to do the same thing with Zachariah Dickerwell in Samuel
Woodworth's *The Foundling of the Sea*.[14] This coldly received play
was withdrawn after the third performance. Zachariah Dickerwell
is a foundling, a survivor of a Nantucket shipwreck who was brought
up in Vermont by a Canadian family. At the end of the play he
finds his father, but not until he has become entangled as a helper
in a love plot in which he saves the life of the heroine and falls in
love with Lititia, her confidante. On the way he meets Madame
Truelip, a "blue-stocking" on a visit to the United States to study
our domestic manners and write a book. She turns up with two
husbands, an Englishman and a Frenchman, but departs with only
one when the Englishman rejects her as a shrew who talks nineteen
to the dozen.

Madame Truelip is a primary attraction here. She is, of course,
Frances Trollope in pale disguise. Woodworth undoubtedly included
her as an obvious competitor to Mrs. Wollope, Hackett's character
in *Life in New York* and his current *Lion of the West*. Of equal interest in this play is Zachariah's peddler's status. Woodworth undoubtedly borrowed the peddler idea from Yankee literature of the
day. His play failed but the character survived in a redevelopment
which Hill worked out with another playwright a few years later.
The Yankee Pedlar would have another setting, another plot, and

---

[14] Odell, *Annals*, III, 622, reports a preview on May 5, 1833, and performances
on May 14, 16, 18, and November 7. Performances are recorded in Philadelphia
for October 17, 1833, and April 30, 1834 (Durang, *History of the Philadelphia
Stage*, Series III, Chapter 29). For an extended summary see *Mirror*, X (May
18, 1833), 363.

the Yankee would have another name, but the character idea would
be the same. Of equal interest is the gimmick of a Yankee foundling.
Did Cornelius Logan borrow this for *The Wag of Maine*, which he
wrote for Hackett a year later? The similarity is too striking to be
ignored. In Yankee theatre a play could fall by the way, though
sooner or later pieces of it would turn up elsewhere. In the commercial game for survival there were no rules for give and take.

The Foundling of the Sea is a "prize" play. The circumstances
surrounding its writing and Hill's acquisition of it specifically illustrate the actor's difficulty in building a workable repertoire. As in
the case of Hackett, who had given $250 in prize money for *Lion
of the West*, Hill's action did not spring from any latent idealistic
support of American drama but from hardheaded expediency in
providing a much needed acting piece in a period when few professional writers could afford to devote time and energy to writing
plays for little or no pay. And like his colleague in Yankee theatre,
Hill regarded a play as a capital investment to be as jealously
guarded as any valuable personal possession. Offering a cash prize
for a play included the possibility of turning up several pieces
adapted to his own particular style. He would therefore be in a position to negotiate for the losing plays as he saw fit. The publicity
value was highly useful, both in the public's anticipation of seeing
a prize play and in the admiration of the actor as a benefactor of
the playwright.

Hill offered four hundred dollars for a play containing a Yankee
character. He selected a judging committee of Messrs. Verplanck,
Webb, and King, highlighted with that magic personality Washington Irving. When these four men looked at the thirteen plays
submitted they thought none of them merited an award. Only when
Hill strongly urged special consideration of Woodworth's play did
they award the prize to *The Foundling of the Sea*. We do not know
how many other pieces from this competition Hill picked up for
later use. In all likelihood his four-hundred-dollar investment at this
stage of his career was a good one, for it undoubtedly helped to
elevate his prestige as an actor. In 1836 he wrote Woodworth, not
without piety, patriotic fervor, and an eye on the box office: "I am
pleased to hear you have done something more for the American
drama; let authors and actors work for each other in our beloved
country, and the time is not far distant when we shall build a dra-

matic fame among us, which will be the envy of the world."[15] A
Yankee businessman in the world of the arts was without peer.

4

In his work with Jones and Woodworth in the spring of 1833 Hill
laid the foundations for a growing repertoire. On October 1 at Philadelphia's Chestnut Street Theatre he added *Josh Horseradish, or
the Lying Yankee*[16] to his growing list of plays. This sketch with a
cast of three—Josh, young Bliston, and Mrs. Bliston— was "written
by a gentleman from Philadelphia." Like so many others used by
Yankee actors, it survives only in the listings of playbills and press
notices. In recording that it met with success, Durang pushes it
aside as "merely the vehicle of Hill's Yankee drolleries." How Hill
acquired this script we do not know, though the billing of its authorship again points out that playwriting was either a lowly sideline
that could scarcely be acknowledged by established writers, or an
amusing pastime for gentleman dilettantes.

No author at all is credited with *Ovid and Obid, or Yankee
Blunders*, another new piece Hill first performed in Philadelphia
on April 30, 1834. He had just returned from his first western tour
to New Orleans and the Ohio valley cities, and he may have picked
it up along the way. Again it probably served as a device to put
Hill's country Yankee, this time Obid Bigelow, in a typical comic
situation with Mr. Invoice, Ovid Doggrell, Thady, Mary, and Ellen.
There was undoubtedly ample opportunity for stories, Yankeeisms,
and other comic devices. Hill kept it in his repertoire for a brief
time and then dropped it.

John Augustus Stone's *The Knight of the Golden Fleece* had
quite a different fate. Yankee Sy Saco quickly won audience approval on his first appearance at the Park on September 10, 1834,
and became one of Hill's most-played roles. Again a Yankee playwright comes together with a Yankee actor to set out the American
idea. Stone was also a New Englander. Born in Concord, Massachusetts, in 1800, he was the son of a cabinetmaker and a descend-
ant of Gregory Stone, who came from England in 1635 and settled
in Watertown, Massachusetts.[17] He began an acting career in Bos-

---

[15] *Life*, p. 47.
[16] This play was sometimes billed as *East and West*.
[17] *Dictionary of American Biography*, XVIII, 77.

WEDNESDAY EVENING, Oct. 21, 1835,

WILL BE PRESENTED THE COMEDY OF

JONATHAN

IN

ENGLAND.

Solomon Swop, - - - - - - - - - - - - - - Mr. HILL

Sir Larry........................Mr. CONNER		Heartley........................Mr. BRITTENHAM
Torrent........................Mr. PORTER		Hogmore........................Mr. STANLEY
Barford........................Mr. REED		Carrydot........................Mr. COLLINGBOURNE
Henry........................Mr. J. G. PORTER		Fanny........................Mrs. KNIGHT
Oldskirt........................Mr. MESTAYER		Mrs. Glassonbury........Miss ANDERSON
Andrew Bang........................Mr. HADAWAY		Amy........................Miss CHARNOCK

After which the New Drama of the

KNIGHT

OF THE

Golden Fleece;

Or, The Yankee in Spain.

By Saco, a Travelling Yankee from Provincetown, Cape Cod, Mr. Hill

Orsorino-Knight of the Golden Fleece....Mr. CONNER	Harquebuss............a Banditt............Mr. STANLEY
Don Emanuel........an Old Noble............Mr.COLLINGBOURNE	Hebanon............his Companion............Mr. MESTAYER
Havier............a Spanish Veteran..........Mr. PORTER	Abbot........................Mr. REED
Blabastro............an Old Domestic............Mr. KNIGHT	Ronquillo........................Mr. FISCHER
Sig. Malvenuto-a Napolitain Commander-Mr. MUZZY	Boy........................Miss BRITTENHAM
Gomez........a disbanded Trooper............Mr. BRITTENHAM	
Olmedo........Officer of Body Guards..........Mr. J. MESTAYER	Donna Constantia....wife of Orsorino....Mrs. KNIGHT
Ali............an Algerine Bondman............Mr. WHITE	Vittoria-a Portuguese Nun of La Trappe-Mrs. MUZZY
Benedicta............	........................Mrs. CONWAY

TO-MORROW, Mr. HILL'S LAST NIGHT

Playbill (October 31, 1835) of George Hill in
Jonathan in England and *Knight of the Golden Fleece.*

ton, and then moved to New York, where he specialized in acting old men and writing occasional melodramas. *The Knight of the Golden Fleece* was first performed three months after Stone drowned himself in the Schuylkill River at Philadelphia.[18] During his short career he made rapid progress as a playwright, showed much promise, and was generally thought to be one of the theatre's brighter lights. He not only drew a Yankee for Hill, but he also sketched an Indian for Edwin Forrest in *Metamora* and redeveloped a backwoodsman for Hackett in the second version of *Lion of the West*. In his work with all three types Stone stood alone. Durang recalls the playwright as a small man, slight in figure, but genteel, a description that might have been made of "Little" Hill.

Unfortunately *The Knight of the Golden Fleece* was never printed, nor has a manuscript version turned up. Any projection of its contents must therefore be made from book and press mentions. The *Mirror* thought Sy Saco was one of the best Yankees seen on the stage up to that time, and the play full of business, bustle, and laughable occurrences. The main point of the play, in the *Mirror* view, lay in the "striking contrast of national character, which exists between the dignified and haughty Castilian, and the 'downeast chap' of our own country."[19] By inserting a Yankee in the Spanish world of Orsario de Luna, Malvento, and Don Emanuel, a romantic environment directly in line with the popular melodramatic tastes of the day and the spectacle drama he had developed in several plays for the Bowery Theatre, Stone provided a piece rich in all the popular ingredients. Here is a curious blending of reality and romance, patriotism, and native character in a far-off, imaginary world.

At this point in Hill's career the *Mirror* recognized his progress in a profile reporting his work and praising his merits as an actor.[20] The engraving published with the article shows us the Hill of this

[18] Rees, *Dramatic Authors*, p. 9. The suicide occurred on May 29, 1835. "It was most deliberate, having made two attempts by throwing himself from Spruce Street wharf into the Schuylkill; from the first he was rescued, and led those who saved him to believe it was an accident. A few hours afterwards his body was found floating in the dock. Mr. Stone was a man of nervous temperament, and had occasionally displayed symptoms of incipient insanity."

[19] *Mirror*, XII (August 16, 1834), 55. This notice was written after an advance look at the playscript a month before the Park opening.

[20] *Mirror*, XII (November 22, 1834), 161.

period—a boyish face, framed by curly hair, with large, soft eyes, a well-shaped nose, and a smiling mouth. There is something in this face of wide-eyed innocence and naïveté, something of the smiling schoolboy, who while he evokes sympathy leaves a warning of slyness and deceit. The *Mirror* writer, after lauding Hill's professional accomplishments, concluded, in the highly flavored journalistic rhetoric of the day, that Hill was "no less esteemed as a man than admired as a comedian, being an exemplary member of society, liberal, high-minded, and social, an affectionate husband, and an indulgent father." No Victorian could hope for a better card than this.

5

Though the *Mirror* recognized that Hill had reached a fair level of success, he had much more to do to insure its permanence. His activities in the next two years before he went to England in the fall of 1836 are much the same as they were after the Park opening. The record for the winter months of 1834–1835 is incomplete, but he was again performing in New York and Philadelphia in May and June, 1835. For the first time he acted *Jonathan Doubikins*, the comedy which Peake had written for Mathews and which Hackett had borrowed and revised. Hill had also two new pieces to offer his public. The first of these was the original version of *Old Times in Virginia, or The Yankee Pedlar*, first performed on May 8, 1835, at the Walnut Street Theatre in Philadelphia. Hiram Dodge later became one of Hill's best characters, though not until the play was prepared in a second version by Bayle Bernard for Hill's London debut in 1836. The play is of much interest in connection with that event, because the tryout and reworking process to which *The Yankee Pedlar* was submitted is a fine example of the treatment Yankee-theatre plays were given before they settled into the permanent repertoire.[21]

A few days after he introduced *The Yankee Pedlar*, Hill tried *Lion of the East, or Life in New York*. Because of its topical interest and the spreading fame of Jack Downing—Hackett was already

---

[21] A third version in which the action was compressed and some of the characters renamed was prepared for Dan Marble when he added the play to his repertoire. Finding material to suit individual talents was the main problem. Hill's energies in this direction enabled him to turn up more acting pieces than were collected by any other Yankee actor. It undoubtedly accounted for his continuous success in the character to the end of his life.

acting a play with the same character—[22] Hill paid Mr. Blake, adaptor of the play and treasurer of the Park Theatre, two hundred and fifty dollars. This was not an original play with an original character as the others had been, but it brought onto the stage in talk of politics the most famous Yankee in the literary works of the day. Hill immediately saw its possibilities, made it his stage property, and proceeded to turn it into an audience favorite that survived in his repertoire for a number of years.

So successful was Hill with his new plays in May and June that he decided to try a new series in November. This time he chose the Park Theatre for his new productions, and there he staged them within a few days of each other. On November 14 he tried *Ephraim Smooth*, probably no more than a sketch. Four days later he played Abner Tanner from Cape Cod in *The Adventure, or The Yankee in Tripoli* by J. S. Jones. On November 27 he not only acted Abner Tanner but also showed New York for the first time the character of Dr. Lot Whittle in *Casper Hauser, or the Down Easter* by H. J. Finn. How different Abner and Lot were we have no way of knowing, but the fact that Hill played them side by side on the same evening indicates some sort of contrast, such as a youthful Abner versus an older Lot. Both of these pieces subsequently formed a major part of Hill's programing.

Since we have already seen Hill at work with Joseph Jones, it is Henry James Finn who is of primary interest. As in the case of *The Knight of the Golden Fleece*, Finn's play was not preserved in print or manuscript and we must rely on other sources for our knowledge of it. H. J. Finn is vastly interesting in this whole context of Yankee theatre. He seemed to touch it all around the edges as an actor-performer and comic essayist without actually becoming a part of it.[23] There was no one more qualified to provide it with a body of genuine comedy than Finn. Yet he never did. He certainly influenced its general directions, but his specific contributions are small.

Though not actually an American by birth, born as he was at

[22] See Chapter 8.

[23] H. J. Finn merits a major study to evaluate his contributions to the American theatre of this period. Brief accounts are available in Phelps, *Players of a Century*, pp. 138 ff; Clapp, *The Boston Stage*, pp. 203 ff; Alfred Bates, *The Drama*, v. 20, 40; Rees, *Dramatic Authors*, p. 83; Durang, *History of the Philadelphia Stage*, Series III, Chapter 27.

Cape Breton in 1795, Finn spent most of his lifetime in America and became well acquainted with Yankees and their ways. His father was an officer in the British Navy. When the family moved to New York young Finn enjoyed the advantage of a better-than-average education, including a brief period at Princeton University. He studied law in the office of Thomas Phoenix, United States attorney for the District of New York, read Shakespeare, and went to the theatre. When Finn's father died—again here is the lack of the strong hand of a male parent who might have discouraged theatre interests—young Finn went with his mother to England, where he taught school, did some miniature painting and some scene painting for a group of strolling players, and eventually made a debut as a comic actor in London. Back in New York in 1818, he worked at the Park Theatre as a property man, copyist, and actor. He then moved to Savannah, Georgia, where he worked briefly as associate editor of a newspaper. During the next few years, which included a return to London in 1821, he appeared regularly on the stage and gradually developed a reputation as a star performer in the 1830's. His years on the stage saw him in many of the classical comedy characters and in a few from serious drama. He was a favorite in Boston, where "his spontaneous flashes of wit and merriment which sparkled through all his personations" were particularly praised. The *Mirror* thought his style of playing broadly ludicrous, and his delineations generally correct, though original and "sketched with a strong and masterly hand" and though sometimes incomplete (only "rough likenesses").[24] As a dramatist Durang thought he wrote with "taste and elegance, eschewing all immorality or that gross licentiousness so contaminating to youth."

Henry Finn's touch with Yankee theatre grew out of his love for the stories and songs of dialect comedy. As an actor he tried entertainments similar to Mathews' *At Homes* and had developed a reputation as a song writer and comic satirist, particularly as editor of the *American Comic Annual*, published in 1831 with illustrations by D. C. Johnston in the Cruikshank style. Frances Trollope, who cited it as the only work of "mere pleasantry" she had seen in America, was much entertained by its liveliness, its "biting attack upon us, particularly upon our incapacity of speaking English."[25]

[24] *Mirror*, IX (July 16, 1831), 11.
[25] Trollope, *Domestic Manners,* pp. 321–322.

She quotes Finn's satirical treatment of Captain Hall—or is it Charles Mathews—thinly disguised as Captain Maudeville Cockaigne: "From Lunmeur; a pretty-considerable traveller; a collector of Fiction, and recollection of Fact—smiling on the Yankees here, and sneering at them at home; the personification of a steamer, upon the low pres-sure system, that sails across the Atlantic, for the purpose of issuing smoke, in two thick volumes."[26]

It was this background that H. J. Finn brought to *Casper Hauser*. He found his story in the newspaper reports of a real Casper whose unknown origin and unexplained murder had made him an object of world-wide mystification. In the play Casper is the lost heir of a noble family, his uncle being the Baron Rhemfeld.[27] The Baron's only daughter, Eva, discovers the wild boy in his lonely retreat and takes him back to civilization. They fall in love and are to be married. On the eve of the wedding Casper is stabbed by a rejected suitor. The murderer is discovered through the activities of Yankee Dr. Lot Whittle. In this play we see that Finn, like Stone in *The Knight of the Golden Fleece*, put together a curious potpourri of romantic thriller-drama and low-comedy. The Yankee was described as an "anything-arian," quick, resourceful, and clever. The humor was apparently broader than in previous pieces, and in performance Hill sang two songs and told several stories. It was much more than a framework for his drolleries, as the sketches so frequently were, and Hill found warm receptions wherever he played it.

6

An over-all evaluation of George Hill's first ten years as an actor presents several problems. Hill's autobiography is most useful in filling in the personal details about his movements, but primary evidence for basis of a detailed knowledge of the plays he performed is lacking, and any evaluation of his innovations is only weakly

[26] Finn, *American Comic Annual*, pp. 49–59.

[27] The play is not extant. A brief summary appears in the London *True Sun* for January 1, 1837, when Hill played it at the Queen's Theatre. Finn played Doctor Lot Whittle in Mobile, Alabama, on February 4, 1835. Noah Ludlow (*Dramatic Life*, p. 427) did not think that "Mr. Finn added anything desirable to either his acting or his reputation as a writer by the exhibition; and yet the piece did not lack interest, but Mr. Finn was not as happy as usual; the character was not suited to his style."

ON THURSDAY EVENING, JULY 7, 1836
Will be performed, the Drama of

KASPER HAUSER.

OR,

The Down Easter.

Doctor Lott Whittle,	- -	**Mr. Hill**
Kasper Hauser,	....	Mrs. Hilson
Baron Rheinfelt,	....	Mr. Isherwood

His 1st appearance at this Theatre.

President Van Fuerback,	Wheatley
Professor Daumer,	Clarke
Grippswald,	Richings
Anselm,	Povey
Hans Hoffmeister,	Fisher
Michael,	Nexsen
Servant,	Harvey

Servants, Waiters, &c. &c.

Eva,	Mrs. Asbury

Her 2d appearance.

Lois,	Gurner
Madame Daumer,	Conway

To conclude with the Comedy of

THE GREEN MOUNTAIN BOY.

Jeddediah Homebred,	- -	**Mr. Hill**
Mr. Tompkins,	....	Mr. Isherwood
Mr. Sandford,		Clarke
Edward Merston,		Wheatley
Joe Shakespeare,		Fisher
Wilkins,		Richings
Terence M'Nab,		Harvey
Mrs. Squamish,		Mrs. Wheatley
Ellen Tompkins,		Gurner
Lucy,		Durie

Park Theatre playbill (July 7, 1836) of George Hill
in *Kasper Hauser* and *The Green Mountain Boy*.

supported. Only one of the four major plays he introduced after his Park opening is extant. In Hackett's case the early scripts are readily available and we can follow his innovations and inventions; but with Hill we must wait for the London trip and the script evidence in the Lord Chamberlain's Collection from that period. Nor do we have any body of criticism before 1836 from which his style of acting can be assessed. The record after that date will be much more fully complete, and we can get a closer look at Hill's actual accomplishments.

How did he differ from James Hackett? The comparison is not only inevitable but most valuable in showing the scope of Yankee theatre. Any theatre form which cannot move in a variety of directions is doomed to failure. The life of Yankee theatre lies in its capacity to stretch and adjust while still remaining within certain predetermined limits. Hill's proponents have frequently advanced the view that if he did not actually precede Hackett as a Yankee impersonator he certainly developed concurrently with him. The evidence is otherwise. Hill may have told Yankee stories as early as Hackett, but the latter anticipated him by at least three years in the acting of the character in plays, and much of Hackett's course in exploration and development had been traversed before Hill seriously took up the role. Any evaluation of Hill's contribution must therefore date from his first attempts to build a repertoire.

Nevertheless, as a stage performer in the Mathews' line of story-telling Hill's early contribution is valuable. He came to it with originality, and, unlike Hackett, who soon abandoned storytelling except as one device among many in fully developed plays, Hill clung to it as a major aspect of his style throughout his career. In the sense of being a solo performer, Hill was much closer to Mathews than was Hackett. His love of songs, whistling, and comedy flute playing also indicates much more of the vaudeville performer in Hill than in his fellow comedian, who, after his first flurry with imitations, became a conventional actor. Perhaps the more radical strain of the entertainer in Hill lowered his discipline and kept him from the solid achievements and wider range of the other actor. As a warm, impressionable stage personality Hill is unrivalled. His delicate style, based on the experience to particularize it, dates from his period of storyteller and itinerant actor.

Hill is no satirist. In this respect, Hackett was much more tied

COMIC OLIO.

FOR ONE NIGHT ONLY.

MR. HILL,

THE CELEBRATED YANKEE COMEDIAN,

Respectfully announces to the Citizens of Bangor, that he will present, on THURSDAY Evening, August 15th, at the TOWN HOUSE, a COMIC OLIO, part of which is selected from the popular Comedies of JONATHAN in ENGLAND, GREEN MOUNTAIN BOY, and THE FOREST ROSE as Performed by him at the PARK THEATRE, New York, and all the principal Theatres in the U. S. with decided approbation.

PART I.

YANKEE STORY. Solomon Swap in the Pantry, from the Comedy of JONATHAN in ENGLAND. Arrival at Uncle Ephs.—Courting Betsey—Ike Marble's trowses—Folks at supper—Dropping Pumpkin Pie on Sal Barters 'new gown—Nancy Slocum blushes—Solomon sits into the Custard Pudding—Pepper-sauce falls down—Door flies open, &c. &c.

COMIC SONG. Chit chat for the Ladies.

YANKEE STORY. Jonathan Ploughboy's call at Washington, from the pastoral Comedy of the FOREST ROSE, Mahogany Desk—Meeting with Zeph Daniels—writing to Jedide—NULLIFICATION QUESTION—Confusion among the "BIG BUGS" and visit to the Theatre.

COMIC SONG. The Country Bumpkin.

YANKEE STORY. Jedediah's Journey to the Genesee Country, from the new American Comedy, entitled the GREEN MOUNTAIN BOY—start from home on the Old Mare—arrival at his 3rd cousins—orchard with one tree—stony farm—talk with the family—marriage of Father—how he got his learning—Uncle Bill—the Temperance Society, &c. &c.

COMIC SONG. If you will list I vow.

PART 2.

YANKEE STORY. Old JOSH ADAMS and his 76 coat—dinner with Lafayette—Gus getting the Coat. Shaved down—Old Man crying—the wild Beast Show—stories about the Revolution—Zedediah Homes and his Bunker Hill Back—laugh at the British Officer, &c.

COMIC SONG. A man of business.

YANKEE STORY. Ichabod's newyear in New York.—The man that slept with him—the 'Calathumpian' Band—Negro Meeting—Concert of Cats—Courting with Sunday Clothes on—Mrs. Wiggins and her husbands shop.

COMIC SONG. Down a green valley.

YANKEE STORY. Zephaniah Tearall and the Sea Serpent. Man with Spectacles on the ladder—went where he was and he wan't there—music sets him crazy—Josh stands a treat—Sea Serpent is seen—they all look "streaked"—bowl of Lemonade—Music makes him run—foot on the orange peel—fall into the bowl—Clothes cut to pieces and left in trouble.

The whole to include with Mr. Hill's much admired Song, called

A HIT AT THE FASHIONS.

PERFORMANCE WILL COMMENCE AT 8 O'CLOCK, DOORS OPEN AT 1-2 PAST 7.

Single Tickets 50 cents. Tickets to admit a Lady and Gentleman 75 cents, to be had at the Penobscot Exchange and at the door. Children with their parents 25 cents.

PROPER OFFICERS ARE ENGAGED TO ENFORCE DECORUM.

Bangor (Maine) Theatre playbill (c. 1834)
of George Hill in several stories, songs, and characters.

to Mathews and the traditions of English comedy. The evidence of Hackett's early experimentation definitely tells us that this was his notion of the comic spirit on the stage, and he pulled away from it only as he broadened his comedy for a less-oriented audience. To Hill, reproductions from life were more in the nature of reporting what he saw without specific overtones of meaning. The comic spirit to him was laughing together with an audience at the vagaries and eccentricities of humanity as he saw it. His laughter was warm, gentle, and usually sentimental. And so the plays he chose to act were story plays of sentiment and melodrama. He turned to *The Forest Rose* because he saw the possibility of quiet fun with a country boy. And when Samuel Woodworth had provided another sentimental drama in *The Foundling of the Sea*, he snatched it up and brought it to the stage. *The Green Mountain Boy*, *The Knight of the Golden Fleece*, and *Casper Hauser* were much of the same conventional design. Hill had no axe to grind with the English, no strong feelings about the meanings of native American difference, no genuine desire to search out American character and put it on a pedestal. James Hackett is clearly the satirist; Hill is much more the conventional performer-comedian.

Probably this strain of conventionality in Hill made it much easier for him to accept and act the plays of conventional design provided by Dunlap, Woodworth, Stone, Jones, and Finn. Their plays certainly would have been available to Hackett also had he wanted them, but he seems to have been looking elsewhere, with his mind fixed on a more objective view of American life to show on the stage. Which one was the more conventional: Hackett, who deliberately borrowed the English tradition of satire; or Hill, who picked up the sentimental-comedy tradition and worked with plays of a highly conventional mold?

As a born-and-bred New Englander, Hill certainly felt an affinity for localisms of which Hackett literally had no notion. Hill's "country-boy" character certainly could seem to derive from the early plays—*The Contrast* to *The Forest Rose*—but it was undoubtedly freshly conceived in terms of personal experience. Down-East really meant something to Hill, and he turned to his fellow New Englanders in Woodworth, Jones, Stone, and Finn for materials he could breathe life into. Seba Smith's Major Jack Downing was no general American but a cider-and-applesauce character out of the peculiar and eccentric qualities of New England life. This quality is more fully developed in later plays, but here the direction is already clearly determined.

In 1836, when George Hill prepared to go to Europe, he had accumulated ten years of valuable stage experience which had put him before every sort of audience from that of the fashionable Park to a country audience at Bangor. During six of those years, spent in the hard work of an itinerant or stock performer, he had learned much about audience tastes and how to control them. After his success at the Park he could declare his own direction, and he moved through the full experience of the star actor. In the winter of 1836 he made a second tour of the Southwest, and then returned for final engagements in New York and Philadelphia. In the latter city on May 26, 1836, he tried, apparently unsuccessfully, to perform the character of Peleg in *Fall of the Alamo*. Not even the topicality of this play, hard on the heels of the actual massacre in San Antonio, could save it from disaster. Beyond this one performance he never played it again.

Hill apparently passed the summer in upstate New York but was back in the city for a testimonial dinner in his honor at the City Hotel on August 8, 1836.[28] He was highly praised for his contributions to the American stage and was presented with a silver pitcher inscribed in recognition of his success. Within a few days he boarded the packet ship *Oxford*, with Captain Rathbun in command, and was on his way to England.

[28] *Life*, p. 38.

chapter 11

Yankee Hill in London

G EORGE HILL was twenty-seven when he went to London. His rise had been so rapid and the acclaim so continuous and wide-spread after his Park debut in 1832 that he had scarcely had time to reflect on what it all meant or to see himself in any perspective. On the voyage across the Atlantic in the jovial company of Charles Murray he amused himself and the other passengers by issuing a daily newspaper with the Hill touches of stories, jokes, and humors, but after he docked in London he settled to his work in a serious frame of mind. Success at Drury Lane was a necessity, he felt, because of its important bearing on his fortunes at home. As he underwent the long wait from late September until his scheduled appearance in November, he worried about the outcome. Yankee dialect comedy was known in London only by those who had seen Hackett in his characters four years previously, and the failure of the comedian at that time loomed before Hill and increased his worry. With Hackett's example before him he knew that success would depend on something much more solid than the mere delivery of quaint sayings in a strange and peculiar dialect. What amused audiences at home where the New England Yankee was to be seen, even in the more remote parts of the Union, was just as likely to confuse and perplex London playgoers. Hackett had already proved that eccentricity and realistic description were not comedy in them-selves but needed the artful and perceptive illuminations of the comedian to turn them to advantage. The only solace Hill could find, and this was a slight one, was that if London did not receive him well, it might also reject the other American actors that had made the crossing that season. What had encouraged such a migration to London was not immediately evident, but there they were, ready to appear in strength: Hill, the Yankee comedian; Edwin Forrest, America's top tragedian; and T. D. Rice, black-faced variety entertainer of Jumping Jim Crow fame. James Hackett had crossed earlier during the summer, but now he had returned to play his Yankee characters at the Park while his rival was in London.[1]

Hill was most anxious to play but not before he knew the score. He spent much of his time seeking the advice of those who had watched Hackett fail in 1832 for lack of a good Yankee piece to reveal his talents in the character to best advantage.[2] We note his concern in a letter on October 20, probably to J. S. Jones. "I have not yet played, as I am to have a new piece written for me for my first appearance. I wish you were here to take some hints and put them on the track for me. There are clever playwrights everywhere, but they do not understand the nice points of Yankee character."[3] And as he strolled about London and noted its many differences from American life he began to understand why. He visited the shops in Holborn and the Strand, and watched the trading in the markets near St. Paul's or around Drury Lane Theatre. More than once he felt the Yankee in him stick out all over, and he longed for some "notions" with which he could dicker with John Bull traders. But though he noted that London dealers were as shrewd and sagacious as any in the world, he thought Englishmen as a body were warm and friendly, "without that eternal ghost of trade haunting them and obtruding the unsocial question of 'How much can I get out of this fellow?' at every new introduction" as there was too often at home. Englishmen appeared to deal with a customer honestly, so he thought, and consider the inducements to trade as matters of honor. John Bull might worship the mighty dollar as much as Jonathan, but he seemed less anxious to get it unfairly and was not too tenacious of it when he did obtain it.[4] What irritated and

[1] See Chapter 8 for the peculiar circumstances surrounding Hackett's trip.
[2] That Hackett made a lively success of his backwoods character in *The Kentuckian* should not be forgotten. This followed in the spring of 1833 and probably made the grade because Bayle Bernard had rewritten it especially for the London showing.
[3] *Scenes*, p. 128.   [4] *Scenes*, p. 131.

embarrassed Hill more was the behavior of some of his American friends who, when at home, denounced all things "aristocratical," but in London toadied to their tailors and bootmakers "to get a squint at patterns of noblemen's coats and pantaloons, or the sight of their persons" when undergoing the operation of being measured. "And such a splutter and fuss as they make to get into a club, or to dine with any of the nobility, would be awful to think of at home, particularly about election times, when everybody is so democratic and have such a 'mess' of feelings for the dear people." In his light sarcasm, Yankee Hill, the Jacksonian democrat, begins to sound a bit like Frances Trollope or even Basil Hall.

But though the fresh and exciting environment of London made Hill see American things more clearly, he still took his Americanism seriously. His rhetoric is often touched with patriotic fervor, as familiar as New England cider and Yankee dialect. How else could he have made such a thoroughbred, unpretentious, symbolic stage character, as he did in the Yankee, without feeling strongly those attitudes and feelings which tied him to American life? As an actor who moved about continuously meeting all sorts of people, and as a city resident when at home, Hill was no provincial. But like the English qualities that stuck out all over the well-bred-man-of-the-world Charles Mathews, so Hill's Americanism was obviously reflected in Hill. "You know there is none with a greater love for his own country, and the things it contains, than I have," he wrote to Mrs. Hill. "I am a good democrat, and glory in a Republican form of government." Nevertheless, he could also criticize American weakness.

You will have to believe me that, in spite of some preconceived notions not in favor of John Bull, I think from what I have seen that Englishmen are ahead of Jonathan in many matters that Americans do not fairly "acknowledge the corn" about. I am happy that I am an American, and not less so that I descended . . . from the sires who came from the "fast-anchored isle."

One wonders, if Englishmen of the day had seen Hill's statement, whether they would have been grateful for his generous acknowledgment or merely amused at the odd-fellow Jonathan they had reared in the "fast-anchored" land across the Atlantic?

2

Hill chose *Old Times in Virginia, or the Yankee Pedlar* for his opening and immediately set about the reworking process with playwright Bayle Bernard. The comedian has not told us why he chose this playscript. He had played it only a few times in Philadelphia,[5] and certainly other pieces in his repertoire had been much better tested before audiences, and he had readjusted and enriched them as performance experience dictated. Furthermore, a new piece for a London audience unacquainted with any of his work would hardly have been necessary merely to give them fresh material. In reviewing his chances for a positive reception, very likely with Drury Lane Manager Alfred Bunn, who had participated in Hackett's dreadful fiasco,[6] Hill must have decided that *The Yankee Pedlar*, especially if rewritten for London audiences by a playwright acquainted with its vagaries, would present the best advantage for showing Hill's peculiarities of style. Its setting on a plantation in Virginia could sharply delineate the eccentricities of the down-East country peddler from the Southern types in the play. In trying to protect Drury Lane's interest, Bunn may also have asked Bayle Bernard to sit in on the conferences, though Hill undoubtedly had made early contact with this writer as the best qualified person to help him prepare his materials. At any rate the choice was made and Bernard set to work quickly to prepare the script for the opening.

Hill's choice of Bayle Bernard was expedient, for he was the only playwright in London who had a direct touch with America. After Hackett's failure with his own Yankee materials, he had employed Bernard, on John Howard Payne's recommendation,[7] to work on *Lion of the West* and *Rip Van Winkle*, and the new versions had been successful. Hackett had also brought home *Job Fox*, and American audiences had liked it too. Though only a year older than Hill, Bernard had already made his mark, not as a gifted writer, but as a solid workman with professional skills.[8] His best

---

[5] Performances are recorded for May 8, and December 17, 1835; May 9 and 14, 1836. Hill had apparently not tried it in New York.

[6] See Chapter 8.

[7] *Mirror*, XI (February 22, 1834), 270.

[8] The catalogue of the British Museum lists forty-four titles of published plays accredited to Bernard. None have survived in literature.

claim as an "American" playwright was his heritage. He was born in Boston in 1808 while his father was manager of the Federal Street Theatre. The family returned to England when he was still a baby, and he was brought up there. His knowledge of America was therefore largely secondhand through his father's anecdotes and his diaries, which he left at his death. Nevertheless, Bayle was still close enough to the source to be more useful to American actors than any other writer. His early career as an actor also helped his view, especially in the area of low comedy, where the playscript, in this age, was secondary to the manner in which it was performed.

It is entirely possible that in preparing *The Yankee Pedlar* Bernard found the paragraph in his father's diaries that actually supported Hiram Dodge with firsthand observation.

This visit of the pedlar is regarded by the Southern trader in the light of a visitation; he may be truly said to have Yankee-phobia, and to look upon a "Connecticut chap" as a commercial Scythian, a Tartar of the North whose sole business in life is to make inroads upon his peace and profit. He ranks him in the list of plagues next to the Yellow Fever, and before locusts, taxation, and a wet spring; indeed, some go so far as to suppose that a shower of Yankees was the crowning pestilence which made Pharaoh give up the Israelites.[9]

Bernard, the son, may have been brought up an Englishman, but in his father's journals he had the best of primary sources. *The Yankee Pedlar* was the first of three collaborations with Hill in Bernard's efforts to make the real Yankee he saw through his father's eyes come alive on the stage. No other English playwright could claim the same position, though several subsequently tried their hand at Yankee eccentricities. When R. B. Peake wrote *Jonathan in England* he was making a play for an English actor to be spoken from an English stage to an English audience; he had not intended it for American use. Hill's request of Bernard undoubtedly assumed that if workable in London, the play would be used in America, and since it was prepared specifically in collaboration with an American actor, it ought to be much more American in attitude and feeling.

Bernard's version undoubtedly used the idea of the playscript

[9] Bernard, *Retrospections*, p. 41. See also the Introduction of Bernard's work for biographical material on the son.

Hill had tried out in Philadelphia, but he probably altered it in much of the specific detail.[10] In Bernard's three-scene farce Yankee peddler Hiram Dodge becomes involved with the household of Colonel Bantum, a plantation owner and horse racer. Dodge craftily maneuvers himself into a position between the Colonel and a rival planter so that he can control a horse race and help the Colonel's daughter marry the man she wants. Dodge lets the young man win the race while he rides the opposition horse to defeat. As we would expect, we see a clever Yankee outsmart a Southerner.

With the script ready, Hill prepared for the opening. He was not quite sure of himself, but he was resolved to give the audience the best performance within his capability.

3

George Hill's London debut in *The Yankee Pedlar* was scheduled for the evening of November 1, 1836, to follow, in the afterpiece position, *The Maid of Cashmere*. The house was full and the response to the melodrama was better than usual. After the entre-scene music, the audience quieted with expectancy for the first appearance of the celebrated delineator of Yankee character in "a characteristic sketch."

As the curtain rose the audience saw on one side of the stage a low tavern beside a road that wound off at the back into some woods. Before the tavern hung a sign with the inscription: The Jefferson

[10] How much of the original playscript which Hill used in Philadelphia was retained in the rewriting we do not know. Two manuscripts of the London version are available in the Lord Chamberlain's Collection. The second one, in the order of filing, contains minor alterations from the first and seems to be a corrected copy of the first. See L.C.C. No. 42939 (1836) and L.C.C. No. 42944 (1837). The only explanation lies in Alfred Bunn's note on the peculiar circumstance created when *The Yankee Pedlar* was produced without the Lord Chamberlain's license during a period of misunderstanding, "and without (of far more importance to the groundlings of his office than all the licenses which he ever signed) the payment of fees." As a result, "an intimation was sent to the theatre by the officials that no further licenses would be granted Drury Lane Theatre until the regulations of his Lordship's Office were complied with" (Bunn, *The Stage*, II, 35). Apparently the formalities were completed and a copy of the play submitted. Since the first copy (1836) in the file was licensed to the Olympic Theatre when Hill played it there in early January, 1837, the second copy (1837) may actually be the original script Bernard prepared, with the Olympic copy reflecting the changes made during and after the Drury Lane performances. The changes are of a minor nature, however, and the play's content stands clear in both.

Head, and on the porch asleep was Mr. Cowpens. Across "the road" on the other side of the stage was the house of Colonel Bantum. The Colonel was also sound asleep on two chairs. Their snores are suddenly interrupted by a group of plantation Negroes who come down the road singing a song.

> De easern State him fall of corn,
>   De Wessom full of guinea,
> De middle good for pickle pork—
>   But non like old Virginny.
> Him sile so rich it nebber mind
>   What seed um got to bear, Sirs;
> If massa plant a coffee pot,
>   Up come de cups and sarcers.[11]

The Colonel and Cowpens shake themselves awake and talk about a horse race in which the Colonel will race Brimstone against Mr. Slingsby's colt for a winner's purse of a thousand dollars. The Colonel has promised his daughter Nancy to Tom Roanoke if, as the Colonel's jockey, he wins the race. When the Colonel learns that a Yankee peddler is on the plantation, he denounces all Yankees for selling wooden nutmegs, pitcoal indigo, and red-flannel sausages. His anger abates with the arrival of a stranger, but the stranger is Moreland, who is secretly in love with Nancy and has put on a disguise to gain entry to the house. As the Colonel and Moreland go inside, we hear offstage the telltale "Fancy Ware!" and Hiram Dodge bounces on with a wooden clock under his arm and a basket in his hand. Immediately the stage is full of shouting and laughing women and children as the plantation pours out to welcome the peddler and buy his wares. On hearing the racket, the Colonel angrily threatens to "cut up" Dodge if he does not depart in a hurry. He punctuates his threat by rushing out for his rifle. When Sam Slouch arrives with a letter from Slingsby about the horse race, Hiram asks for the job of delivering it to the Colonel in order to get inside the house and mollify its angry owner.

In the second scene, as the Colonel and the disguised Moreland discuss a new horse, Hiram arrives with Slingsby's letter, which discloses that Roanoke, for a hundred-dollar fee, is going to ride

---

[11] Punctuation has been added, and the last line edited from "Up come up cups and sarcers."

Slingsby's horse instead of the Colonel's. Moreland and Nancy now declare their love and sing a sentimental duet. As they embrace, Dodge suddenly returns, sees them, collects five dollars to keep quiet, and then collects another five from the Colonel, who, arriving just in time to see the lovers leaving together, is suspicious of their behavior and willing to pay to find out about it. When Cowpens brings news that Dodge has also gone over to Slingsby, the Colonel tries to trick Hiram into delivering a note to his overseer with the message "tie up the beaver and give him 100 lashes." But the Yankee, never outsmarted, gives the note to Mr. Slingsby, who innocently delivers it. When the Colonel hears Slingsby yelling offstage, he knows Dodge has fooled him. Nancy ends the scene with another love song.

The plantation is now "railed in" for the horse race. Slingsby reports that the Colonel will double the stakes if Roanoke does not ride, and he offers the job to Dodge, who accepts. The Colonel has engaged Moreland as his jockey. When the young lover fears he may lose, Dodge assures him he will win the race and get the girl the Colonel has promised the winner.

The crowd now gathers, and the race begins with clatter and excitement. It is reported to us by Nancy, Cowpens, and other spectators. Moreland finally wins when Dodge is thrown over the hedge, and he immediately asks for Nancy's hand. The Colonel first refuses, then capitulates when reminded of his promise. Moreland explains to the happy Colonel that Dodge fell off the horse to punish Slingsby for offering Moreland one hundred dollars to throw the race. A group of Negroes now carry Dodge onto the stage, stretched out cold on a hurdle. The Colonel is so contrite he offers forty dollars to see the Yankee alive again. "Done Squire," says Dodge popping up like a Jack-in-the-box. So amused and grateful is the Colonel that, in place of the forty he offered, he gives the Yankee one hundred dollars. Hiram ends the sketch with a speech and song.

Well, now I swow if that an't grand enough for the King of Great Britain. Why that draws out love like Maple Sugar. Well, this an't turned out no bad day's trade. I rather think I feel about as lively as a stump'd tail bull in fly time. Now I an't got but one more pint to settle. What do the folks about me say to all my doings if they dont think they're too tarnal bad to see agin. Perhaps they won't altogether object to another visit from a

Yankee pedlar

Tho in others' affairs I'm a meddler,
Pray don't condemn a poor pedlar.
My effort has been to achieve a good cause,
But all is in vain if denied your applause.

OMNES. Though in all our affairs he's a meddler,
Pray don't condemn the poor pedlar.
His effort has been to achieve a good cause,
But all is in vain if denied your applause.[12]

The plot of *The Yankee Pedlar* has been recounted here in detail because it contains all the ingredients of many a Hill play: the loose plot to permit expansion with stories and Yankeeisms; a number of songs, and one particularly for the Yankee; the Yankee character placed in sharp contrast to other types around him to display his cleverness in getting the best of the bargain; the Yankee assisting the young lovers in the *commedia dell' arte* tradition of comedy. But the significance of this sketch does not rest on these points alone. Either Bayle Bernard, or the author of the first version, in selecting the Southern plantation with its Negro life as the scene of the play provided the environment of the first completely indigenous American theatre form, the minstrel show. If not the first, *The Yankee Pedlar* is certainly among the earliest plays to bring together in a single setting the two best-known areas of American folk life. Shortly after *The Yankee Pedlar* had opened, London would see also T. D. Rice in his black-face character. In the clever and enterprising Yankee, the relaxed, horse-racing Southerner, and the singing-dancing plantation Negroes were Hill and Bernard merely capitalizing on the Londoners' broad curiosity about American life? They were certainly presenting a kaleidescope of America as Europeans saw it.

4

The reviews of Hill's evening began appearing the next day.[13] Within a short time the general verdict was complete: Hill was a first-rate comedian, one of the best London had seen, but Bernard's

[12] Punctuation has been added in both the speech and the song.
[13] The opinion in this section is a composite of the reviews in London newspapers and weeklies. Many of the reviews were collected in *Opinion of the*

farce was poor stuff. Many reviewers, perhaps with consideration
for Bernard's collaboration as a playwright-mechanic with Hill,
and with the attitude that since the evening was an amusing one
much censure of the play itself was not in order, turned it aside
with a bare mention. Others labeled it nonsense of the worst sort,
"vapid," a "stupid farce," a "farago of rubbish," with a line of
characters "somewhat below the highest" on the stage. One was
angry that Drury Lane stage was nightly disgraced by this combination of nonsense. Comment varied from the mild report that the
Yankee was unknown in dramatic literature and his Yankeeisms not
well understood, making judgment difficult beyond recognition of
its freshness and novelty, to the overt statement that the play was a
failure and the writing in it very bad. "The very tiger behind our
cat shall write a better, ay, though his pencil was a wet piece of
chalk occasionally brightened by a dip in a bottle of Warren's jet."
On the other hand, the report on Hill's performance was quite the
opposite. Bad notices were buried under the avalanche of favorable
report. The reception of Yankee Hill, to say the least, was highly
enthusiastic.

In the reviews of *The Yankee Pedlar* and other plays which he
subsequently played in London, Edinburgh, and Glasgow, we have
an enlightening picture of the style of acting Hill had been formu-
lating for several years. He is occasionally compared to Charles
Mathews, now dead for over a year. One reviewer noted that
Mathews' Jonathan seemed a caricature beside Hill's, and that the
American had surpassed the English comedian in his dry, rich, and
quaint humor. Others made comparisons with Knight, Keeley,
Liston, and Tyrone Power. Hill was closely linked to Power—
though the characters the two played were quite different—in his
refreshing quietness and entire absence of any stage manner. And
like Power, who had been criticized in America for drawing his
characters on too quiet and small a scale, and for not exaggerating
and making "hits" of his comic points, some critics thought Hill's

---

British Press on the Performances of G. H. Hill, collected by a Friend. The same
group also appear in *Life* and *Scenes*. One review from Edinburgh and one from
Glasgow are also included. This list has been amplified by searching some of
these reviews for further comment not included in the original compilation, and
by adding other sources such as *The Drama, Figaro in London, The Times,* and
reviews for Hill's performances in January, 1837, at the Queen's and the Olympic Theatres.

humor almost too quiet for an English public, that he should at least speak a little more loudly and not drop his voice when he came to the essential words of a joke.

The concurrent success of these two comedians at this time leads to the conjecture that the new style in acting, for comedy at least, which the audience was intuitively seeking was something more approximate to everyday life than it had been seeing on the stage up to this point. The acting of classical comedy with its artificialities appeared to be passing in favor of this new folk form, so full of images familiar to the new popular audiences made up of country-come-to-the-city people. Incidentally, it was during this season that Madame Vestris introduced London to the realistic box setting, with its rugs, drapes, and everyday furniture. Revolution was in the air and comedy was in the forefront of the change.

Hill's style, the reviewers noted, though comparable in part to others, was unique. His appearance was prepossessing: a slight figure with good features, a peculiarly pleasant countenance, a smile that mingled gravity and grins, and a capital voice. His expressive eyes were continually mentioned—their rich comical expression, their slyness, their shrewdness and cunning, their quiet humor. Against one reporter who saw Hill "open his mouth wide, run around the stage like a wildcat, jump like a ring-tail monkey," were the many others who found his lively style captivating in its laughing, bustling, lounging, solemn, chattering, easy, and natural animal spirits. Quietness was pointed to as the distinguishing feature that made his style eminently chaste and simple, with no resource to mimicry or the appliances of buffoonery and grimace. His strong point was in his sly look, with a droll impudent stare. All was devoid of vulgarity. When these London critics described Hill's characterization of Hiram Dodge, they saw no caricature but only finished pictures, with nature in every line. There was no straining after making a point. The humor was dry, quaint, witty. Hiram Dodge was a thoroughbred Yankee, sly, fraudulent, cunning under a mask of simplicity, a smooth, slick peddler, and an accurate, truthful image. Hill's taste and discrimination made a Yankee with no humbug about him, with an indescribable twang, a self-possessed expression, and an amazing cunningness.

In the overview the reviewers conceded Hill the position of a first-rate actor in the comedy line, with one notice labeling him the "only" comic actor furnished by the United States. His humor was irresistible in its effect and his pictures accurate. Except for Irish Power, Hill had no rival in telling a story. He was a talented actor of admirable command, of considerable mark and likelihood, with a peculiar and original style. And not the least, he could keep an audience always in the best of humor and frequently in roars of laughter. As a comedian he was truthful to life, subtle and quiet in manner, with a freshness London seldom saw.

Before Hill left Europe for home in March, 1837, he played engagements at two other London theatres, and in Edinburgh and Glasgow. So much was London taken with Hiram Dodge that, in addition to the many performances at Drury Lane, Hill played the character twenty-one times at the Olympic Theatre. And during this engagement, so much was he in demand, the managers of the Queen's Theatre arranged several appearances at that house, to be performed simultaneously with the Olympic's.

At the Queen's, Hill tried to break the pattern of continuous performance in *The Yankee Pedlar*. Such a long run in the same role had not given him a chance to present his repertoire. There he played *Casper Hauser* on January 9, and a new play, *A Down-East Bargain, or Love in New York*, later in the month. Little is known about this last play, nor are we able to enrich our knowledge about *Casper Hauser*, for Hill seems to have performed both plays without obtaining licenses from the Lord Chamberlain. Neither appear in the Lord Chamberlain's collection, as do the other London plays performed by Yankee actors. Newspapers must therefore be relied on for information about their production.

A Down-East Bargain, which introduced Zephaniah Makepeace, "a Down Easter out of place and in love with Nabley," was probably written by W. T. Moncrieff, a busy London hack playwright like Bernard. In connection with its first New York performance, George Odell hints that it may have been borrowed from Woodworth's *The Foundling of the Sea*, with Zephaniah Makepeace an English spelling for Zachariah Dickerwell. The lists of characters for the two plays are quite different, however. What suggested his inspiration, Odell does not say. If it was a reworking of Woodworth's play, it was in line with what Bernard had done with *Pedlar*. At any rate, Hill showed it in London only once or twice, and only a few times in the States.

After this attempt to sell more Yankee wares, Hill left for a successful tour of the provinces. He received equally enthusiastic notices wherever he went. By the middle of April the Yankee comedian was on his way home in the *United States*, Captain Holdridge commanding.

What a contrast this London reception was to the one given James Hackett in 1832. After the opening, word of Hill's London hit was carried back to New York and the *Mirror* enthusiastically played it for all it was worth. In January, after noting that it had examined nearly all the London papers reporting Hill's acting, the *Mirror* stated flatly that Hill deserved all the commendations showered on him. But in expanding its statement it also implied a great deal more. Hill's quiet and striking style in portraying the Yankee, the *Mirror* mentioned, had helped to improve the crude and incorrect notions Englishmen still had of America and Americans.[14] This was very high praise if it was true. If others were dubious, at least the *Mirror* thought its American theatre ambassador had partially fulfilled its long-held hope.

George Hill's venture onto the boards of Drury Lane had put him at the top in London as well as at home. *Knickerbocker Magazine*, which had followed his career for several seasons with active interest, saluted his merits as an actor and a man—"in the exhibitions of the quiet, dry humor, peculiar to the Yankee, par excellence, he stands unrivalled. His acting is nature itself."[15] It was always the *Mirror*, however, with the neatest word: " 'A clever man is Yankee Hill,' says the London *Literary Gazette*, and ditto the *New York Mirror*."[16]

14 *Mirror*, XIV (January 21, 1837), 240.
15 *The Knickerbocker*, May, 1838.
16 *Mirror*, XV (April 14, 1838), 334.

chapter 12

After London: Hill's Success and Decline

T HE YEARS between George Hill's first London journey and his death in 1849 constitute a curve in his career: during the first half of the period, a continuous rise in his development and contribution as an actor as he broadened and strengthened his theatre activities; and then a gradual falling off and decline in the last few years as his purposes wavered. The mature Hill that gradually emerged from the boy of the 1832 Park debut is not always the disarming, smiling, charming nature we glimpsed earlier. As the simple, country-boy Yankee in him gives way to the actor of affairs, ambition strikes him and he moves with confidence and independence. No Yankee actor enjoyed such a full measure of success by acting a single eccentric character, but no Yankee actor was exposed to the unusual opportunities open to George Hill.

The biography of Yankee theatre outlined in this book is not a personal story of the usual sort, with close and penetrating examinations of human motives and directions. It is primarily concerned with the product and the description of that product rather than with the intimate lives of the people who made it. Personal treatment of individuals is important in this account only when it would reveal a specifically relevant background, explain an action taken, or declare a direction pursued in the total view of illuminating Yankee theatre. Yet one cannot work in this material without being caught up by the personalities who made it, and occasionally the close view helps our understanding. What caused George Hill's decline at thirty-five, when his most productive years as an actor should have been still ahead, is a relevant question. If we could answer it we might discover much about the problems in making a career of a single comedy type. The example of James Hackett, who dropped the Yankee character as he moved into a much more diverse pattern of acting, has already been noted. But Hill's direction seems to be determined a great deal more, not by technical and professional decisions growing out of a change in his actor's purpose, but by character traits within the man which basically ordered his actions.

No one has been more complimentary of Hill's abilities than Francis Wemyss. In his capacity as manager in Philadelphia, Baltimore, and Pittsburgh he not only saw Hill perform frequently, but dealt with him in the actor-manager relationship, where he could watch Hill closely. He greatly admired Hill's quiet natural manner which delighted an audience, giving it "full employment" while the comedian was on the stage. Wemyss very frankly credited Hill as the best actor of American comedy and thought his London success well merited. He further complimented Hill for his contribution of several good acting pieces to the American theatre, and he praised him as one of the most attractive stars audiences had seen for many seasons. But then Wemyss changed tack, giving us another view of Hill. He forgot, argued Wemyss, what he had been, and what he was, and "aimed at an unenviable notoriety out of his profession" which injured his future success. "Had Mr. Hill been a man of education, he would have supported himself with credit in the position he had suddenly reached. Having boldly breasted a storm which threatened to annihilate his claims as an actor and triumphed over it"—Wemyss is probably here referring to the Drury Lane test—"an overweening vanity has proved more detrimental to his fame than all the artifices of his enemies could ever have accomplished."[1]

What Wemyss specifically had in mind rests in obscurity, but the last period of Hill's life brings into focus much of what Wemyss had to say of the actor. Part of what happened to Hill might be explained, as Stone explains it,[2] through gossip and personal stories.

[1] Wemyss, *Twenty-Six Years*, I, 203.
[2] Stone, *Personal Recollections*, pp. 225–227. While in London, Hill had an affair with "a fascinating but very *artful* young actress of the name of Miss R——s, whom he brought with him to this country. . . . While in the city of

But much can still be learned about George Hill through established
events and facts.

2

The curve of George Hill's success pattern continues a fairly steady
rise through 1843. Immediately after his return home from the
London journey he proceeded to reap what reward he could out of
the new labels he could attach to his name. He opened at the Park
Theatre with *The Yankee Pedlar*, proclaiming it had been played
fifty nights in Europe and identifying it further "as performed by
him at Drury Lane."[3] During the summer as he toured from New
York to Albany and Boston, south to Washington and Richmond,
and west to Louisville and Cincinnati, the billing and the newspaper puffs praised his fame. In Cincinnati where Mrs. Trollope
was still very much remembered, Hill's friendly ambassadorship in
England was pointed out—"a credit to his country"—along with
his remarkably versatile comic powers.[4]

Back in New York in September, the busy Yankee comedian
staged three new pieces to take advantage of Simpson's offer to use
the strength of the Park company as he wished. The first was a new
Bayle Bernard play, *Speculations, or Major Wheeler in Europe*,

---

Washington, which was during John Tyler's . . . administration, she produced
so decided a sensation among the magnates of that city by her cunning manoeuvr-
ing, coquetting, and shrewd strategy, as to actually succeed in controlling the
appointment of many a 'scurvy politician' to an office in some of the government
departments at Washington, as well as elsewhere. 'Bob' T——, it was strongly
suspected, had been inveigled in the meshes of this artful girl, which may in a
measure account for the influence she had in controlling affairs to the extent she
did. It was through the wiles and intrigues of this young actress that Hill was
ultimately driven to an utter state of despair and final ruin! 'Women and
wine,' so often the ruin of young men of the present day, was the cause of de-
stroying poor Yankee Hill! . . . He died . . . leaving an amiable and very exemplary wife and several children . . . Hill once owned a beautiful villa at
Batavia, located near the New York Central Railroad depot, situated on an ele-
vated plot of ground, commanding an uninterrupted view of the beautiful village
of Batavia and surrounding country; but whether this property was saved from
his wrecked fortune and secured as a home for his wife and children, we have
never been advised."

[3] Odell, *Annals*, IV, 129.

[4] Hill performed a piece during this engagement titled *Wandering Boys*. Since
this is the only time this title seems to have appeared, and since no evidence
exists to substantiate it otherwise, historians of the theatre assume it to be an
alternate title for one of the regularly performed works in Hill's repertoire.

and this he played on September 4. On the eighth he tried an anonymous sketch titled *Turn Out*, featuring a Yankee called Gregory. And a week later, on September 16, he played J. Moncrieff's *A Down-East Bargain* for the first time in the States. *Turn Out* soon falls by the wayside and *A Down-East Bargain* has already been mentioned. *Speculations*, with its enterprising Major Enoch Wheeler, "a speculator with a few new inventions" from Penobscot Bay, State of Maine, became a permanent part of Hill's repertoire.

Bernard apparently wrote *Speculations* for Hill while he was in London, but because of the unusual demand for *Pedlar* it was never played.[5] As we have already noted, Hill declared that the material for this play took form on the trip he took to Raynham and Taunton with Joseph Jones in the summer of 1835. As he discussed possible play ideas with Bernard, Hill undoubtedly described the character he had in mind, and together they thought up a plot to set off the Major. Portsmouth, England, was the setting, which again placed the Yankee in a foreign environment where he would be clearly contrasted. Since the sketch was also intended for English audiences, the local setting was of further value in providing familiar and nonconfusing background for Hill's eccentricities and Yankeeisms.

Again a comic intrigue was woven around the plight of a girl who was denied by a guardian the right to marry the man she wants, and assisted by the Yankee to win the man of her choice.[6] So often is this same basic plot repeated, one is forced to conclude that, as with the modern "Westerns," the delights for the audience lay, not in the plot itself, but in the detailed way in which it was evolved and the acting which brought it alive. Major Enoch Wheeler of the Penobscot Militia, State of Maine, has just landed at Portsmouth, England. In trying to sell some Yankee "notions" to Edward Markham, he learns that Markham is much in love with Ellen, whose guardian, Mr. Ledger, had forbidden Markham to enter the

---

[5] Hill played this at the Haymarket Theatre in London on July 21, 1838, during his second European tour.

[6] The script is extant in the Lord Chamberlain's Collection. The story line has appeared so frequently in the Yankee plays that it has the aspects of a major theme. Since other plays of the period also used the same idea, it could possibly be regarded as basic folk profeminist propaganda. Certainly it is tied into the idea of independence and freedom.

house. The guardian intends to marry Ellen to his boyhood chum, Major Jungle, who is scheduled to arrive that day from India. Wheeler offers his help to Markham, and the plot begins to turn. In an intrigue of confused identities, Wheeler is taken for Jungle, is warmly welcomed in Ledger's home, given Ledger's smoking jacket to wear, and is royally entertained. The confusion is uncovered when Ledger arrives home from London, but not until Major Wheeler has found a letter in Ledger's jacket which he uses to force the guardian to let the lovers marry. In the meantime he has trapped all of Ledger's friends into buying stock in his Yankee speculations. The three scenes are placed successively in front of "a marine view," in an apartment in the house, and in a drawing-room.

Speculations gave Hill his usual opportunities. It was not so much a plot as a framework for the comedian's bag of tricks. When it was later performed in London (July 21, 1838) reviewers characterized it as "barely dramatic," "rather a narrative than a farce," "a novelty," and very slight material "without epigramatic neatness." One critic thought Hill's playing of a "very *quiet* description," and the wit of the farce "equally peaceful."[7] Nevertheless, the framework was solid enough for Hill to move his character about as he pleased. So we see "a little odd-looking man with large eyes who stares about at everything as if he was going to make a catalogue." And he sells Yankee notions: "a waterproof hat made of mad-dog skin; a Patent castiron self-action Horse Persuader; and horse spectacles."

At the party of Ledger's friends, on hand to welcome Major Jungle in the last scene of the play, Hill arranged an opportunity for one of his best pieces of business—playing the flute. Several jigs are indicated here, and Hill undoubtedly made some fine comic moments of them, varying the business as he saw fit.[8] Whether he had used the business before, we do not know, but he would repeat it later in other plays. Here it is clearly marked, and for the first time we note his specific use of musical instruments as a comic device. In the property inventory made when his estate was settled

---

[7] *Figaro in London*, July 28, 1838.

[8] Ludlow, *Dramatic Life*, p. 675, reports hearing Hill on the flute. "I heard him once, between a play and a farce, perform one of Nicholson's most difficult concertos for the flute, for which he deservedly obtained great applause."

after his death, several musical instruments are listed: "1 Eight Keyece flute ($5.00); 1 old Com. flute (.75); 1 old violin (.25); 1 Bassoon (1.00)." The "Com." flute was evidently a property—a comedy flute—for business only the imagination can project. When the goods were sold, the Keyece brought $9.99, which indicates that it was a playable instrument; the other only 25¢.[9] Such is the epitaph to a Yankee comedian.

When Hill played his third engagement at the Park in November, that busy year, he tried a fourth play New York had not seen. This carried the title *Peaceful Pelton, or the Vermonter* and was authored by H. A. Buckingham "of this city."[10] Was this one of the plays Hill had turned up in the prize contest that had produced Woodworth's *Foundling of the Sea*? Beyond knowing that its principal character, Peaceful Pelton, was a "professor of psalmody and phrenology" and that the play contained a "misanthrope" and a "pair of rogues," critics are ignorant of its nature; so the play rests forever as undisturbed and peaceful as its title suggests. In the spring of 1838 Hill played it in Philadelphia, to end its career. A week later he was back at the Park with another new sketch, *A Day in France* by Charles Selby.[11] Again a foreign environment is indicated for Yankee Josh Higgins, but what the New Englander did on this occasion also remains a mystery.

3

At the end of May, 1838, George Hill again sailed for England, this time accompanied by Mrs. Hill, for a visit that lasted over a year. His first engagement at the Haymarket featured him in daily performances from July 13 through September 8. Then he toured the provinces, as he had done before. On January 23, 1839, he gave two entertainments in Paris at the theatre where the English company played, and there he also attended a masquerade ball in the costume of one of his Yankee characters. Back in London, he opened a new play by Bernard, *Wife for a Day*, which, after a month's run, gave

[9] Inventory made by Cordelia Hill, Hinman Holden, and Branon Young, filed December 17, 1849, Batavia, New York. Among the other "assetts" listed were a bird cage and bird; one spittoon; one case of surgical and dental instruments; 4 trunks, 2 carpetbags; 1 case of curiosities. Total money value of all items: $182.68.

[10] Odell, *Annals*, IV, 194.

[11] Robert L. Sherman, *Drama Cyclopedia*, p. 126.

him full standing as a member of the Haymarket Theatre's acting company. He added other Yankee plays to extend this run of performances, interrupted by illness, until the end of May. In July he moved to the New Strand where he again played nightly for a month, supported by another new piece, *Seth Slope, or Done for a Hundred*, which Joseph Sterling Coyne authored for him. Not until September, 1839, did Yankee Hill return to the States.

Wife for a Day and *Seth Slope*, new additions to Hill's permanent repertoire, were admittedly novelty pieces for the sake of displaying his comic capacities. Reviewers thought them good-humored and laughable, with the second more like an "ordinary, bustling farce" than the first.[12] Both were made of contrivances which could place the Yankee characters in strange and laugh-provoking situations.

In *Wife for a Day* country virtue is victimized but finally wins over city pretension, fraud, and dandyism, as Yankee Nathan Tucker is brought into contact with Mademoiselle Angelique, a French seductress, and Kezy Whiting, a Yankee country girl, the feminine counterpart to a Yankee boy. It tells the story of two brothers: Nathan, the Yankee country boy, and Montagne, a Yankee dandy who has been sent to Paris for medical training by his social-climbing mother. The parents have split over the children: Mrs. Tucker despises Nathan as a country bumpkin, and Mr. Tucker despises Montagne as a citified dandy. When Montagne returns home secretly married to a French opera dancer he tries to protect himself—and the fortune he will receive from his mother— by talking Nathan into pretending for a day to be the husband of the French chorine. In a series of situations in which Nathan is subjected to all kinds of embarrassments, Montagne's scoundrelly past is exposed. But Nathan protects his brother to the end, even to losing girl friend Kezy Whiting temporarily, by paying the chorine's hotel bill out of his own pocket, fighting a duel, being charged with a thousand-dollar debt, and enduring a beating by the sheriff who has come to arrest Montagne. Nathan's masquerade is finally exposed, Montagne is apprehended, and Mr. Tucker settles an estate

---

[12] Criticisms and comment on plays performed during the 1838–1839 season in London are again a composite, and are drawn from the following sources: playbills for the Haymarket Theatre, *Morning Advertiser, Morning Herald, The Times, Morning Chronicle, Morning Post, Sunday Times, The Spectator, Figaro in London.*

TREMONT THEATRE.

☞ PRICES. ☜

Bozes 50 *cents;* *Pit* 25 *cents;* *Proscenium Bozes* $1; *Third Tier* 37½ *cents;* *Gallery* 12½ *cents*

MR. HILL

(ALIAS)

YANKEE HILL'S BENEFIT

AND LAST APPEARANCE.

Mr. Rice - as - Bone Squash!

＼Received Nightly with enthusiastic applause.

☞ Doors open at 1-4 before 7 o'clock and the Performance will commence at 1-4 past 7 precisely.

This Evening (WEDNESDAY) Sept. 21, 1842,

Will be acted (first time in this City) a new Drama, in 3 acts, written expressly for Mr. Hill, entitled

FREE TRADE!

——OR——

THE YANKEE IN TRIPOLI

ABNER TANNER (a Yankee Trader from Marblehead)	-	-	-	MR. HILL
Ali, Bashaw of Tripoli	-	Mr. Ayling	Jack Gale, a Yankee Sailor, out of his reckoning. - }	Mr. C. Howard
Timur -	-	Haynes		
Ben Agan -	-	Chapman	Slaves and Soldiers	
Janar -	-	Benson	Marania, a Greek - -	Miss McBride
Banda -	-	Mullikin	Mulicka - - - -	Mrs. Smith
Ezzan -	-	Ring	Pummelda - -	Mrs. Gilbert
Officer -	-	Parker	Grapyosa - -	Miss Parker
Slave -	-	Thomas	Dancing Girl - -	Miss F. Jones
Alcany -	-	Howard	Attendant Ladies	

DURING THE DRAMA,

A TURKISH DANCE - - MISS F. JONES.

＊Sich a Gittin Up Stairs, (by desire) - - Mr. Rice.

To be followed by the first act of the laughable Piece of

SETH SLOPE

OR...DONE FOR A HUNDRED!

SETH SLOPE (a Yankee Traveller, partial to hard dollars and soft bargains)	-	MR. HILL		
Belmont - - - -	Mr. Leman	Miss Skinner - -	-	Mrs. J. Greene
Boots - - - -	Thomas	Miss Trainer - ' -	-	Miss Parker
Waiter - - -	Ring	Miss Crump - -	-	Mrs. Gilbert
Emily Leeson - - -	Miss McBride	Betty - - -	-	Miss F. Jones

In the course of the Evening, MR. HILL will sing his original and popular Comic Song, entitled

"THE WHISTLING BOY,"

AND PLAY

A FAVORITE SCOTCH MELODY ON THE FLUTE.

on Nathan. Here are enough comic shenanigans to satisfy the most demanding Haymarket gallery gods.

Seth Slope, or Done for a Hundred is a repetition of the same tired plot we have encountered before. A young and wealthy girl is prevented by her guardian from marrying the man of her choice, and the Yankee cleverly thwarts the guardian. But in the detail there is much to remind us of Eldon Thomas' *Charlie's Aunt*, the celebrated English farce of the nineties. Seth Slope, a Yankee traveler, meets Belmont in a Cheltenham hotel and discovers the young man cannot marry Emily because her guardian has promised her to his own son in order to keep her fortune for himself. Seth resolves to aid the helpless Belmont for a fee of £100. His scheme to bring the lovers together takes them, disguised as aunt and niece, to a girl's boarding school where Mr. Doodle has hidden Emily. There they are entertained at tea by the lady teachers. When Belmont inadvertently kisses Emily as Seth is being conducted to the bed chambers by the decorous spinsters, their ruse is discovered. Seth continues his plotting and turns up at Doodle's house, where Emily is now concealed under the eye of governess Miss Crump to await her marriage to Doodle's son Augustus. Seth now masquerades as Professor Slikelbow, a musician, and hides Belmont in the piano. When again the ruse is discovered, Seth plots with Sally, a maid in the house, and arranges a subterfuge that sees old, false-wig Crump meeting Augustus, who thinks he is meeting Emily, in the garden, while Emily escapes with Belmont.

Again the plotting is contrived, but the opportunities for fun are quite obvious. Both plays, *Wife for a Day* and *Seth Slope*, were apparently good enough to bring large audiences to the Haymarket and the Strand for the longest runs a Yankee actor had ever played to that date. A major event for Hill occurred on April 2, 1839, when young Queen Victoria attended a performance of *Wife for a Day*. She was so pleasantly entertained that she encouraged other nobility to support the playhouse.[13] In the parade of names were the Duke and Duchess of Beaufort, the Marquis of Normandy, the Duke and Duchess of Cleveland, the Earl of Chesterfield, the Earl of Kilmorey, the Earl and Countess of Lichfield, and the Earl of

[13] *Sunday Times*, April 7, 1839, April 21, 1839.

Errol. Yankee Hill's antics were not the only thing on the program, but they made a strong part of it. Was the English aristocracy taking a "serious" look at America through the eccentric comedian they saw on the stage? If so, Yankee Hill was carrying more of a burden as the favorite ambassador of democratic America than he ever imagined, even in his fondest dreams.

4

The period between Hill's return home in early October, 1839, and the beginning of his decline in 1843 is marked by a number of unusual incidents for a Yankee actor. It is during this time that Wemyss' accusation of "overweening pride" in George Hill begins to take on meaning. While in London he made an agreement with James W. Wallack to appear at the National Theatre on his return to New York. Such a decision is a rather startling surprise, especially as Simpson was aboard the *British Queen* on Hill's return trip and tried to persuade the comedian to give up the National and come to the Park as he always had. Hill refused. In the years following, except for a few benefit performances, including one for his old friend Mr. Simpson, he never played at the Park again. The hold which that theatre had on stage affairs in New York was beginning to waver, but Hill's action goes unexplained and we conjecture that he saw more opportunity in Wallack's offer. At any rate, Hill opened in Philadelphia, then he returned to the National, where he played his only engagement at that theatre in November. During his remaining years, all of Hill's subsequent appearances in New York were either in locations which were booked for a single performance, or in isolated engagements at the Olympic, Palmo's Opera House, and the Bowery Theatres, or at the Chatham Street Theatre, where he performed many times and was given the title of "Chatham comedian." Hill's own theatres are the exceptions.

Why George Hill took up theatre management at the very peak of a successful acting career is hard to explain. Within a year after his second London venture he is competing with Simpson and Wallack. Had he failed to make the mark he aimed at after returning home? Did he simply think he could make more money alone than as a star for other managers? During the spring of 1840 he brought out at the Chatham Theatre in rapid succession four new

pieces, but none of them made a hit.[14] On March 19 he played
Ebenezer Fish in *The Tourists*; on April 1 he tried Peleg Rowan in
Diamond Cut Diamond, or The Wolf of Brazil; ten days later he
showed Peter Funk in *Shabby Gentility, or Sailors on a Lee Shore*;
and the next day, April 11, he tried *Zekiel Homespun*, with the
Yankee bearing the name of the title of the piece. In the fall of that
year he decided to operate on his own. Did the illness that had
showed itself several times in the past two years and which he
believed to be a heart ailment turn him, in a search for security,
away from dependence solely on his own acting? Had his experience
at the Haymarket given him the idea that a comedy theatre was
possible in America? Was it a driving ambition to make a mark of
the most impressive sort, to do what Hackett had already tried to do
but had failed at? There is no way to answer these questions. At
any rate, George Hill opened the old Franklin as Hill's Theatre on
October 12 and kept it operating, with declining business, until
November 23, when he gave up.

The prospectus for Hill's Theatre was good. It was redecorated in
a most comfortable and elegant manner,[15] with the old pit converted
into a handsome parquet. Further, he warned that "no females
would be admitted to any part of the house unless accompanied by
gentlemen," which, of course, banished the offenses of the third
tier. A strong sense of middle-class respectability is at work in Hill
as he tries to elevate the acting profession and the position of the
playhouse. What Hill had learned at the Haymarket was evidently
being applied here. But could a comedy theatre succeed? Was
American comedy extensive enough to provide the wide range of
programs necessary to continuously lure audiences into his theatre?

As the company began performances on October 12 with a string
of Hill's own pieces,[16] he prepared a number of new sketches and
gave them strength by billing them close together. Ikey Seekout in
The Conspiracy, or Who Tore Your Coat? on October 30; Colonel
Slimmerkins in *The Veteran of Seventy-Six* on the next evening;
Sober Second-thoughts in *OK* on November 4; and Return Strong in
Cut and Come Again on November 16. Where did all these anony-
mous pieces come from? Except for a scattered few playings, they

[14] Odell, *Annals*, IV, 385–386.
[15] *The Knickerbocker*, November, 1840.
[16] Odell, *Annals*, IV, 506.

are never heard of again. They were unable to support the failing fortunes of Hill's venture. On November 23 he closed the house and went to Philadelphia to play for three weeks at the Arch and Walnut Street Theatres. After this respite he again returned to New York, where he tried another sketch, Weazle Wideawake in *Catch a Weazle Asleep*, on January 16, 1841.

The period from February to September, 1841, holds a new surprise. In Boston, under the influence of Joseph Jones, Hill took up medicine. He bought a set of surgical instruments[17] and showed serious intentions of getting a Harvard medical degree. Such a venture is almost as fantastic at this point in Hill's career as any in which his most eccentric stage Yankees ever became involved. He attributed this startling decision to illness.[18] One wonders if the failure of his managerial adventures had anything to do with it. His strange move, however, did not last long. When he was submitted to the rigors of the operating room, the would-be physician fled in horror and disgust midway through his first experience.

By September, 1841, Hill was back at his old work again. At the Chatham on January 17, 1842, he tried Zephaniah Twang in *The Vermonter, or Love and Phrenology*, and a week later he played Jebel Judex in *Of Age To-Night, or Natur's Nature*. Neither brought the box-office returns he wanted. To support his fortunes during the spring, he made several one-night appearances, telling stories, singing songs, stringing personal anecdotes and true stories of Yankee life together into a potpourri he labeled *Lectures on New Englanders*. This he presented at the Lyceum in Brooklyn, at the Society Library, and finally at the New York Museum. At the Museum Hill made his second attempt at management. Either his idealistic faith that a theatre completely devoted to light comedy could work or his eagerness to succeed as a businessman lured him on. But again the venture was short-lived. Apparently he had learned very little from his management of the Franklin, for this new venture ended about as quickly as it had begun.

5

Something now happened to George Hill that was important to the broader fortunes of Yankee theatre. On December 17, 1842, at a

[17] Note that these are listed in the inventory of his estate.
[18] *Scenes*, p. 148.

Park Theatre benefit, he played for the first time Solon Shingle in Joseph Jones' *The People's Lawyer*.[19] Hill had not uncovered a play in the three years since his return from England that was more than a passing novelty. In bringing Solon Shingle to the stage he started the chain that tied Yankee theatre to the "new" stage Yankees of the 1860's.[20] John Owens revived this play twenty years after Hill's first performance and turned Solon Shingle into one of the most famous stage characters of the 1860's.

This play is important because it clearly reveals the growth and change in the Yankee character and the play of which he is a part. It is a long way from the experiments of James Hackett's early days. Solon Shingle in *The People's Lawyer* was an ingenious variation of the accepted stage Yankee.[21] Instead of the vitality and exuberance of the country boy, Solon offered the simplicity and wisdom of age. His name spoke his character: "Solon," the wise, and "Shingle," the unfinished rustic. He was a back-country farmer on the loose in Boston to sell a load of applesauce. And it is his adventure in the city that Jones weaves skillfully into the main plot, melodramatic and sentimental to the core, yet accurately reflective of the life of its time. Solon is a fully drawn character, amusing in the drollest manner, often clever, and sometimes apparently stupid. Under his outer shell, however, is the same basic-type character present in all the Yankee plays. He is no fool; yet, by contrast to city people, he appears to be one. In Solon Shingle, Jones is laughing at the eccentricities of old age in conflict with the directness and naïveté of youth. The play is more solid comedy than the usual Yankee fare, and this may account for its long life in the hands of such successful comedians as Hill, Burke, Locke, and Owens.

The story of *The People's Lawyer*, though usual in its exaggerated treatment of right and wrong, is intriguing because it represents one of the earliest attempts to show on the stage the conflict between the new city mechanic, including the office worker, and his "superior." There is something faintly reminiscent of *The London Merchant* in this story of "crime does not pay." To conceal a forgery, Hugh

[19] Celia Logan claims that her father, C. A. Logan, wrote this play, and that Jones merely revised it for Hill (*Dictionary of National Biography*, XI, 357).

[20] See Chapter 15 for the discussion of this new direction.

[21] *The People's Lawyer* was printed by William Spencer (Boston) in 1856. How close this version is to the one Hill acted in 1842 we do not know.

Winslow, a rich, respectable merchant (he is a leader in the local Temperance Society, does not believe in dancing, staunchly adheres to work and thrift as the only purposes in life), tries to force Charles Otis, his clerk, to lie about the signature on a check. When Otis refuses Winslow dismisses him from his job and arranges to frame the overly honest clerk to invalidate his court testimony. He induces a weak gadabout, John Ellsley, also in his employ, to put his watch in the clerk's pocket. The watch is discovered there, Otis is arrested, and appears to be lost. But to the rescue comes Robert Howard, the People's Lawyer, in the disguise of a working man. In the courtroom Howard forces Ellsley to confess his complicity in the frame-up and proves Winslow a forger. He also induces Otis' sister Grace to become his wife. Charles is released and all ends happily.

Solon wanders in and out of this plot, never touching it directly, but always remaining the important figure in the play by the strong contrast he provides to the seriousness of the other characters. He is attached to them through a series of amusing episodes: his struggle with the flour and lampblack in Winslow's store; the theft of his applesauce, which urges his attendance at the trial in search of the thief; his appearance at Howard's home at the end of the play to join in the general celebration. Perhaps his most amusing scene is that showing the courtroom conflict with Mr. Tripper, the prosecuting attorney, whom Solon always outwits.

The other characters and situations in *The People's Lawyer* also offer variety and interest. Virtue (Otis) is pitted against evil (Winslow). Howard's battle cry—"Fear not, our laws are just; our judges honest men; our jurors are our equals. The right will prevail"—is pure faith in democracy. The warped ethics of the businessman, as exemplified in Winslow, is disapproved. Only when virtue and courage are joined, as in Howard, can material wealth be acceptable at all. And then Howard adds, "Still I lose not, I trust, my right to the title of gentleman, because my hands are hardened by labor." Such ringing sentiments seem naive to us today, but they undoubtedly had special meaning to an audience of clerks and mechanics eager to declare their own freedom and independence. They must have responded warmly to Howard's challenge: "Hugh Winslow, do right; though you pile heaps of gold as stumbling blocks in the path of Justice, still will the righteous judgment overtake the evil doer." How pretentiously moralistic and melodramatic it sounds to our ears, but how better could the popular faith in the future be phrased than in Howard's speech, "What should hinder the son of toil, when genius stimulates, from acquiring the highest fund of knowledge that science gives. Our country is a free one, and education flows from the public fountains for all who thirst for its refreshing streams."

6

The People's Lawyer marks the end of Hill's contribution to the theatre form he had helped so much to shape. During the last five years of his life he appeared regularly in eastern theatres, made a trip to the West in the spring of 1844, and still continued to introduce new pieces. None of the five which appear after *The People's Lawyer*, however, are of any significance. On September 25, 1843, he showed *The Pilot* with Sergeant Drill to Chatham audiences; on November 6 he tried Content Jones in *The Spy in New York;* a week later he impersonated Jobes Crampton in *Honest Roguery;* on April 26, 1846, he attempted *The Doom of the Tory Guard;* and finally we note his last new piece on June 15, 1846—Joel Dean in *The Western Heir.* All are of anonymous authorship and all disappeared almost as quickly as they were seen. At the same time, Hill continued his solo evenings, with audience response much as it had been during his early years. Late in March, 1849, in one of his last appearances, shortly before his death, he played alternate evenings as an entertainer with Fanny Kemble at Stuyvesant Institute. How strange that their paths should cross again at the end of Hill's career. They probably recalled those nights in 1832 when they had played together and found success.

George Hill still wore the crown as the best Yankee impersonator in the world of Yankee theatre. But in his private world his fortunes were turning out poorly. He had borrowed money over the years —one of his creditors was actor Sol Smith—to purchase property and establish an estate in LeRoy, New York, where he had first met Mrs. Hill. These obligations he could not meet. Legal suits for recovery began in the spring of 1849, including such personal items as food bills. During an engagement at Saratoga Springs, where he had gone in the summer of 1849 to recover from illness, he played for the last time. Yankee Hill was scarcely forty years old when he died on September 27, 1849.

In the overview what was George Hill's contribution to Yankee theatre? Later discovered facts have not much changed the image he showed in 1836,[22] though they have filled it in and authenticated it. Through his continuous efforts to find actable material, he brought over forty pieces to the stage, far more than any other Yankee actor. He gave the Yankee story prominence and built it into a major aspect of Yankee theatre. He delighted London and won prestige for the stage Yankee through his artful, low-key, subtle delineations. And through his innate capacities as an actor he helped to convince London critics that the American stage had begun to find itself.

His principal contribution, however, lay in his method of approach and the style of acting it effected. Every description of Hill's performance tells us that his style was realistic. As a New Englander he caught the innate, local qualities of the down-Easter and brought them to the stage so that audiences thought they were seeing the real thing. At Bangor, Maine, Hill tells us, he appeared in a musical olio in which he represented his usual country boy. A local farmer in the audience insisted that the character on the stage was not Hill at all, but Seth Snow, a son of one of his neighbors. Only when Hill had removed his make-up and wig did the rustic see his error. "Look here, Mr. Hill," he said, "I hearn the hull of your talk inside there, but I don't think much of that, cause I hear that stuff every day, to hum."[23] This is an anecdote and therefore suspect as qualified criticism. Nevertheless, the point of view in it is so thoroughly supported by objective evidence elsewhere that its validity is admissible, and it becomes symbolic of Hill's achievement as an actor.

By going to life, as Hill tells us he did in his tour with J. S. Jones, he was able to discover those eccentricities of behavior, manners, and speech which could be artfully translated into stage terms and still give the impression of a believable reality. Many of the scripts he chose to act were romantic in style, with complicated stories and scenic effects. But genuine comedy can never stray far from the realities of everyday life, and Hill was a genuine comedian. So he revealed the images of New England life he saw about him in the context of melodrama or artificial incident. Yankee Hill was a Realist in a period dominated by romantic drama. Like Hackett, his

[22] See the final section of Chapter 10 for a comparison with Hackett.
[23] *Life*, p. 23.

intention was to reveal life as he saw it in the tradition of all great comedy. Unlike Hackett, however, he gave it no satirical overtones, but reported honestly and in specific, localized detail his notion of New Englanders. He gave new direction and climax to Yankee theatre in his quest for the real thing.

part 4 Change and Decline

chapter 13

Dan Marble and the Western Hybrid

T FIRST GLANCE Danforth Marble, the third Yankee impersonator to come on the scene, looks like a slick Yankee trader who
sees a good thing, buys it cheaply, and then sells it for a smart profit.
Unlike Hackett, who largely abandoned the Yankee character to
others in the 1840's and found his fortune elsewhere, and Hill, who
left debts behind him, Marble made a marked financial success with
the Yankee, leaving to his widow, after his death from yellow fever
on an acting tour along the Mississippi in 1849, an estate of $25,000.
Sol Smith reports that as manager of the St. Louis Theatre he alone
paid Marble $40,000 over a ten-year period. And after 1838, when
the actor had achieved something of a national reputation, accented
by a modest success at the Park Theatre while Hill was in Europe,
no other actor in Yankee theatre could claim as popular a following
as he enjoyed, whether it was at New York's Bowery Theatre or in
New Orleans or St. Louis. On the basis of recorded performance Dan
Marble was clearly the national Yankee comedian in the 1840's.
Hackett's extensive gallery of native character types certainly retained for him the title of top American comedian, and Hill still
held his position of "first" Yankee in the eastern cities, but in the
national view Marble was the popular delineator of the stage New
Englander. When he performed in London in 1844–1845, though
his repertoire of pieces was bluntly dismissed as insignificant, his
powers as a comedian were admired and his Yankee characters admitted to a place beside Hill's.

But what a Yankee his was! More aptly it could be called a "Western" Yankee, so far had it departed from the near-to-life delineation of Hill's down-Easter. Marble used a similar dialect and similar story-telling techniques, and drew his costume from the common wardrobe, but the Yankee that emerged from all of this was a general American—part Jonathan, part Davy Crockett, part Mike Fink. In copying Charles Mathews, Hackett had tried to be more explicit than the English comedian, pinning his character to New England tradition as he understood it from his fringe position in New York State. Hill had borrowed Hackett's model, but he went much further, forging a specific and localized New Englander out of his own heritage and his more subtle notion of native comedy. Marble, too, made an original contribution. By coming to the character after the first strong impulses and creative energies toward native identifications had already begun to wane, and as the character of the West had come more clearly into focus, Marble found a new brand that gave fresh life and scope to expression of the native character on the stage. J. S. Jones argued pointedly that Marble could not act a Yankee at all and did not know what the character was all about. To frontier audiences in St. Louis, Cincinnati, or Louisville, however, Marble's local Yankee was still an eccentric New Englander, yet possessed of characteristics they could readily recognize in themselves. The distinction between a Yankee from Massachusetts or Connecticut and a Yankee from Maine had disappeared completely, if it had ever really existed, and a clever, country-boy-wheeler-dealer who was closely identified with the making of the new frontier had replaced both of the older types.

If Marble's personation today appears more romantic, more exaggerated, less tied to reality, it may well be because our vantage point prevents us from readily seeing what remained of satire in the Yankee, so thoroughly is it inherent in the stories of the playscripts. Hackett's satiric pointings were obviously arranged, but Marble's audiences, so it seems, were expected to take a great deal for granted. London's total rejection of Marble's pieces, so successful when played in the western towns of Cincinnati, St. Louis, and Louisville, may possibly be the best evidence that an inherent American meaning was obscured in the playscripts for everyone, except to those who knew what was going on. As literary pieces they were utterly worthless, but as acting instruments for showing Marble's notion of the Western-Yankee American they were ingenious frameworks. They did not immediately die when Marble died, for J. H. McVicker of the Chicago theatre bought them from Mrs. Marble and continued to play them during the fifties. Marble's contribution to Yankee theatre has been obscured and underrated through imperceptive interpretation of his apparent generalization and romanticization of the character. A close look at his work, however, gives him a distinct position in the hierarchy of early American comedians.

2

Dan Marble's Western Yankee can be partially explained by reference to his early years as an apprentice actor. He was a genuine New Englander, born in 1810 at East Windsor, a small town a few miles north of Hartford. His family, from Vermont, had a small furniture business.[1] Dan began his fortunes in Hartford, first in a dry goods store and then as an apprentice silversmith, a craft that soon found him a job in New York near the Chatham Theatre. There he made many friends and began to appear frequently as a super in mob scenes. He joined an amateur acting group, played Carwin in *The Orphan of Geneva*, abandoned his regular employment as a silversmith, resorted to odd jobs for a living, and finally on April 11, 1831, arranged a Chatham Theatre appearance. For the privilege of the starring role of William in Jerrold's *Black-Eyed Susan* he paid Mr. Spear, whose benefit it was, a cash fee of twenty dollars. Audience reaction to Dan's playing ranged from mild to indifferent, but it was favorable enough to win him a job with John S. Potter's stock company in Norfolk, Virginia. There he played a wide variety of roles and told his first Yankee stories, the latter undoubtedly picked up from what he had seen of Hackett's and Hill's shows in New York. Within a few months (April, 1832) he was again back in New York, telling Yankee stories at the Richmond Hill, the Chatham, and the Bowery Theatres. Though he tried for a time to establish himself as an actor of serious roles, the comedy line emerged as his strongest asset, and in 1834 he contracted with Charles R. Thorne to play low-comedy roles in a strolling tour

[1] Marble is the only actor to acquire a contemporary biographer. Jonathan F. Kelly wrote his account of the actor, *Dan Marble: A Biographical Sketch*, under the pen name of Falconbridge. Much of the background material in this chapter is drawn from this source. Again, as in the case of Silsbee, facts must be constantly checked against other standard sources. References to this source hereafter will be denoted as Falconbridge, *Dan Marble*.

through western New York State and lower Canada. This was the beginning of Marble's western apprenticeship, that kept him out of New York theatres for nearly three years.

Dan Marble shares with T. D. Rice, the ingenious Negro impersonator, the honor of being the first native American to emerge as a star actor from the Western theatres. Sol Smith and Noah Ludlow, together with a few others, had certainly achieved no little fame along the rivers in the twenties and thirties, but none had risked their reputations in New York, certainly not in London, as did Marble and Rice. Rice's development of the Negro character was a natural evolution out of the River culture, where Jim Crow was as common in everyday life as Jonathan in New England. Marble's American was far from original, but his work with it moved in a fresh direction as he modified the Yankee under the pressure of Western audiences who bluntly told him in their reactions what would go and what would not. The stage Yankee of Hackett and Hill had developed largely from the city tastes of the Park Theatre audience, and it had undoubtedly been modified by similar reactions in Philadelphia and Boston. But Marble's "new" Yankee was a sharp contrast. What audiences saw was a broad, simply stated comic figure, sometimes capable of pathos in quieter moments of sentiment, usually clever, even sly, but certainly something of a hearty, practical joker—Jacob Jewsharp, Curtis Chunk, Lot Sap Sago, Deuteronomy Dutiful.

Marble's adventures with Thorne's company as it made its way first to Newark and Paterson, then up the North and Hudson Rivers and west on the Erie Canal, was probably not unlike those Hill had encountered a few years earlier, though now the flourishing and hospitable canal towns had improved the traveling actor's lot. Marble was engaged to play whatever tragedy roles he could handle, as well as sailors and Yankees, all in support of Mr. and Mrs. Thorne, Miss Celeste, William Graham, Frank Fremont (the brother of Colonel John C. Fremont), and two other young actors. Marble anticipated Francis Wemyss' later advice to all young actors to go west for experience, by beginning his serious training in such busy western towns as Rochester, Lockport, Batavia, the Canal terminus at Buffalo, and even Toronto. When the tour ended he returned to Buffalo, where he was hired by Dean and McKinney for the Eagle Street

Theatre[2] company. From this time forward he made that city his permanent home. There he married Anna Warren, daughter of William Warren of Philadelphia's Chestnut Street Theatre, and bought a home on Main Street. There too he was buried in the local cemetery.[3] Evidence indicates that under Dean and McKinney's management Marble told Yankee stories during this period in cities as far west as Detroit.

3

Sam Patch, Marble's most famous stage Yankee, was born in Buffalo. Among the twenty or so Yankee characters that the comedian from Hartford eventually played, none better illustrates the broad direction he was to take with this comic type. Sam Patch so caught the imagination of American audiences of that day that Marble kept him as a core character in his repertoire for the rest of his stage career.

Whether Marble himself first thought of the stage possibilities of Sam Patch and commissioned the first play (two others were later written around the character), or whether E. H. Thompson, a Buffalo attorney credited with its authorship,[4] worked it out and offered it to Marble, we have not yet discovered, but with its first playings at the Eagle Street, where it was given a top production with new scenery, Marble quickly saw that he had a potentially big hit in

[2] The *Mirror* for October 17, 1835, describes this theatre, an excellent example of the provincial theatre of the period. Buffalo at that time had a population of 15,500 and was a busy city because of its strategic position at the western end of the Erie Canal and as a port on Lake Erie. The pit was forty-two feet wide and twenty-eight feet deep. Four rows of boxes surrounded the house, which was decorated in blue and gold. Gas candelabras, fastened to the front of the boxes, lighted it. The act curtain was painted to represent rich drapery, and at the top of the proscenium was a medal pendant on which was painted a buffalo. The stage and its machinery were constructed under the direction of Mr. Thomas Daines, an experienced stage carpenter.

[3] *The Commercial Advertiser* (Buffalo, New York), November 15, 1836, records the marriage. Marble first appears in the *Buffalo City Directory* for 1835; Mrs. Marble is last listed there in 1852. They lived at 524 Main Street. *The Daily Courier* (Buffalo, New York), May 21, 1849, carries the announcement of the funeral. Anna Marble and a W. Marble are listed in the McVicker's company when it played in Davenport, Iowa, in 1859 (Joseph Schick, *Theatre in Eastern Iowa*, p. 71). W. Marble is probably Dan's son.

[4] The *Buffalo City Directory* for 1836–1837 lists Thompson as an attorney, with offices at 156 Main Street. Also Falconbridge, *Dan Marble*, p. 88.

Sam Patch, the Yankee Jumper. That this piece should be played first in Buffalo was entirely logical, for Sam Patch was a real person whose adventurous life was highlighted by a leap over Niagara Falls from Goat Island on October 6, 1829.[5] Later he jumped the falls of Passaic River, and then abruptly ended his life in a similar adventure on the Genesee at Rochester, New York. Such devil-may-care daring had made him a notorious celebrity, and after his abrupt demise his exploits were colorfully lauded in story and ballad, despite such attacks on the public's idle curiosity as George Morris made in the *Mirror:* "Enterprises like those of Patch should be discountenanced; they are unproductive of good and conduce too much positive evil." Even Mrs. Trollope, when she visited Rochester shortly after Patch's fatal accident, could not resist telling the story.[6] H. J. Finn gave him full comic treatment, in dialect, in the *American Comic Annual* for 1831, and Seba Smith wrote a ballad of twenty-six stanzas to make Jack Downing the official biographer of Sam Patch in verse.[7] Imaginative sources beyond the full and colorful newspaper accounts were thus available to Marble and Thompson when they arranged the character for the stage.

Unfortunately no playscript of this first piece has yet been uncovered, so its contents must be put together from playbills and brief critical mentions. George Odell's report from the July 31, 1838, program of the Park Theatre,[8] where Marble played it after a big success at the Bowery in May, describes Philip's attempt to carry Katherine across the river in a terrific storm and "flying leaps among the fancy—through a window by Sam." Mrs. Trollope and Sam are also matched in a scene. There is a discussion of "Steam Doctors" and Yankee courtship. The climax was, of course, Sam's wonderful leap over Niagara Falls in a "union of courage and virtue—proving 'some things can be done as well as others'." It was announced that Marble would leap from the extreme height of the theatre, "a feat never attempted by anyone but himself, and prove that 'cold water

---

[5] For an extended account of the real Sam Patch and his later treatment in literary form see Richard M. Dorson, "The Story of Sam Patch," *American Mercury*, 64 (June, 1947), 741–747. See *Mirror*, VII (September 26, 1829), 95, for an early notice of the jump over Niagara.

[6] Trollope, *Domestic Manners*, p. 377.

[7] Smith, *Life and Writings of Major Jack Downing*, p. 235.

[8] Odell, *Annals*, IV, 321.

don't drown love'." This is certainly a conglomerate for the stage, broad enough to suit any Western theatregoer.

The scene with Mrs. Trollope suggests much to the imagination. She was such a familiar and ridiculous figure to American audiences that comedies seemingly could hardly do without her. Did the Buffalo version contain the scene or was it added in Cincinnati, Mrs. Trollope's home ground, where Marble shortly played it? The discussion of "Steam Doctors" indicates a possible Yankee story. It must have been a pale moment, however, in comparison to the big jump from the flies to beneath the stage, with Sam "coming up in a bubbling river of spray and foam."

How the jump was managed tells us much about spectacle drama in the theatre of this period. A large trap was opened on the stage behind set pieces of water and waves, so we are told by Marble's biographer, and the actor jumped through this trap, often from a height of forty feet, onto a spring bed softened with shavings.[9] When well arranged, the illusion was excellent; when poorly done, as in London, it was completely ridiculous. At the Haymarket, we are told, some blankets and canvas were clumsily arranged to represent Niagara, and Marble leaped upon a bed of straw in the middle of the stage which snapped and crackled with his weight.[10] Another reviewer thought Niagara Falls looked like the "boiling over of a vat at the soap-boiler's."[11] But however good or bad the illusion, there was no denying the danger of Marble's jump. On one occasion at the Bowery Theatre the comedian was seriously injured, though he managed to limp through the remainder of the performance.

What sort of Yankee did Marble make of Sam Patch? Here was a true-life story that had already been fictionized and romanticized when Marble began playing it. Yet he probably gave it a vestige of the real thing. He undoubtedly wore the costume, spoke the dialect, told the stories, and set out the American love of superiority. In an interview with a St. Louis reporter shortly before his death, Marble tells us that he modeled his first stage Yankee—probably not Sam Patch—on real life by remembering a specific person he had seen and patterning the character after him. He found a hat, a coat, some

[9] Falconbridge, *Dan Marble*, p. 93.
[10] *Morning Herald* (London), October 15, 1844.
[11] *Morning Post* (London), November 5, 1844.

trousers, and some boots exactly like those of his model, and then mimicked him in his gait and other mannerisms. "I was more like him than his shadow, for his shadow couldn't say nuthin."[12] Yet, real as Marble might have supposed himself to be, when compared with Yankee Hill's subtle, quiet personations, Sam Patch must have seemed more like a Kentucky "screamer" than a down-Easter.

We get a clearer view of this contrast when we look at the Sam Patch play Marble commissioned in England for his London engagement in 1844. Unfortunately, the second play in the series, *Sam Patch in France*, put together for Marble by fellow comedian J. P. Addams and played infrequently during the forties, is not extant. The English playscript survives, however, and we can measure it against its reception by the London play reviewers. Its discussion here is pertinent, though it means jumping an eight-year gap from the Eagle Street Theatre to the London theatres.

Sam Patch the Jumper (1844)[13] is a hastily written farce-melodrama of undeclared authorship about a young man who is being disinherited by a scheming steward and is saved at the last moment when Sam Patch discovers the villainy and jumps Niagara Falls to murder the steward. The plotting is full of intrigue, becoming so involved that it is not without confusions. Yankee Sam Patch has come to Henry Somerville's twenty-first birthday celebration. It is a most important occasion for the young man because, according to his father's will, on this day the family fortune will pass to him. But Henry's steward and his accomplice, Mrs. Mouser, in order to get the fortune for themselves, have forged a letter, purportedly from Henry's mother, granting Henry permission to marry Victorine. This action, by virtue of provisions in the will unknown to Henry, will disinherit him, and cause the fortune to revert to the steward. The couple are married just before Henry's mother discovers the steward's crime, and she is forced to tell him that he is disinherited because Victorine is poor. In the meantime, wealthy Colonel Bradville, in searching for his long-lost daughter whom he had been forced to abandon in the neighborhood years ago when he was pursued by bandits, discovers that Victorine is his child. The steward learns of this fact and determines to murder Bradville. Hiring some ruffians, he sets an ambush at the foot of Niagara Falls,

[12] Falconbridge, *Dan Marble*, p. 203.
[13] Lord Chamberlain's Collection, British Museum.

And Sam approached those awful Falls,
And leapt them like a frog.

Seba Smith's *The Life and Writings of Major Jack Downing*
Sam Patch Leaping Niagara Falls.

where Bradville is attacked. Sam Patch arrives in the nick of time and jumps the Falls to save Bradville. When confronted later by the still-living Bradville, the steward pulls a knife and rushes the Colonel. Sam saves him a second time by killing the steward.

It is easy to see why London reviewers dismissed the play as confused and overly complicated, even in an age when involved plotting of this sort was the general style for melodrama. The new piece looks suspiciously like a discarded play on which the Sam Patch business is engrafted. Purportedly the action takes place in New England near Boston, but suddenly Sam is standing atop Niagara Falls four hundred and fifty miles away. The plot is thoroughly English. The other comic servants, Bridget and Gaspard, are only vaguely related to American comedy, and even Sam, as delineated in the script, is a pale copy of all other Jonathans. Except for the leap over Niagara, the piece has no distinguishing identity.

The London criticism[14] of this artificial contrivance sounds like the 1832 outburst against James Hackett's *Militia Muster*—a poor affair, a miserable piece, indiscernible plot; a most incoherent mass of vulgarity, an absurdly deep and lugubrious attempt at domestic tragedy, memorable badness; vilest conceivable compound of trashy melodrama and vulgar farce, play of such poor quality as to swamp an actor of less merit; hackneyed material jumbled together; rubbish; ludicrous earnestness. A description of the jump over Niagara through the eyes of one reviewer vividly accents its failure in performance. "This monstrous absurdity at once settled the fate of the piece. Mr. Marble crept from under the carpets, and for a time was inaudible. Finding words and deprecatory shrugs equally ineffective, he tried a nigger dance, with which he left the stage to take care of itself." Another critic thought it a bad, coarse, extravagant scene. That Marble survived it at all is a testimonial to his capacities as a comedian. Why did he try it? One reviewer declares, with what seems to be more than simple conjecture, that Marble himself wrote it. There might possibly be a grain of truth in this assertion, but since no other evidence supports it, we are left to conclude that

---

[14] The criticism cited here is a composite of reviews in *The Morning Advertiser, Morning Herald, Morning Post, The Examiner, The Spectator, Sunday Times, Weekly Dispatch, Morning Chronicle, The Sun, The Observer, The Court Journal, The Globe.*

Marble either had it in hand when he arrived or commissioned it in England. The comedian engaged Leman Rede to rewrite *Yankee Land* at this time, and it is entirely possible that the same writer could have provided the new Sam Patch play.

4

When Dan Marble first played Sam Patch in Buffalo in 1836, Yankee Hill together with T. D. Rice and Edwin Forrest were creating a sensation in London. At that time transatlantic performance was far from Marble's mind, for he had yet to declare fully his line of acting roles and his individual style. Stardom at any time means success at projecting radiant individuality across the lamps, and Marble was still an undeclared stock actor. During the next few months in the river towns his particular fund of humor would quickly take shape, and his special eccentricities would be molded into the experienced performer in the Yankee line. Sam Patch's success in Buffalo was only the beginning, and Marble had much to learn from audiences out of touch with the local interest in the Falls jumper. Besides, he also had to discover much more about the craft of low comedy, though his experience at the Eagle Street Theatre had taught him richly.

Marble's rise to stardom is a matter of a few months between his departure from Buffalo in November, 1836, and his appearance at the Bowery Theatre on May 1, 1837. His tour took him to Columbus, Ohio, for two weeks, then to Cincinnati, and on to Pittsburgh. At Francis Wemyss' suggestion, he added *The Forest Rose* to Sam Patch. In St. Louis he made his first contacts with Sol Smith, who positively encouraged him. After St. Louis came Memphis. Then, with success ringing in his ears, he swung back East to Wheeling and Baltimore. In the latter city he "borrowed" Hackett's old piece, *Sylvester Daggerwood*, to provide a framework for Yankee stories. A side tour to Washington and Richmond occupied him for a time before he returned to Baltimore and the swing north to New York. No evidence supports the five-night run at the Walnut Street Theatre in Philadelphia recorded by his biographer, but since William Warren was Marble's father-in-law, he may have played with the company in a minor capacity.

A fully recognized star status was not far distant, however, for shortly he was in New York. There on May 1 and subsequent nights he played Sam Patch at the Bowery Theatre.[15] Later, he tried his wares in Boston, and in December he played several nights in Philadelphia. This time again he is indebted to Hackett. He "borrowed" Solomon Swap to add to the ever resilient Sam Patch and Jonathan Ploughboy. Charles Durang tells us that *Sam Patch* failed because it was a "wishy-washy affair, without the least rational substance and dramatic claims . . . a melange of nonsense," but he counters it with an enthusiastic compliment to Marble's Jonathan Ploughboy—"hit off to the life."[16] On January 2, 1838, the comedian played for the first time Jacob Jewsharp in *The Maiden's Vow, or the Yankee in Time.* J. P. Addams, who was playing in the Walnut Street company, not only authored it but acted the role of Charles Cariton to Marble's Jacob.[17] No copy of this play survives nor is its content known, though Marble played it frequently for the next few years. Of much more importance is the play Marble introduced when he again returned to Cincinnati in May.

The Vermont Wool Dealer, which Marble first played in Cincinnati on June 4, 1838, became the principal farce in the comedian's lifetime repertoire. Like *Sam Patch*, it was a "Western" play. We have met its author before: Cornelius Logan, the actor-manager who had written *The Wag of Maine* for Hackett in 1835[18] to begin his association with Yankee theatre. Logan is an example of the nineteenth-century actor-manager who wrote stage pieces for fellow actors in return for a modest fee of a few hundred dollars. The short farce he now devised gave Marble a Yankee afterpiece with which he could make a standard evening's entertainment.

The Vermont Wool Dealer, or The Yankee Traveller is a reverse on the usual theme of the Yankee outsmarting the city slicker. In this extant comedy the country boy, who thinks he is a clever sharper, is outwitted in the city by a girl. Amanda Waddle, a rich heiress, has just arrived in New York from Saratoga Springs with her father, her mulatto maid Betty, and her suitor, Captain Oakley.

---

[15] Odell, *Annals*, IV, 167.
[16] Durang, Series III, Chapter 52.
[17] *Ibid.* See also Arthur Wilson, *A History of the Philadelphia Theatre, 1835–1855*, p. 184.
[18] See Chapter 8 for a discussion of Logan's background.

Yankee Deuteronomy Dutiful, also on the steamboat, thinks he is
in love with her and has pursued her to the hotel with the intention
of marrying her and winning her fortune. Oakley discovers the competitor, challenges Dutiful to a duel, and arranges to meet him in
Hoboken. Amanda's father intercepts the Yankee's love letter to
Amanda and also arranges a duel. When Dutiful proposes to Amanda in a comic love scene she at first rejects him; but on learning of
the duels, she decides to prevent them by plotting to elope with him
that night disguised in Betty's clothes. Her father and Oakley discover the plot, waylay the veiled "Betty" when she appears, only
to discover that it is the real Betty. Dutiful is confused. When another veiled Amanda appears, the men think they have caught the
real thing, but find it is Negro Bob, the waiter, dressed up in
Amanda's clothes. Waddle and Oakley, in laughing at Dutiful, so
provoke him that he is ready to throw the unsuspecting Bob at them.
Amanda discloses her hoax, accepts Oakley's proposal, and kids
Dutiful about being the American Blue Beard. Laughing at the joke
she has played on him, the Yankee stands them all to champagne
that he has just acquired cheaply in a sharp deal.

That it is a contrivance is obvious. Yet here are all the ingredients of a Yankee stage piece: a Negro waiter for jokes about color;
a mulatto maid for a disguise plot, reminiscent of *The Forest Rose*;
a singing, comic, Irish drunk in Con Golumby, the waiter; the traditional barkeep in Slap; an irate, possessive father type; and two
lovers. The Yankee as the central character ties the rambling plot
together with Yankee stories, a string of Yankeeisms, a comic love
scene, and the surprise joke at the end. Dialects are indicated for
both Negro Bob ("Wall, now, is dat any reason 'cause you ain't goin'
wait on de gentleman?") and Irish Con Golumby ("Och! If your
honor plase to believe me, I'm the innocentest man"). The Yankee
refers to Bob as "blackee" and as an Ethiopian: "He ain't white, no
way you can fix it, unless you turn his skin inside out, and then I
reckon it would be flesh color."

Deuteronomy Dutiful exhibits the usual characteristics of thrifti-
ness:

Well, you see, I havn't got time to make a long courtship of it, because
my business is all out o'kilter, and has to go on in Vermount without

me; besides this seems to be a pretty dear tavern, and you know everyday I spend staying here courting you, is so much out of your pocket
after I marry you, for I swan, if you don't marry me right away, I'll
charge the extras to you. I will. Honor bright.

We also see the trader: "I sell notions o' all sorts by hullsale." And
again: "Well, let's see if we can make a trade." When he is called
"coward" he blazes forth:

Want to use fire weapons, I'll fight you with rifles loaded to the muz-
zles with three cornered slugs, and rammed into each other. Get my
Ebenezer rig, and you'd think somebody was blowin' rocks! . . . Get my
dander up, and you'd think it was the Cape Cod sea sarpant in con-
vulsions.

But except for the general image, there is much that does not sound
like the New England of Yankee Hill or even of Hackett. There is
a broadness, an obviousness that is less defined. Again the unmistakable flavor of the Kentucky backwoodsman or the riverman seeps
through the external gloss. Logan's Yankee was certainly a general
American of the lower order, and Marble aided the picture with his
broad style of acting.

With Sam Patch, Deuteronomy Dutiful, Jonathan Ploughboy,
Jacob Jewsharp, and Solomon Swap, Marble now had his gallery of
Yankee characters, and he was again ready to assault the East. In
July, 1838, he tried his string at the Walnut,[19] and at the end of the
month he got his call from the Park Theatre. With Hill and Hackett
in Europe, Marble had the field to himself. He had won Bowery
audiences the previous January, and now he was "discovered" at
the Park. From this point forward his career followed the usual
course: adding plays, cementing his public reputation on all fronts,
traveling eventually to London, making the popular return with national tours from Boston to New Orleans.

Of the new pieces he added to his repertoire, a few are of special
interest. *The Backwoodsman, or The Gamecock of the Wilderness*
attracts attention because it seems to be Marble's answer to Hackett's
Nimrod Wildfire. Marble's piece is not extant, but brief mentions
indicate that Marble first played the central character in St. Louis
(October, 1840) as a "Ranting, Rousing Kentuckian." Of curious

[19] Wilson, *Philadelphia Theatre*, p. 193.

interest is the designation of the character when Marble played a rewritten version in New York on May 12, 1846. The Yankee character in that version is called Samson Hardhead, *a Vermonter*. Had Leman Rede, who did the rewrite while Marble was in London, made this change? From what we have seen of Marble's "Western" tendencies, the actual geographical location of the character would have made little difference. Hardhead was probably a "Westerner" in both versions. *Life in New York* (October, 1840, St. Louis) gave Marble a chance to play Jack Downing. Had he "borrowed" Hill's play? *A Home in the West* (1847, Boston), which provided a stuttering Yankee for Marble, was written by Colonel Bradbury, a "talented" editor and printer of Cincinnati and an intimate friend of the actor.[20] In *Our Jedidiah, or Great Attraction* (New York Olympic, February 28, 1849) Marble played Curtis Chunk, a stage-struck Yankee, and in *Oregon* (New York Park, March 17, 1846) he acted the national character of Uncle Sam.

Only one play in this later group—*Yankee Land*—has any special distinction. This is the second version of Cornelius Logan's *The Wag of Maine*.[21] Dan Marble first played it at the Bowery Theatre on November 19, 1842. The plot in the printed version of this play, probably Logan's rewrite for Marble, has been vastly improved in detail over the original draft of *The Wag of Maine*, though the basic story remains unaltered. Lot Sap Sago, an orphan country boy brought up by Mr. Malson, discovers that he is the long-lost son of Sir Cameron Ogleby, a wealthy Englishman. But before the discovery comes out the audience follows the wicked Malson through a series of incidents: a threat of mortgage foreclosure, to force Lieutenant Ostrand to let him marry his daughter Josephine; an attempt to murder Lot's father, which Lot thwarts in the nick of time; and his attempt to escape from the police. Surprise discoveries at the end reveal that most of the characters in the play are related to one another.

The plotting can be more easily followed than in *The Wag of*

[20] Falconbridge, *Dan Marble*, p. 189.

[21] It was later adapted for Marble by Leman Rede under the title *Hue and Cry*. This version cut the play to one act of nine scenes. All of the essentials are retained but some of the comic detail is lost. This version is available in the Lord Chamberlain's Collection. See also the discussion of *The Wag of Maine* in Chapter 8.

Maine, and the characters are more sharply etched, especially
Yankee Lot Sap Sago. A country lad, extremely independent, with
no occupation except hunting and occasional farm work, Lot is a
strange mixture of wit and half-wit. Marble actually played him
as a half-witted Yankee orphan with the intention of provoking the
sympathy of the audience. Lot is as ready to like others as he is to be
liked himself, and he indulges in his practical jokes in the simple,
unaffected manner of a small boy on a spree. His frequent references
to the open life of frontier country often hint at his special individuality. He calls Manikin a "crocodile hunter," a Colonel Nimrod
Wildfire label, and his speech is filled with what appears to be the
Western idiom. "I had a fowling piece, and the infernal machine
never had a bullet in it afore, and its stomach seemed to turn agin
it, for it squirmed and twisted so like the devil, that I was glad to
fire it off to ease it." And again: "I rather guess he must have melted
away, and his whiskers have soaked up the fat." How mindful this
is of Mike Fink or Davy Crockett. "She squirreled me up all one-
sided," or "A strange critter that's got hair enough on his upper lip
to stuff a cart saddle," are a far cry from the quiet, unobtrusive talk
of *The People's Lawyer* or *Wife for a Day.* The occasional references
to wilderness and to bear and skunk hunting, and the exaggerations
in speech and story give *Yankee Land* a decidedly Western feeling.
Lot speaks Yankee dialect, of course, and he is a cunning, sharp
bargainer in the usual Yankee tradition. But underneath he has more
Kentuck in him than Yankee—a Western hybrid.

5

When Dan Marble sailed for Liverpool on the *Acadia,* Captain Harrison in command, in September, 1844, he had a solid American
reputation to support him. He had been accepted at the Park and the
Bowery, and he had a strong following in every principal city in the
States. Like Hackett and Hill before him, Marble did not undertake
the London journey for money but for added reputation at home,
which the London appearance—a necessity for all American stars
—could provide. His repertoire could also be overhauled and perhaps embellished with a piece or two by an English "play-wright."
He opened at the Strand Theatre on September 30, played there
regularly for over a month, and then moved to the Haymarket for
several performances. A tour through the provinces kept him occu-

pied until the end of February, 1848, when he returned to the capital to play a benefit performance before embarking for America.[22]

The best single source of comment on Marble's capacities as a low comedian, as with the other Yankees, is the record of his London reception. What the reviewers thought about *Sam Patch the Jumper* has already been noted. Their opinion of *The Vermont Wool Dealer* was not much better. One critic rather caustically remarked that it was "almost as uninteresting a farce as any we ever saw." *Yankee Land* fared somewhat better. One viewer thought it was not as outrageous as Jonathans usually are, and another noted that it was not "ill-contrived or ill-written" but could succeed for a time on its own merits. A third thought it was on the dubious side—a mere trifle made up of commonplace characters and commonplace incidents. A fourth argued that it contained some genuine feeling. A fifth labeled Lot a backwoodsman and thought he bore the stamp of truth. A sixth held the opinion that it was slovenly constructed, dull, and uninteresting. The consensus was that the American actor had greatly risked his reputation by appearing on the London stage with such poor material, and one reviewer flatly stated that Marble should be advised on what would go and what would not. Without his unusual comic talents Marble would have been hissed off the stage as Hackett had been in 1832, instead of being shouted and laughed off, as he was in *Sam Patch*.

When the reviewers considered his capabilities as a comedian independent of the plays they applauded him as enthusiastically as the Strand and Haymarket audiences that warmly cheered him and loudly laughed at his Yankee eccentricities. They agreed on his effectiveness as a comic actor: "Marble is the farce," an excellent performer, a very clever actor, with a twinkle in his eye and a sly smile. They thought his Jonathans exceedingly amusing, seasoned with quaint and dry humor, and a faithful picture of one form of American life. One reviewer estimated that Marble could be a favorite on the English stage in the most touching characters of English comedy, so well did he express the common feelings and passions of man. "Unmistakably legitimate" was the compliment for his dialect, and the quaint nasal tones and droll actions were recog-

[22] *The Times*, February 27, 1845, advertisement. The benefit was for Mrs. Coleman Pope at the Strand Theatre. He played *The Stage-Struck Yankee* on this occasion.

nized as the real thing. One critic lauded Marble for his illumination of character, and others praised him for his fine comic abilities, the quality of his humor, his original images of nature and life, and his first-rate acting.

The comparison with Yankee Hill was inevitable. From it Marble emerged in the eyes of one critic as the better, because of his capacity to delineate his characters with breadth and force, yet without exaggeration. While Hill was praised as a fine talent, he was thought to be too quiet and subdued, and the traits in his picture too fine and delicate to project to any except to very close and attentive observers. Marble, on the contrary, dashed on his colors with a bolder and firmer hand, and with a more decided and striking effect. Had audience tastes in London also shifted towards a broader acting style? The critics liked also Marble's fresh Yankeeisms—"sufficient to excite the laughter of the gravest philosophers"—and they praised such stories as the one about the bashful young man, who, upon taking a kiss from a pretty girl, blushed so red that he burned his shirt collar; or another about an individual who had land so far east that he was obliged to cut through the trees to let the sun rise; or the one about a cow so obstinate that her milk would not yield cream.

Some critical comment is particularly revealing of Marble's individual acting style. One reviewer asserted that Marble's comedy, borrowed in part from Davy Crockett, was for a while amusing but at length grew tiresome and vulgar. Another was disgusted when he saw the actor "pull a fowl to pieces with his teeth, limb by limb, without flinching." Is this a genuine Yankee? A third declared that Sam Patch was as "familiar and smart as it was possible for any New World man to be, but he went too far—it was overdone. The perpetual motion and the odd mode of expression soon became flat and unprofitable." The busy activity set the spectator in motion, with roars of laughter, hisses, shouts, and hootings. So frequently is the Marble humor referred to as Kentuckian—half horse, half alligator—that the Western flavor is unmistakable. Englishmen of the time would have made little distinction between a true-bred down-Easter and his Western cousin, and the confusion in their statements about Marble's Yankee indicates clearly the direction he took in the character. But one thing was certain. American humor was distinct from that of any other country, and Marble's representation of it, despite the great poverty of his repertoire, had afforded a high degree of enjoyment. The *Court Journal* declared it a success "as gratifying as it was decided and deserved."

6

The comedian's return to America met the usual hearty welcome in New York, Boston, Philadelphia, and the western cities where he toured as extensively as before. The high opinion of his acting had not changed; it had only intensified. American audiences everywhere found him "excessively funny." Henry Stone thought him good enough to "draw a laugh from the ghost of old Job Gould."[23] Joe Cowell believed him to be much better as an actor than the public acclaimed him and capable of making anyone laugh "no matter if you have the toothache, the headache, or the heartache," and superb enough to "make you laugh at a funeral."[24] With better pieces, the southern theatre manager commented, Marble could have held his own as a superior actor in the general field of comedy, both in England and America.

But in the overview of comparison, how different Marble's Yankees must have been from Hill's or Hackett's. His speech and action were characterized by a lazy drawl whose coolness and deliberate quality projected the cunning, conceited, selfish characters of his Yankees. And though he did not at all project the subtle delineations of the down-East flavor of speech, and mixed and modified the strict Yankee type, his other actor's talents brought out a comedy considered "perfectly killing" to many in an audience. He was a capital storyteller and costume improviser, and when offstage he delighted in practical jokes highly reminiscent of his onstage fictional creations. A liking for serious parts, a taste that failed to diminish even when he had become an established comedian, urged Marble to examine his characters in depth, with the results that scenes of pathos and emotion stood in sharp contrast to those of his usual sure-fire comedy. What Dan Marble brought to the Yankee character was the openness, the freshness, and a good deal of the bombast and rugged individualism of the frontier.

[23] Stone, *Personal Recollections*, p. 193.
[24] Cowell, *Thirty Years Passed among the Players*, pp. 99–100.

chapter 14

Joshua Silsbee—A "Go-Ahead" American

M̲R̲. S̲I̲L̲S̲B̲E̲E̲ is a decided "hit." Imagine the essence of all the stories of soft Yankee suitors and 'cute Yankee pedlars, of all the impossible jokes and unjustifiable jargons, of all the Sam Slickery, and Pegleg Wheelery, all the Mrs. Partingtons, and the other elaborated witticisms of down-East editors—and, in short, of all that is shrewd, and quaint, and all besides that is helplessly nonsensical, in the American comic literature—incarnated in the person of one individual, and let that individual be a plump, or more than plump, personage, whose eyes are capable of much expression, from the stare of stolidity to the twinkle of cunning, and the muscles of whose decidedly plain face are under complete command—let his other developments, more especially those manifest when the actor is not turned toward the spectator, remind the latter of the Listonian conformation—and you have some idea of the artist who made his *debut* last night, and who kept the theatre in a shriek of laughter during the whole time he was on the stage.

In this review in the London *Morning Chronicle* for September 24, 1851, the writer set out the full meaning of Joshua Silsbee's relationship to Yankee theatre. He was no more enthusiastic and warmly laudatory than others had been that morning after the American comedian's sensational opening in Samuel Woodworth's *The Forest Rose* at the Adelphi, but no others saw the actor in such all-inclusive perspective or labeled him so definitely as the epitome of all that had gone before. Josh Silsbee was to play one hundred and twenty-three performances of *The Forest Rose* at the Adelphi —the longest consecutive run of any Yankee theatre play—before he turned to another piece. The *Chronicle* reviewer tells us why this could happen with the oldest play in the Yankee-theatre repertoire and in the hands of the fourth major actor of American comedy to visit London since Hackett had taken the first step in 1827.

When Silsbee crossed the Atlantic, Hill and Marble were both dead, Hackett seldom played the Yankee, and Englishmen seemed to have grown weary and bored with the flood of eccentric American humor. Yet here was Josh Silsbee—a copyist of the first order; an open purloiner of Hill, Marble, and Hackett's repertoire of plays; a Westerner by birth and experience, with only a secondhand knowledge of Yankees; an American star comedian who had not even played at the Park Theatre; an ambitious, self-pushing, aggressive competitor who openly declared that he was clearly the best of the Yankee line; an actor who took everything and gave little to the comedy line he had borrowed—here was Josh Silsbee evoking roars and shrieks of laughter from London audiences whose forebears had completely rejected Hackett's New Englander, warmly applauded Hill's, and accepted Marble's as interesting though considering his plays impossible. To the Adelphi audience of 1851 Joshua Silsbee was the Yankee comedian *par excellence*. The few voices who spoke out against him, who thought him limited, who, after they had seen him in a second part, thought it the same as the first, were scarcely heard amid the enthusiasm and excitement. There is much irony in all this.

What had brought about such complete acceptance? Had London begun to understand what American comedy was all about? Was the general state of its own theatre at a lower level than it had been in the thirties? Was the melodrama-loving audience at the Adelphi of a more popular, less demanding sort than those at Covent Garden or Drury Lane? Had the level of play reviewing changed for the worst? There is no doubt that Silsbee was a genuine talent, that he knew how to entertain and control an audience, that he was possessed of a funny face and figure comical in themselves, but his capabilities alone could not account for his huge success. It is more likely that the prevailing notion of the American had changed, as well as the attitude toward the nature of comic entertainment. The American was certainly no longer the strange oddity he had been to Englishmen in the thirties, and his stage image, if drawn on a broad scale, was easily recognizable. His "pointless" stories, that somehow had begun to take on point, and his Yankeeisms were expected paraphernalia. No longer were they the queer, eccentric, puzzling things of Hackett's day. What had been new was now old, and with age there was mellowness and fond acceptance. Was Silsbee's Yankee a real American or a fantasy? Was it a caricatured image of what Englishmen thought it ought to be? A look at Josh Silsbee's family background and his training in acting can tell us much.[1]

2

Though all of the Yankee-theatre actors were native Americans, Silsbee's antecedents seem to have more of the aura of indigenous America about them than do those of the other actors. Perhaps it is because he was born and raised on the frontier, whereas the others came from much more settled areas. In the story of Silsbee's life we see something of the pattern of westward expansion, settlement, development of the arts, and the relationship of the West to Eastern culture.

When Joshua's grandfather, Enos Silsbee, first pushed northward from Pennsylvania into New York State in the general flux of movement and expansion after the Revolutionary War, he found a broad wilderness barely opened to settlement. Western New York State in 1794 was active frontier country. Its Indian problems only recently had been brought under control, and European titleholders operated extensively through land agents. Except for a few rivers and a rough wagon road cutting westward across the central part of the state and not reaching much beyond Canandaigua, transportation was awkward and undeveloped. When Enos Silsbee made his land arrangements with Captain Williamson, the land agent for the estate of Sir William Pulteney with offices at Bath, Canandaigua,

---

[1] Silsbee's background must be pieced together from a variety of sources. Among these are *Tallis's Drawing-Room Table Book*, pp. 43–44; W. W. Clayton, *History of Steuben County*, pp. 425–426; brief mentions in Walter M. Leman, *Memories of an Old Actor;* Francis Wemyss, *Chronology of the American Stage;* T. Allston Brown, *History of the American Stage;* George C. D. Odell, *Annals of the New York Stage;* Joseph Ireland, *Records of the New York Stage from 1750 to 1860;* William W. Clapp, Jr., *A Record of the Boston Stage;* Falconbridge, *Dan Marble: A Biographical Sketch;* Noah Ludlow, *Dramatic Life as I Found It;* Oral S. Coad, *The American Stage.* Part of the New York State background has been filled in through local research.

and Geneva, he was one of the many new settlers on the move westward out of New England or northward from Pennsylvania and
New Jersey who came with bag and baggage in search of new land
and the riches it promised. He brought his wife and three children,
and settled in the rich, fertile valley between Crooked Lake (now
known as Keuka Lake), with its aura of Indian legend, and pond-
like Waneta Lake to the east. To the north the turnpike ran toward
Penn Yan, an abbreviation for Pennsylvania Yankee in description
of its first settlers, and to the south, scarcely eight miles distant, to
the village of Bath on the Cohocton River.

Scarcely two years after Silsbee bought his land, the township
round and about had developed into a settlement named Fredericks-
town. In 1808 it was renamed Wayne in honor of the famous Revolutionary War general, the name the town bears today. The new
town was an ideal location for an enterprising settler because of its
fortunate position on the main pike, less than a mile distant from
the lake and the transport it afforded. It was in the midst of excel
lent farming land, and Silsbee was not long in realizing his opportunities. He opened the first hotel in the Wayne territory, built the
first ashery, and developed a large acreage in wheat and other
grains. In partnership with a Mr. Fitch, he turned storekeeper to
supply the booming territory with tools and other conveniences. He
passed this enterprise and ambition along to his eldest son, John,
who continued to enlarge the fortunes of the family by opening up
new land and building and operating the first sawmill in the area.
In 1812, John was elected to the office of town clerk, an extra job
which provided enough income for marriage and settling down on
a farm near his father's home. Joshua, the second of nine children,
was born there on December 1, 1813.

Of young Silsbee we know nothing. Reared as he was of good
Presbyterian stock, we can well imagine that his early years followed the usual pattern of country family existence: hard work
during the months of the growing season, school during the four
snow months, occasional visits to Bath or Penn Yan, swimming,
fishing in the lakes, hunting for fox and bear, and when he wanted
to be alone a run to the heights that overlooked Crooked Lake and
the slopes of the huge bluff across the water. He probably saw his
first theatricals in Bath, for it was through this town that actors,

such as Samuel Drake's company,[2] passed on their way to Olean and
the Allegheny River, which could carry them to the South and the
West via the Ohio and the Mississippi. By the early 1830's, when he
must have been contemplating what work he would do, the country
around Wayne was busy and open. As the second son in the family,
Josh probably had to make the not uncommon decision of seeking
his fortune elsewhere. By the mid-thirties we find him along the
rivers trying his hand at acting.

Our first record of Joshua Silsbee's specific interest in the stage
turns up in 1836, when he was engaged as a stock actor in the company of the Nashville Theatre. This was to be followed by work
under the same management in the theatres at Montgomery and
Mobile, but when the season opened, the new actor did not appear.
Furthermore, he showed no cause whatever for breaking the engagements.[3] It is reasonable to assume that he worked during this period
somewhere along the River as a stock actor, though his biographers
date his debut a year later at Natchez, Mississippi. We have already
noted Tyrone Power's surprise and pleasure at the highly receptive
audience of "gentle folks" he found at the theatre there during his
1835 tour. The gentlemen sat in the pit, he tells us, and several
groups of pretty and well-dressed women sat in the boxes. Twenty-
four–year–old Silsbee must have made something of a hit at Natchez,
for two years later we find he is a specialist in fops and juveniles
in Thorne and Scott's National Theatre company in Cincinnati. In
Frances Trollope's town he married Mrs. Trowbridge, who, like
himself, had been playing the western circuit. She had first acted
with Dan Marble at Columbus, Ohio, in 1836, shortly after she came
to the States from her native England, and in 1838 she had joined
the Cincinnati company. Since Mrs. Silsbee was to act with him in
many of his Yankee plays, it is pertinent to mention here that she
was a popular leading woman in the river towns, "a *model* wife, a
lady-like, kind and pleasing woman, and a fine mental actress,"[4] an
ideal compliment in a robust theatre in which personal reputations
were frequently in question.

[2] See Noah Ludlow's lively account of the movement of Drake's acting company westward in 1815.

[3] Douglas Hunt, "The Theatre in Nashville," *Birmingham Southern College
Bulletin*, XXVIII (May, 1935), 57.

[4] Falconbridge, *Dan Marble*, p. 102.

It was in Cincinnati that Josh Silsbee made his first hit as a Yankee comedian. How appropriate this event was. No city in the West could boast so large a proportion of real Yankees as could this crossroads town, citizens thoroughly characterized and caricatured by Mrs. Trollope. Two performances of *The Forest Rose* are advertised in the *Advertiser and Journal* for March 28 and April 11, 1840, but who played Jonathan is not noted. Nor is any mention made of Silsbee's telling a Yankee story at J. M. Scott's benefit on May 27, a story which one biographer declares the immediate hit encouraging him to exploit further this brand of eccentric humor.[5] Yet we know he had been busy in the low-comedy line. On September 1 Silsbee is mentioned in a review of a performance of *Rochdales*: "Old and young" Rochdales as played by "Messrs. Silsbee and McConachy shewed a strong family likeness—which is all we may say of them."[6] This barbed and pointed negative was sharply reversed a few days later in a report of *The Forest Rose* performed on September 3. Silsbee could scarcely have hoped for more.

In the person of Mr. Silsbee, one of the "stock" actors of this establishment, we behold a new "star" just appearing above the horizon; which, as far as appearances indicate, is not unlikely, at no very distant day, to attract no inconsiderable notice in the theatrical world; this, however, depends much on study and industry, as it is in the delineation (*sic*) of national character judging from the specimen presented on Thursday evening. . . . We have seen but few who could surpass him. The audience present on the occasion, one and all, evidently endorsed this opinion by its rapturous and simultaneous burst of applause.

The extent of Silsbee's success is reflected in the bills of the next few days. On September 5, according to the *Advertiser and Journal*, he played "a very creditable performance" of Solomon Swap. On September 10 he tried *The Lady of Lyons*. This time the newspaper's notice of Silsbee's acting of the fop, Glovis, is far from complimentary: "He so far overacted his part, that . . . he presented a disgusting caricature. . . . This description of character is evidently so far out of his line, he had better not attempt it any more." At least the reaction from the sidelines was not indifferent. But Silsbee's Yankees were another story. That they were "all the go" is

[5] *Tallis's*, pp. 43–44.
[6] Cincinnati *Advertiser and Journal*, September 1, 1840.

indicated in his acting of Obediah Whitaker in *The Foundling, or Yankee Fidelity* "by R. C. McLellan of Philadelphia" on September 7.[7] On September 11 for his benefit night he performed all three Yankee plays and told some Yankee stories. This was repeated the next evening. On the eighteenth he again acted Swap, and a week later three new characters: Pardon Dodge in Louisa Medina's great Bowery success, *Nick of the Woods* (September 26); Jerry Jenkins in *Battle of Chippewa* (September 30); and Bill Ball in *Liberty Tree* (October 1).

The success at Cincinnati could mean only one thing—Silsbee had jumped the hurdle from stock actor to star. With abrupt decision he purchased two or three Yankee pieces and set out for the East to begin the career of the wandering star performer. At first he played the small towns, enriching and embellishing his style in accordance with his sensing of audience reaction, then he turned to Philadelphia (Arch Street, September, 1841),[8] Boston, and finally, after many months of seasoning, to New York (Chatham, June, 1843).[9] We find a side note on his own opinion of himself in a correspondence with Sol Smith. From Silsbee to Smith on June 26:

I have a better set of pieces than Marble—besides they are generally new. You may think I am boasting—but I can bring letters from—Joe Jones—Thorne—Charlotte Cushman and others if necessary that they consider me No 1   Easy—on the same nights for four nights & Hill withdrawn & I was engaged.

From Smith to Silsbee on July 6:

You are perfectly correct in supposing that we may think you are a little given to boasting—But never mind—business is business. If you are considered *here* better than Marble . . . you will do well.[10]

Silsbee's view of himself as better than either Marble or Hill was not without some foundation. In June, 1843, he alternated nights with Hill at the Chatham, while Marble played at the Park, in a Yankee theatre festival unequaled in New York. And Sol Smith,

[7] *Ibid.*, September 7, 1840. Advertisements appear for this date and others also in *The Daily Gazette.*
[8] Wilson, *Philadelphia Theatre*, p. 249.
[9] Odell, *Annals*, IV, 646.
[10] Quoted in William G. B. Carson, *Managers in Distress*, pp. 236–237. Original in possession of Missouri Historical Society.

sharp Yankee trader that he was, arranged a similar bout for Silsbee and Marble in St. Louis the following September. What a battle for the West that must have been, with the combatants in the guise of New England Yankees!

3

What did Silsbee contribute to the Yankee theatre repertoire of plays? It would be unfair to say that he gave nothing. Yet, with some qualification, this evaluation is not far from the truth. Of the thirty-five or so Yankee pieces he played during his stage life, more than a dozen were "borrowed" from other Yankee actors. The others are of only nominal interest. Among the "borrowed" plays are the two perennials in the public domain, *Jonathan in England* and *The Forest Rose*, and two Marble pieces, *Yankee Land* and *The Wool Dealer*. Apparently Marble did not own these last two plays, and Silsbee probably played them with permission of the author (Cornelius Logan). We have no way of assessing the truth of Durang's comment that Silsbee appeared in all of Hill's pieces, "either the original, or founded on his plots and stories," but it is clear that after Hill and Marble died Silsbee added most of their major characters to his repertoire.[11]

From the major group—Silsbee's original acquisitions—not a single character or play of importance is added to the general body of Yankee theatre pieces. It is true that none of his plays reached publication, a highly limiting factor in evaluating their worth. But on the other hand, none of them were acted by other Yankee actors, a fact which indirectly assesses their value. Only five of them have acknowledged authorships, the others being of anonymous origin. R. C. McLellan's *The Foundling* has already been mentioned in connection with Silsbee's Cincinnati debut. Could this possibly have been an adaptation of Woodworth's *Foundling of the Sea?* J. S. Jones' *The Battle of Lake Erie* was probably a stock piece, with a Yankee as a minor character. It appears that Silsbee played the other three with some regularity—Silas S. Steele's *The Rebellion in Canada*, C. A. Logan's *Celestial Empire, or Yankee in China,* and

---

[11] Advertisements in *The New York Times* August 15–30, 1853, show that Silsbee acted *The Forest Rose, Wife for a Day, The Yankee Pedlar, Green Mountain Boy, New Notions, Seth Slope, Yankee Land, The Wool Dealer, Yankee in France, Yankee in Time.* These plays were either Hill's or Marble's.

J. P. Addams' *Redwood, or Connecticut Curiosities.* Among Silsbee's more frequently played anonymous pieces are *Sam Slick, Courting in Connecticut, Boston Tea Party, Nick of Time,* and *Bumps, or Yankee Magnetism.* How all of these sketches differed we do not know, but they must have provided the comedian with an assortment of situations for stage impersonations which, if we are to believe those who saw them, varied little if at all from piece to piece. The plays which sustained him most were the borrowed ones, and these he acted regularly in most engagements during the forties.

In the overview Silsbee emerges as primarily the actor and not the fully developed theatre artist which Hackett and Hill certainly were, and which Marble became to a certain extent. In 1850 the ambitious Silsbee was billed as "the gem of Yankee comedians par excellence—the man of many parts."[12] This may have been a Yankee pun, though it is supported by Charles Durang, who thought the comedian brought to the stage "some original racy drawings of the passing follies of the day, which often were satirically just and true."[13] If businessman Silsbee saw no need to work hard at developing a solid body of individualized Yankee materials, he at least was not without flashes of originality. He might exploit the materials already on hand, but he was possessed of certain undeniable talents as a performer.

Borrowing of repertoire was not the only way in which Silsbee imitated the other Yankee comedians. He also tried his hand at management. On December 25, 1848, he became owner and manager of the new Athenaeum National Museum in Philadelphia. We can anticipate the result of this imitation: it survived for scarcely a month.[14]

4

Josh Silsbee's image as a Yankee delineator is nowhere set out in such full relief as in the chatty and highly enthusiastic newspaper reviews of *The Forest Rose* in London.[15] A dozen different sources,

[12] Durang, *History of the Philadelphia Stage*, Series III, Chapter 101.
[13] *Ibid.*
[14] Wilson, *Philadelphia Theatre*, p. 116. The company included Mr. and Mrs. J. S. Silsbee; Mr. and Mrs. D. P. Bowers; Misses E. Eberle, Hull, West, and Young; Messrs. Barnford, Crocker, E. Dean, J. M. Field, J. R. Hall, R. Johnson, McMinn, E. Thompson, Walters and West. D. P. Bowers was stagemanager.
[15] Comment on Silsbee's style and capabilities is a composite of reviews drawn

some of considerable length, paint the first impression in vivid colors, and they at once not only tell us about what Woodworth's play looked like to Englishmen,[16] but they also give us a vivid picture of a working American comedian at mid-century.

A look at the licensed version of the play in the Lord Chamberlain's collection[17] reveals that while Silsbee retained the plot outline, he definitely threw Jonathan into prominence by random cutting. The play seems to have lost by that time any individuality it ever had. Its generalized characters could have been extracted from all nineteenth-century domestic pieces. The villainy of the city types in this version is even more sharply focused to contrast vividly with the virtue and industry of William and Jonathan as country types. This version still locates the action near New York, but Taunton, Massachusetts, is mentioned frequently, indicating a possible tie to George Hill. The play now gives Jonathan the principal position, with two opportunities to perform country dances, as well as tell a story of Connecticut courtship. The piece is arranged in two acts (nine scenes).

When the London play reviewers saw Woodworth's pastoral opera they emphatically separated it from the comedian in its principal comic role. Poor Woodworth! His picture of American country life was not only a quarter of a century old, but it had been hacked and rearranged to suit an actor of a different type and style. In addition, it was of American authorship untouched by London hacks. With such an American label, even when the London competition that week was of such dubious merit as *The Housekeeper, The Duke's Wager, Court Beauties, Mazeppa,* and *Turning the Tables,* it would scarcely survive the onslaught of those who protected the theatregoer's interest. One reviewer thought it reminiscent of English sentimental comedies and ballet opera of the eighteenth century, with many situations and speeches actually taken from them. Another declared that it did not possess plot, originality of any sort, or decent composition, that it provoked nothing but utter contempt for the abilities of its author. Jonathan

---

from these periodicals: *The Era, Morning Post, The Spectator, Sunday Times, Morning Advertiser, Morning Chronicle, The Times, Illustrated London News, The Examiner, The Globe, The Standard.*

[16] See the detailed analysis of this play in Chapter 3.

[17] Lord Chamberlain's Collection No. 43037.

was seen as a low-class character around whom a number of non-descript personages revolved for no purpose except to set off the Yankee. The piece was as clumsy as dramatic ineptitude could make it, with dull, pointless, weakly sentimental scenes leading to nothing. "The kindest thing one can do," wrote one reviewer, "is to forget the fact." The Adelphi company were complimented for performing well in parts much beneath their talents.

How different is their view of Joshua Silsbee, whose stories, chuckles, and capers kept the audience in a storm of incessant laughter, despite his creaking vehicle. As they looked at him they saw a homely, good-natured face with little, cunning, blue eyes and a self-contented smile. His body was thickset, the perfection of ungainliness with every movement an offense against elegance. A nasal twang, high-pitched in tone and monotonous in delivery, characterized his voice, and he spoke in a dialect marked by peculiar pronunciations, expressions, and words, which he rattled off with an air of quiet gravity and with a sense of unctuous enjoyment. On his head he wore a flaxen wig, combed back, and his costume consisted of very short trousers and an absurdly cut coat. His figure thus presented a mixture of stolid stupidity and wide-awake cunning.

When the reviewers considered his capacities as an actor they tended to characterize him as a comic speaker rather than a comic actor, with most of the laughter deriving from what he said rather than what he did. They found his humor broad and racy, and sometimes coarse and vulgar. This his prudish Victorian audience allowed him because he portrayed Jonathan in all ways with such characteristic extravagance. At points his manner was quiet, with a roguish cast in his eye; at other places his actions were eccentric and exaggerated. He told his stories in such an irresistible manner that screams and shrieks from different parts of the house actually interrupted their drollery. And when he danced his Cape Cod Reel he flung himself about in a frenzy, throwing his legs up behind and raising his head and shoulders as much as he did his knees.

How real was he? Little attention was given to this matter, in spite of its pertinence when Hill paid his visit to England in 1836. Did Londoners no longer care whether this was the real thing? The few reviewers who mentioned it were divided in opinion. Some thought that Silsbee must be the real thing because he was so consistent in what he did, and that his merit lay more in his close imitation of Yankee dialect and peculiarities than in his artistic excellence as a comedian. The balancing view was that, though Silsbee's portrait was amusing, it was nevertheless an exaggeration of the cute, slick, sly New Englander, and not without a good deal of stage buffoonery.

When the reviewers made their over-all evaluations they did not readily agree. Several thought him a genial, original actor who could give a natural gusto and relish to the old Yankeeisms. One thought him a clever actor with many of the best qualities of a comedian, and another declared his transatlantic comedy was truly remarkable. *The Times* labeled Silsbee the best actor of his class ever seen by a London public.

But set against this were the dissenting notes. One critic held that he could see no evidence of a genuinely humorous imagination, though in parts Silsbee was apparently very truthful in characterization. He looked for but could not find the irresistible flashes that bespoke an original humorous intellect. When Silsbee turned in January from *The Forest Rose* to *The Yankee Pedlar* some reviewers took a sobering second look. The critic for *The Era* had been highly enthusiastic in September, but in the cold of January he found Silsbee a highly limited actor with no variety and no range. "He also does little more than speak, and in acting he is a mere amateur." Hiram Dodge, he thought, was a mere repetition of Jonathan Ploughboy, an opinion boldly stated by two other reviewers. At first, when Silsbee was quite new, whatever he chose to say was tolerated, but a second or third look, apparently, revealed his lack of versatility. He is "used up" already, commented *The Era*'s man.

The comparison with Hackett, Hill, and Marble was inevitable. One reviewer, on seeing Silsbee dance, remembered that Hackett had done much the same thing in *The Kentuckian* twenty years earlier. Another recalled the poor impression Marble had made, and how much better Silsbee was in the part. Hill provided the readiest comparison, because his style was so small in contrast to Silsbee's large, unctuous, and broad manner. But when the critics looked at the latest Yankee in a part which Hill had actually played, they remembered Hill's excellence and could see Silsbee's shortcomings. In the overview, London saw a comedian whose acting kept a bad play alive. And what they had thought was worn out in the Yankee had come alive again in the person of Josh Silsbee. If he made them laugh greatly at the nonsense, he still soberly reminded them that a real America and a real Yankee existed somewhere across the Atlantic. Did Josh Silsbee bear any relationship to the real thing?

5

The last phase of Silsbee's career is completely characteristic of the aggressiveness and ambition that had guided his rise from a western country boy to stardom in London. When his first bright success, after his return home from London to New York, had palled, Silsbee turned again to the West. This time it was not the river country that lured him but California, and there he went in 1855, along with the many who hoped to build a fortune in the wake of the gold discovery. What was recognizable about the stage Yankee in New York and London, Silsbee thought, would also be perfectly clear to Californians. But others had traveled the road before him—minor actors, to be sure—and the market for Yankee eccentrics was not so fresh and lucrative as he had hoped. Still, however, though they thought his pieces old and threadbare, he won them to laughter.[18]

He had a harder time convincing those who took his representation of a New Englander seriously. The river towns, the cities of the East, and even London had tolerated the comedian's broad and extravagant exaggerations, but in California, where Yankees had arrived in great numbers, nothing less than the real object could entirely satisfy. The critic for San Francisco's *Golden Era* granted that Silsbee showed the independence of the Yankee character, but he was disappointed not to find the shy, cool shrewdness, the bargain-driving element. An even greater deficiency, suggested the reviewer, was Silsbee's failure to express true Yankee bashfulness in the presence of a female. The truth of the matter was that Silsbee's Yankee was acceptable stage entertainment of an eccentric sort, but as a representative of New England it was far from the truth.

Joshua Silsbee's death in San Francisco in December, 1855, at the age of forty-two brought to a close the era of Yankee theatre. From Hackett to Silsbee it had moved from a satirical comment on

[18] George R. MacMinn, *The Theatre of the Golden Era in California*, pp. 166–167. See also the San Francisco *Alta* for April 13 and 17, 1855.

vaguely perceived New Englanders to a broad, comic entertainment about Americans in general; from the genuine reality of Hill's creation to the broad, eccentric, romantic image of the Silsbee model. But the eulogy in Josh Silsbee's obituary could have applied to all of them: "a keen and close observer, and a man of great goodness of heart, and mildness, and amiability of disposition."[19]

[19] *Alta*, December 23, 1855.

epilogue

To tightly limit Yankee theatre to the work of its four principal comedians is to arbitrarily declare an unrealistic scope and to lessen its dynamic impact on American theatre. Yankee theatre *was* American comedy before 1850, and its status as such was not disturbed until the appearance after mid-century of the "city plays," with such types as Mose the Fireman. Nor does its influence and its larger context of meaning come to an end when three of its proponents are dead and James Hackett has given up the type. In the total view of American comedy, Yankee theatre is the second and most crucial stage, and, as such, it forms the basis for the third major period, a period strongly marked by the delineation of middle-class elements and the city problems of a more highly integrated cultural pattern. Two questions, then, must be considered in any view of the meaning of Yankee theatre: What was its scope? What was its influence?

Part of the answer to the first lies in its nature as "lower-order" comedy. Royall Tyler displayed both orders in *The Contrast*, but the significance of Yankee theatre, especially in the 1830's, is its mirror reflection of the basic meanings and implications of American democracy in political form as exemplified by a common man of independence, self-assertion, capability, imagination, cleverness, and high potential. Jonathan is a Jacksonian Man. To give him exact, realistic delineation, Hill made him a specific regional type; but the others followed the moods of audiences wherever they found them, and out of this pressure they molded a general American, a native primitive set apart from all other varieties of the English-speaking breed. While such a "lower-order" classification strictly limited the over-all meaning of Yankee theatre, it declared a tight unity of direction and design, and it led to the establishment of a strong acting tradition and a characteristic body of acting pieces.

The range of Yankee theatre outside the work of the four star performers is clearly discernible. All native actors who aspired to rise as comedians had to first traverse the field of Yankee comedy. English actors so thoroughly dominated and controlled the major roles in the standard English comedy that competition in this category almost entirely excluded the American, though he was allowed to play the minor roles. The stock-company assignment system and the traveling English star—Kemble, Macready, Mathews (the younger), for example—also severely limited the possibilities. What remained was American comedy. Once Hackett had proved its box-office possibilities, the training road for the young native comedy actor was fully declared. Alec Simpson's appearance as the first Jonathan in *The Forest Rose* while a member of the Chatham Theatre acting company has already been noted. And we have followed Hill, Marble, and Silsbee as stock actors.

Other native Americans of mention before 1850 who played Yankees are W. F. Gates, E. L. Davenport, and J. P. Addams, and after 1850, G. E. Locke, J. H. McVickers, David G. Robinson, Fayette Robinson, C. K. Fox, Charles Burke, Joseph Jefferson, John Sleeper Clarke, and John Owens.[1] Gates was the Bowery Theatre's low comedian in the thirties, and Addams, already noted as a Yankee playwright, together with Davenport, were first stock

---

[1] John Owens is an exception. He was not born an American but came to this country at the age of five. J. S. Clarke was born in Baltimore in 1833, and G. E. Locke in Epsom, New Hampshire, in 1817. J. H. McVicker bought some of Dan Marble's plays from Mrs. Marble, and in 1851 starred in them on tour. Noah Ludlow (*Dramatic Life*, pp. 732–733) tells us that in 1855 McVicker went to London, where he appeared in four theatres in a series of Yankee characters, playing *Sam Patch in France* for twelve weeks. He eventually became associated with the theatre in Chicago. David Robinson, born about 1805 in East Monmouth, Maine, went to California in 1847 with a medical degree from Yale University. There he became interested in the theatre and began acting Yankees and telling Yankee stories. Fayette Robinson was born in 1818 near Avon Mineral Springs in Livingston County, New York. Brown, *History of the American Stage*, p. 317, tells us that he made his first appearance on the stage "at a school exhibition in his native town as Jonathan Doolittle in *A Yankee in England*." Although Brown does not identify it as such, this could be Humphreys' play.

comedians and then stars in their own right. Davenport took over Gates' position at the Bowery in the forties, and Addams, already noted in connection with Dan Marble as a Yankee-theatre playwright, for a season or two after 1849 tried Yankee pieces, his own as well as others, at Burton's Theatre on Arch Street in Philadelphia and at the National Theatre and Brooklyn Museum in New York.[2]

When Hill's and Marble's Yankee pieces became generally available after 1850, Locke, the two Robinsons, McVickers, and Clarke played the characters from New York to San Francisco. Burke followed Gates and Davenport at the Bowery, and made a hit with Hill's role of Solon Shingle.[3] John Owens later picked up this character in the sixties and turned it into a major stage portrait. C. K. Fox was the first Gumption Cute in *Uncle Tom's Cabin*, a role which Jefferson also played before he made his first major break-through with Yankee Asa Trenchard in *Our American Cousin*. This general catalogue of actors who played Yankees would be incomplete without mentioning four actresses who were commonly associated with the Yankee plays—the first Mrs. Hackett, her sister Mrs. Sharpe, Mrs. Joshua Silsbee, and Mrs. Mestayer. And all stock actors before 1850 played roles in Yankee pieces at one time or another in the general assignments of the "acting-line" tradition.

The popularity of Yankee comedy can be gauged by examining the incidence of the star comedians in New York between 1833, when Hackett and Hill first began their competition, and 1845, when the others have joined the field.[4] With the exception of the 1838 1839 season, when Hackett and Hill were both in Europe, major Yankee actors could be seen during five or six months of every season, with a yearly average of seven engagements each of several performances, the number rising to a peak of ten in the 1837–1838 season, when Marble first entered the New York competition with Hill and Hackett. Similar studies in Philadelphia and Boston would probably result in similar histories for both these locales, though other cities had to be content with two or three

---

[2] See Odell, *Annals*, V, 25 ff.; VI, 41 ff., 104 ff.

[3] Burke was born in Philadelphia on March 27, 1822, and died in New York on November 10, 1854. See Moses, *Actor Families*, pp. 73 ff. for more detail. Ludlow (*Dramatic Life*, p. 714) records Burke's playing *The People's Lawyer*, *The Forest Rose* and *The Vermont Wool Dealer* in New Orleans in April, 1851.

[4] Odell's *Annals* is the primary source for this frequency-of-performance study.

engagements a season as the various actors made tours to the inland theatres. On not infrequent occasions in New York, and probably also in Boston and Philadelphia, engagements were arranged in which one comedian followed on the heels of another; and at rare moments, particularly in bad business years, two might play simultaneously, alternating nights as programming permitted. When star comedians were scarce local actors would sometimes try a new Yankee piece by themselves in the interest of satisfying audience craving for Yankee productions. In this way apprentice low comedians could be given a chance to act such a piece, and local writers, actors, or stage managers a chance to write one. Telling down-East stories was the usual way for a young comedian to get started.

The "lower-order" comedy of Yankee theatre not only provided a new training ground and career opportunities for low comedians, but it also influenced the wider range of American plays and playwriting of the period. Strictly defined, Yankee theatre plays are those in which the Yankee is the principal character in the dramatic action; his main function in the plot may be to help others, but there is no question of his dominance. When we look outside this category to other plays, especially those of the forties and fifties, after the type had been well established, we find the Yankee frequently as a secondary character. His popularity as a stage type as well as his common tie to American life appear to have made him an indispensable ingredient in native melodrama and comedy. *Nick of the Woods* has already been mentioned. The two temperance dramas, *The Drunkard* (1844)[5] and *Ten Nights in a Bar Room* (1858), and *Uncle Tom's Cabin* (1852) thoroughly illustrate this extension in the use of the type.

In *The Drunkard* all of the country people are Yankees, though it is William who emerges as the close friend and protector of Edward Middleton and successfully defeats the villainous Lawyer Cribbs. In *Ten Nights in a Bar Room*,[6] with its action laid in the New England village of Cedarville, it is Sam Switchel who protects Willie Hammond from the vices of Gambler Harvey Green. Switchel is an easy-going, cracker-barrel, hayseed farmer, full of

---

[5] *The Drunkard, or The Father Saved* by W. H. Smith was not published by Samuel French until the 1850's, but the first performance is dated much earlier.

[6] Brown, *History of the American Stage*, p. 294, claims that W. W. Pratt wrote the play for G. E. Locke.

action and courage when aroused. Mehitable Cartright, also a full-blown country type, is his girlfriend. The play is directly tied to Yankee theatre in its dialect, its songs, its Yankee stories, its bashful love scene between the two Yankee comic figures, and Switchel's clever manipulation in protecting Willie from evil. In both plays the Yankees assist the principal characters and provide comic relief, but they do not dominate the action.

Even less of a participant in the main action of the play is Gumption Cute in George Aiken's version of *Uncle Tom's Cabin.* This Yankee—played by a number of prominent comedians, including Joseph Jefferson and C. K. Fox—was added by Aiken when he adapted the famous novel.[7] Gumption Cute is not really fused into the action but stands outside it as a sort of comic encrustation on the melodrama. In its original form the character was only sixteen lines in length, but its importance as an audience lure is revealed when we note, in its first New York billings, that Gumption Cute was given equal status with Uncle Tom and St. Clair. How this could be justified we do not know, unless the Yankee was extended in the playing. We note a number of years later in another version that the role had reached major status with over eight hundred lines.[8] This latter version undoubtedly became a fully declared Yankee play. In Aiken's original adaptation, the Yankee adds little to the story beyond brief scenes with Topsy and with Miss Ophelia, the New England spinster. He is a rather distasteful, disreputable character —a tramp, a vagrant who appears as a panhandler in a ragged Army uniform. Aiken possibly intended to contrast the slovenliness of a northern tramp with the Southern Negro slave who could not control his destiny. The reality of the other character drawings in the play may have encouraged Aiken to insert something fresh from his own Boston background. The character is not without originality, but he remains something of an enigma in our view.

As the set forms of Yankee theatre reached out to touch the comedy acting tradition and native plays, they became vulnerable to changes from other directions. Something new seems to be in-

---

[7] There were other later versions, but George Aiken's has been generally accepted as the best. Montrose Moses, *Representative Plays by American Dramatists,* pp. 605 ff., notes that twelve versions were available when he prepared his anthology. The Charles Taylor version, the first to appear in New York, ignored both Eva and Topsy in the cast.

[8] Harry Birdoff, *The World's Greatest Hit,* p. 116.

fluencing them in the 1840's, a fresh impulse that would keep a
Yankee on the stage for the rest of the century. The new develop-
ment is first noticeable in Anna Cora Mowatt's *Fashion, or Life in
New York* (1845). In this satire on the follies of social position in
New York, new directions in American comedy are clearly indicated. There is something strongly reminiscent of James Hackett's
The Times, or Life in New York—though it is unlikely that Mrs.
Mowatt had any acquaintance with the earlier piece—and even
something of *The Contrast*. She has caricatured city types, but her
hero, Adam Trueman, is very much related to the Yankees. From
Cattaraugus County in western New York State, Trueman is a
gentleman farmer and a man of strong character. No marked
dialect or Yankeeisms color his speech in the published text. We see
him as an epitome of all that is simple, unpretentious, straight-
forward, and direct, for he provides a sharp contrast to the city silli-
ness of Mrs. Tiffany and the others. He has a sturdiness and a
definition about him which declares a genuine reality. What has
Mrs. Mowatt done with him to make him look so different from the
Yankee country types on the stage? With her talents as a playwright
she has pushed aside the cluttered facade of the Yankee-theatre type
and found something more genuine underneath. She has also drawn
her farmer, not from the lower orders, but from an upper level of
country life. The city types in *Fashion* are caricatures of people
with new wealth, the lower orders of the democracy who have come
into money. The result of this fusion is a middle-class comedy. The
lower order had been parodied by Mathews and the Yankee-theatre
comedians. The upper-order American had not been much seen on
the stage, because, as Mathews had maintained, Americans at this
level differed little from the same class of Englishmen and were not
subjects for low comedy. Mrs. Mowatt has discovered the middle
ground, and with this discovery a new life for the Yankee on the
stage is declared. Had the audience changed? The popular democratic audience of the thirties wanted to see its own image on the
stage and the middle and upper orders who went to the theatre
found his oddities amusing and meaningful. But a new, middle-
class audience seems to be emerging, especially in the cities, and
they want another image. The country type has not disappeared;
he has merely changed his clothes and improved his speech. When
Mrs. Mowatt wrote her play this sort of entertainment was limited

to audiences in a few cities. In the fifties it would grow, and in the sixties and seventies it would declare the direction of the American stage.

The change is undeniably underway. At the very height of Yankee-theatre popularity and influence, the new American stage image is taking shape. It will mean a more mature, more fully developed, more individualized type. And as playwrights of talent work with him, particularly outsiders like Dion Boucicault and Tom Taylor,[9] the old Yankee-theatre character type will seem less and less a reality, more and more as if he never existed at all. A middle-class prejudice will hover over him, and the new American will declare that he is not his cousin at all. We can watch the shift as we follow Joseph Jefferson through the acting of Salem Scudder in Boucicault's *The Octoroon* (1857) and Asa Trenchard in Taylor's *Our American Cousin* (1858). Both characters are Yankees and Jefferson gives them a distinct New England flavor despite their Irish-English authorship. The freedom of the old Yankee actor to "create" his own pieces by expanding, altering, and individualizing plays by English writers is gone. In its place is a solid, much more mature character line. Salem Scudder is only a distant relative of Hiram Dodge, but the outline of the peddler in Virginia is still there in his shrewdness and clever manipulations of life on the Plantation Terrebonne. And in Asa Trenchard, Jefferson created a tall, simple, uncouth Vermonter, with touches of pathos as well as low comedy.

Perhaps the old and the new are best brought together in the work of John E. Owens, though this highly successful comedian of the sixties and seventies was not born an American.[10] It is Owens who is usually associated with the character of Solon Shingle in *The People's Lawyer* rather than George Hill, for whom Joseph Jones wrote the play, because Owens made it his principal role in the sixties. His Solon Shingle, according to Brander Matthews, was a direct, simple picture of a homely New England farmer, loquacious, inquisitive, shrewd, full of his own importance. Mathews thought it recalled Winslow Homer's studies of farm life, that it was

[9] Boucicault was long associated with the American stage, but he is, of course, an Irishman by birth. Taylor was English.

[10] For extensive biographical detail see Mrs. John E. Owens, *Memories of the Professional and Social Life of John E. Owens*. Owens came to the United States when he was five years old.

real and distinct to an extraordinary degree.[11] How mindful of George Hill's acting is this comparison to the real thing. Owens cut the original script, introduced his own, highly individualized business, and elaborated on the comedy in his own style. Yet we can see in this new portrait of the Yankee farmer much of the vestige of the old. A similar link is in the work of Denman Thompson, a native American born at Girard, Pennsylvania, who forged a career out of *The Old Homestead* and its Yankee character of Josh Whitcomb. Thompson's work in the 1870's is the connecting tie to James A. Herne and his New England plays of the eighties.[12] There is something more than coincidence in Herne's naming a character in *Sag Harbor* Captain Dan Marble.

In the overview the influence of Yankee theatre was most extensive. Cut out and fashioned as it was from the coarse fabric of American life, then modified, stretched, and roughly sewn together by hands still crudely unskilled, or borrowed outright from the English theatre, Yankee theatre created an American, sometimes localized but often generalized, that caught the imagination both at home and abroad. In simple, uncomplicated, often broadly exaggerated terms, it told Americans who they were in an age that needed a personal, individualized definition to fit the growing nationalism and the feeling of difference from the European prototypes. Did the American conglomerate, separated from its forebears by three thousand miles of ocean, and varying numbers of years, have a national character? Yankee theatre attempted to define one; and it took what it found abroad, and sold it to the English, who argued its reality, sharply criticized its craftsmanship, and returned it to America, battered but determined. In the specific world of the stage Yankee theatre partially weaned audiences away from a strict diet of English plays and English actors by encouraging the view that native products had inherent merit. It won its spurs in artfully

[11] Matthews, "Americans on the Stage," *Scribner's Monthly*, XVIII (July 1879), 331. William Winter thought Owens' comic acting "rosy with health and redolent of enjoyment" except when he was too literal, too "true to life." At those moments his acting failed, Winter argued. "In becoming literal and photographic, he became monotonous and dull" (Winter, *Shadows of the Stage*, p. 218).

[12] Herne was born in Cahoes, New York, in 1839. Note other Yankee types in Herne's plays: Pitticus Green in *Margaret Fleming*; the whole dramatis personae in *Shore Acres*.

convincing theatregoers that it was solid entertainment. Yankee theatre followed the prevailing moods of the popular audience, withdrawing from satire when it did not work, exploiting the basic product for all it was worth in the Yankee's concept of making money in the easiest and cleverest way. What its craftsmen turned out did not elevate the level of theatre in America, but it did encourage playmakers and occasionally a genuine talent. Yankee theatre declared a new way to bring native actors into the theatre by providing a form the English simply could not imitate. Once it had determined how to train an American actor, the path for native participation on the stage was fully declared, and English domination was weakened.

Yankee theatre was at once an avenue to native and European understanding of the new political democrat called an American, and a way in which native actors and writers could participate in the theatre arts on their own stages. It broke the old monopoly by declaring a new one. Solomon Swap had traded watches with John Bull. The latter still had the case, but the Yankee had the works.

APPENDIXES

APPENDIX A

A Note on Yankee-Theatre Stage Speech

From a scientific point of view, a single "true" New England dialect did not exist during the Yankee-theatre period.[1] Local dialects can be defined only when differences with the standard language are clearly delineated, and this requires elaborate historical speech descriptions based on scientific data. In lieu of such descriptions, we must turn to the literary dabblers in dialect—playwrights, comic essayists, and others— who provide the only record of what was regarded as Yankee speech during this period. These must be looked at with great caution. How many hands retouched the plays before they came to print is impossible to determine. Frequently, many years elapsed between the first production of a play and its first printing. What George Hill or J. S. Jones might have worked out or even taken for granted could have been easily changed as the use of the dialect, or notion of the dialect, altered. Probably we can depend on the plays for only suggesting New England speech, and we must imagine that the actors provided far richer talk, varying with each individual conception of the dialect. Viewed in this manner, it is possible to accept the point of view that some actors were superior to others in their rendition of the characters. What in Hill was considered the "real" thing, probably more closely approached the general conception of New England speech held by the more discerning audiences in the east-coast cities where direct contact with New Englanders was possible. For the most part, Hill as a born-and-bred New Englander was accepted as the standard, and the others were compared to his "genuine" Yankee.

The general similarity of speech in the Yankee-theatre plays indicates not only the influence of certain actors on the several parts they performed, but a rather extensive use of early texts when preparing new plays. Mathews used David Humphreys' glossary as early as 1823,[2] and

---

[1] See George P. Krapp, *The English Language in America*, I, 231.

[2] This is the glossary attached to *The Yankey in England* which Humphreys printed in 1815. See Chapters 3 and 4 for further mention. The glossary itself is reproduced as Appendix B of this book.

other actor-writers probably continued to borrow from it after that date. Printed texts of several plays show an increase in the use of dialect after 1835, with the late plays becoming very rich and elaborate, especially when the western influence had encouraged the use of a more exaggerated vocabulary and of manufactured word-forms. What had been largely word choice and expletive in *The Contrast* became a stereotyped speech exhibiting a large number of sound differences in addition to the usual use of substandard grammatical forms. In large part the printed texts generally confirm Professor George Krapp's opinion that "the New England dialect as a literary form is mainly popular or illiterate American English with a very occasional splash of genuine local color."

Any attempt to draw a brief description of New England speech used in the plays must rely to a large extent on interpretations of spelling. Where words of a certain class are spelled in the same manner a commonness of sound distinguishing these words from words in a different class is usually confirmed, but the exact phonemic description of the sound is a more difficult matter to determine. James Russell Lowell's rules for New England speech have been largely discredited as basic description for a "true" dialect in use during the 1830's and 1840's.[3] Many of the differences he mentions are typical of other parts of the country as well as New England and cannot clearly be labeled Yankee "dialect." However, if we overlook the restricted scientific meaning of "dialect," and give it a loose interpretation, Lowell's rules become more credible and can assist us in making a fair description of the speech employed by Yankee-theatre actors.

A number of vowel peculiarities appear with regularity. Such words as *care, swear, there,* and *where* were pronounced more nearly as *car* and *mar* would be today. The vowel of *end* and *scared* sounded like that in *pin,* and that in *have* was raised to sound more like *end. Daughter* and *sausages* sounded like *father,* and a class of words such as *home, stone,* and *whole,* containing long *o* were shortened to a vowel nearly like that in *cut* and *rut.* And some of those words which today sound like *cut—such, discover, touch, just*—were voiced like *lip* or *bit,* or in the case of *shut* like *bet.* Another large class of words containing *er* or *ear* spellings—*serve, Jerseys, merchant, serpent, earth,* and *learn*— were probably pronounced with the same vowel that *carve* uses today in coastal New England speech. In addition, the *r* sound was usually dropped in such words as *first, horse,* and *girl.* The diphthong in *boil,*

[3] James Russell Lowell, *The Biglow Papers,* p. 38. See Krapp, *The English Language in America,* I, 231–234. See also Frances Trollope's list of American phrases, *Domestic Manners,* pp. 427–428.

spoil, poison, royal, and *point* sounded like the diphthong in *lie* and is still heard today in parts of New England as well as in other sections of the country; and the diphthong in *how, out, mouth,* and *now* resembled the sounds still used in parts of western New England, a sequence of the vowels in *pet* and *put.*

The use of the consonants varied to some extent from present usages. Words pronounced today as *picture, creature, natural, fortune,* and *nature* used only a consonantal *t* in the mid position instead of the sound cluster. The sound of the alveolar nasal *n* was substituted in unstressed syllables at the end of words for the velar nasal, spelled *ng,* as it is today quite generally in New England and the South. The most interesting spelling-pronunciation was the use of *er* to end such words as *tallow, swallow, yellow,* and *widow* (i.e., spelled: *taller, swaller,* etc.), probably indicating the use of the same vowel as the sound at the end of *sofa.*

There are other minor sound differences noted in the printed plays, but this description is sufficient to give an idea of what was required in the way of dialect from the Yankee actor. In addition, he undoubtedly developed a strong nasal twang, perfected a drawl to lengthen the vowels, and learned a long list of general-low-colloquial grammatical forms to give his speech an uncultivated quality. *Gin* was substituted for *give,* as *ax* was for *ask, driv* for *drove, fit* for *fought, throwd* for *threw.* Moreover, he *guessed, calculated, reckoned,* and was *flummixed, consarned,* and *swowed.* Occasionally he found someone *constipatious, contankerous, splendiferous. Tarnal* and *cute* were his favorite adjectives. But from wherever his language derived, it was always employed to the best possible advantage to uncover his own character, or the characters of those persons around him. It was always colorful and frequently vivid. In the hands of the Yankee actor, speech was a weapon, an entertainment, an artifice, and a musical score.

APPENDIX B

David Humphreys' Glossary of Yankee Words

The Glossary appended to the published edition of David Humphreys' play *The Yankey in England* (1815) is reproduced here in facsimile. It was one of the earliest attempts to record the typical speech of western New England, and it served as a specific model for Charles Mathews and Richard Peake when they put together their stage pieces of *Trip to America* and *Jonathan in England* (both performed in 1824). Though no specific evidence supports such an assumption, in all probability James H. Hackett, and others who worked with the Yankee character during the 1820's, found it a useful description of the regional language.

Glossary

Of words used in a peculiar sense, in this Drama ; or pronounced with an accent or emphasis in certain districts, different from the modes generally followed by the inhabitants of the United States ; including new-coined American, obsolete English, and low words in general.

A

Abord, for, on board.
Afeard, afraid.
Afore, before.
Agin, again.
Ant I, probably from, and I, used however rather as a negative.

A-nuff, enough.
Argufying, arguing.
Arter, after.
Atarnal, eternal.
Atarnity, eternity.
Awful, ugly.
Ax, ask.

B

Ban't, } am, or as, or
Ben't, } are not.
Becaise, because.
Berrying, burying.
Beleve, believe.
Bile, boil.
Bin, been.
Bissy, busy.
Bissness, business.
Blud, blood.
Boggling, difficulty, delaying, unnecessarily hesitating.
Boost, raise up, lift up, exalt.
Borrerd, borrowed.

Boot, *to boot*, something given into the bargain.
Bred-stuffs, all kinds of flour, meal, farinaceous substances, grain. In England, corn is used as the generic term. In America, corn is always intended to apply to maize— otherwise called Indian corn—the most abundant and useful vegetable production in the United States, from the extreme northern to the southern boundary.

Briled, broiled.
Brussels, bristles.

Buty, Beauty.

C

Calculate, used frequently in an improper sense, as reckon, guess.
Captivated, captured, taken prisoner.
Cent, 1-100th part of a dollar—a copper coin of the United States.
Clever, relating to moral character,—not skilfulness or dexterity.
Chaffering, holding a long talk.
Chaunce, chance.
Chirk, churk, brisk, lively, in good spirits.
Chares, chores, trifling employments at or near home.

Cleverly, very well.
Close, clothes.
Clus, close.
Concarning, concerning.
Cood, could.
Copper, formerly current money of the value of a halfpenny in England.
Count, (in provincial use,) estimate, reckon,
Cum, came.
Cumfort, comfort.
Curridge, courage.
Critturs, creatures.
Curious, extraordinary.
Cuss, curse.
Cussed, cursed.
Cute, acute, smart, sharp.

D

Darned, old English.
Darter, daughter.
Dasent, dare not.
Despud, desperate.
Despudly, desperately.
Lilly dallying, wasting time for little purpose.
Divil, devil.
Druv, driven.
Dreadful, used often as, very, excessively; even as it regards beauty, goodness, &c.

Du, do.
Dubble, double.
Duds, old clothes.
Dum, dumb.
Dumpish, heavy, silly.
Du pry tel, (exclamation probably from) do pray tell.
Duse, does.

E

Eend, end.
Enny, any.
Enny-wheres, any where.

E'en-a-most, almost.
Extrumpery, extempore.

F

Fairce, farce, fierce.
Fairm, farm, firm.
Farmament, firmament.
Fleering, } terms of con-
Flouting, } tempt, vulgar.
Flip, liquor made of rum, beer and sugar, with a hot poker put into the mug to stir it.
Flustration, extreme agitation.
Fokes, folks.
Forgit, forget.

Forrerd, forward.
Fort, fault.
Fortin, fortune.
Fortino, fortizno, for aught I know.
Forzino, far as I know.
F'rall that, for all that, or notwithstanding, &c.
Friggit, frigate.
Frolics, country festival sports.
Frind, friend.
Furder, farther.

G

Gals, girls.
Gawkey, awkward.
Gimcracks, (nice bagatelles) curious trifles.
Gin, given, gave.
Gineral, Gin'ral, General.
Gineration, generation.
Glib, smooth, easy.
Gownd, gown.
Granny, grand-mother.

Guess, instead of being applied to things conjectural, misapplied to such as are past, present—certain ; believe, think.
Gum, foolish talk, nonsense
Gumtion, sense, understanding, intellect.

H

Han't, } have not.
Havn't, }
Hansum, handsome.
Harty, well
Hectored, bullied, insulted by domineering.
Her'n, her own, hers.

Heerd, heard.
Hild, held.
Hoss, horse.
Huffy, ill-natured.
Hull, whole.
Hum, home.
Humbly, homely.

I

Ile, oil.
Improve, employ, occupy.

Inyons, onions.

J

Jeerings, contemptuous sneers.
Jest, just.
Jeesting, jesting.
Jiffing, or *jiffin*, instantaneously.

Jumping jings, jingoes, expletives indicative of confirmation.
Jurk, jerk.

K

Keow, cow.
Ketch, catch.
Kill-dried, (the preparation of the meal of maize or Indian corn for exportation,) kiln-dried.

Kittle, kettle.
Kiver, cover.
Knack, faculty of doing things with facility.
Know'd, knew.

L

Larning, learning.
Leetle, little.
Lengthy, long.
Licker, liquor.

Lines, loins.
Lovyier, lover.
Lug, (very vulgar) bring, bring in, lift, hand.

M

Mad, (not in the usual sense, insane,) to make angry.
Mainly, mostly.
Mannerliness, good breeding, good manners.
Marcy, mercy.
Massiful, merciful.

Mayn't, may not.
Meb-be, may be.
Munching, (low word,) chewing with a mouth full.
Muggy, sultry, close air, very hot.

N

Naborly, neighbourly.
Nation, very extraordinarily.

Nationality, attachment to clan or country, belonging to, or fondness for a nation.

Native, (last syllable pro-
nounced long,) native.
Neest, nest.
Nice, smart, tidy, spruce.
Nicely, in good health.
Nip, (original American,)
pint, half pint bowl.

Notion, ⎫ used frequent-
Notions, ⎬ ly not in the
Notional, ⎭ English sense
of the words.
Nuther, neither.
Nick-nacks, trifling super-
fluous articles.

O

O, the Dickens, exclama-
tion.
Obstropulous, obstreper-
ous.
On't, on it, of it.
Ort, ought.

Outlandish, strange, foreign.
Overmatch, superior.
Owny towny, (*owny dow-
ny, ounty tounty*) pe-
culiarly belonging to
one.

P

Paerils, perils.
Parfect, perfect.
Parson, person.
Peek, ⎫ to observe
Peeking, ⎬ slily and
Peep, ⎭ sneakingly.
Pertection, protection.
Pertest, protest.
Pestered, very excessive-
ly.
Plaguy, as a degree of
comparison—very—to
enhance the force of the
word with which it is
connected.

Poke your fun, jeer, pos-
ter, plague.
Potecary, Apothecary.
Poorly, miserably, ill.
Prehaps, perhaps.
Presarved, preserved.
Pritty, pretty.
Pluck, heart, courage,
spirit.
Put out, disobliged, of-
fended.

Q

Quarte, quart.
Quiddities, trifling nice-
ties, odd behaviour.

Quiddles, disorder in the
head, moping disease in
horses, dizziness.

R

Railly, really.
Rather, (pronounced narrow on the first syllable) frequently used to diminish or qualify the term to which it is applied—sometimes pronounced *Ruth-er.*

Reckon, calculate, depend on the fact, sometimes nearly in the sense in which guess is misapplied.
Roiled, disturbed, applied to liquors and temper.
Rubbige, rubbish.
Ruff, roof.

S

Saie, say.
Sabba-da, Sabbath-day.
Saisse, or *Sairse,* sauce.
Saisy, saucy.
Sarpent, serpent.
Sarvice, service.
Sarvant, servant.
Sartinly, certainly.
Scart, scared.
Scholard, scholar.
Seed, saw.
Sen, since.
Sheep, ship.
Sha'n't, shall not.
Shabby, } applied to ill
Shabbily, } looks or appearance in dress, vulgar.
Shood, should.
Shugar, sugar.
Shute, shoot.
Shure, sure.
Sitch, such.
Slim, } used in a peculiar
Slink, } sense.
Snap, to break short.
Snappish, petulant, easily provoked.

Sneaking, used in a peculiar sense.
Sparked it, (young men keeping company with young women and sitting by the fire after the the family has gone to bed.) courting.
Spook, (a word used by the Low Dutch in some parts of America,) apparition, ghost, hobgoblin.
Shose, suppose.
Spry, acute, nimble.
Sperit, spirit.
Spunk, courage.
Staggers, horse-apoplexy, wild conduct, madness.
Stan, Stand.
Stickling, hesitating, delaying.
Stiddy, steady.
Strait, straight.
Stur, stir.
Stunded, stunned.
Stump, challenge.
Sumwheres, somewhere.

Swags, exclamation.
Swamp it, ridiculous kind of asseveration.
Swimmed, swam.

Swound, swoon.
Swap, Swop, exchange.
Suzz ! Surs ! a corruption from Sirs.

T

Tarms, terms.
Tarnation, used in a peculiar sense.
Tantrums, Tantarams, do.
Tatterations, do.
Tawking, talking.
Techy, easily irritated, froward.
Telled, told.
Toddy, (beverage) rum, sugar and water mixed together.
To-rights, immediately, instantly.

Trim, habiliments, dress.
Trade, physic, medicine.
Truck, to barter, exchange one thing for another.
Trampoosing, traversing.
Tuff, tough.
Twang, nasal pronunciation.
Twistical, tortuous, not above-board, not quite moral.
Twitted, reproached.

U

Underlin, an inferior animal.
Unpossible, impossible.

Uppish, (vulgarism) proud, arrogant.

V

Vacarme, (French) to make a noise, racket, scold.
Van, exclamation.
Vaggers, do.
Vartuous, virtuous.
Varmount, Vermont.
Varses, verses.
Vittles, victuals.

Venture, offer a bet, lay a wager, stake.
Vouch, vouch it, vouch on't, a species of asseveration.
Vow, do.
Vum, do.
Vumpers, do.
Viges, voyages.

K

W

Wage, or *wager,* to bet.   *Wood,* would.

Y

Yawping, (probably from   *Yit,* yet.
yelping) a noisy fellow.   *Your'n,* your own, yours.

ERRATA.

Prologue—8th line from top, for *Southey* read *Southern.*
Page 30, 6th line from bottom, read *spooks* for *spoons.*
Page 36, 3d line from top, read *yawping* for *gawping.*
Page 49, 21st line from top, omit the word *and.*
Pages 58 and 59, for the word *sheep-stick* read *sheep tick.*

BIBLIOGRAPHY
AND INDEX

BIBLIOGRAPHY
A Note on Sources

Professor A. M. Drummond has contributed greatly to the general study of early American theatre through his encouragement, supervision, and development of several doctoral dissertations in this area. This book is an extensive reworking of one of these unpublished studies, *Yankee Theatre: 1825–1850*, Cornell University, 1948, by the present writer. In addition to the two discussions by Constance Rourke, mentioned in the Acknowledgments, the following treatments of the stage Yankee should be specifically noted: Jonathan W. Curvin, "The Stage Yankee," *Studies in Speech and Drama in Honor of Alexander M. Drummond* (Ithaca, Cornell University Press, 1944); Richard Moody, *America Takes the Stage: Romanticism in American Drama and Theatre, 1750–1900* (Bloomington, Indiana University Press, 1955); Portia Kernodle, "Yankee Types on the London Stage, 1824–1880," *Speech Monographs*, XIV (1947), 139–147; Arthur H. Quinn, *A History of the American Drama from the Beginnings to the Civil War* (New York, Harper & Bros., 1923); Richard M. Dorson, "The Yankee on the Stage—A Folk Hero of American Drama," *New England Quarterly*, XIII (September, 1940), 467–493. Other pertinent and useful studies are these: Jeannette Tandy, *Crackerbox Philosophers in American Humor and Satire* (New York, Columbia University Press, 1925); Walter Blair, *Native American Humor* (New York, American Book Company, 1937); V. L. O. Chittick, *Ring-Tailed Roarers* (Caldwell, Idaho, The Caxton Printers, 1941). Other studies specifically associated with the backgrounds of the Yankee actors are cited in the notes on the chapters devoted to those subjects.

A. YANKEE-THEATRE PLAYS

The plays in this list were acted by the four leading impersonators of Yankee character: James Hackett, George Hill, Dan Marble, and Joshua Silsbee. The list has been compiled from scattered sources. Odell's *Annals of the New York Stage* and Wilson's *History of the Philadelphia Theatre* have been used extensively, with supplementary checks in other area theatre histories where available. Newspapers, magazines, and playbills have also provided details. A title preceded by an asterisk is extant in either manuscript or print. Each entry includes these categories of information: title, author if known, the date (month, day, year) and place of first performance, name of the Yankee character and the actor who first performed it. L.C.C. refers to the Lord Chamberlain's Collection in the British Museum.

Adventure, The; or, The Yankee in Tripoli. By Joseph S. Jones. November 18, 1835, New York (Park). Abner Tanner: George Hill. Hill also played this under the title *Free Trade! or, The Yankee in Tripoli.*

Advertising for a Wife; or, Ebenezer Venture. Disputed authorship (Lawrence Labree or Douglas Jerrold). October 11, 1841, St. Louis. Ebenezer Venture: Dan Marble.

All the World's a Stage. See *Our Jedidiah.*

Backwoodsman, The; or, Gamecock of the Wilderness. First-version authorship unknown. October ?, 1840, St. Louis. Second version by Leman Rede. March 12, 1846, New York (Park). Sampson Hardhead: Dan Marble. The character is advertised in St. Louis as "a Ranting Rousing Kentuckian" but in Rede's version he is definitely a Vermonter. Was this play first used as a competitor to Hackett's *Lion of the West* with its character of Nimrod Wildfire?

Battle of Chippewa. Authorship unknown. September 30, 1840, Cincinnati. Jerry Jenkins: Joshua Silsbee.

Battle of Lake Erie, The. By Joseph S. Jones. April 12, 1843, Boston (Tremont). Jethrod Oaktree: Joshua Silsbee. Was this a nautical Yankee? Jones wrote other characters of this sort. Quinn (*A History of the American Drama from the Beginnings to the Civil War,* p. 430) notes a performance of the play on October 31, 1842, but lists no actor for it; very possibly it was not Silsbee.

Boston Tea Party, The; or, Yankees in 1773. Authorship unknown. April 14, 1843, Boston (Tremont). Bill Ball: Joshua Silsbee.

Bumps; or, The Magnetized Yankee. Authorship unknown. April 15, 1844, Philadelphia (National). Abel Hartshorn: Joshua Silsbee. An alternate title was *Yankee Magnetism.*

Casper Hauser; or, The Down Easter. By Henry J. Finn. November 27, 1835, New York (Park). Dr. Lot Whittle: George Hill. Kendall, p. 94, reports that Finn himself staged the play in New Orleans (Camp Street) in February 1835. See also Ludlow, *Dramatic Life,* p. 424, for a performance in Mobile about the same date.

Catch a Weazle Asleep; or, Love and Starvation. Authorship unknown. January 16, 1841, New York (Chatham). Weazlewideawake: George Hill.

Celestial Empire, The; or, The Yankee in China. By Cornelius A. Logan.

(Quinn, *From the Beginnings to the Civil War*, p. 436) March 4, 1846, Philadelphia (Arch). [Unknown]: Joshua Silsbee. Falconbridge claims this as a Dan Marble play, but there is no record of his playing it. H. J. Conway has also been credited with the authorship. See *Mirror*, VIII (June 18, 1831), 393–395 for a possible source of the play in J. K. Paulding's story "Jonathan's Visit to the Celestial Empire."

Conspiracy, The; or, Who Tore Your Coat? Authorship unknown. October 30, 1840, New York (Hill's Theatre). Ikey Seekout: George Hill.

Courting in Connecticut. Authorship unknown. November 5, 1845, Philadelphia (Arch). [Unknown]: Joshua Silsbee. This may possibly be a story. Silsbee incorporated something of this sort in his London version of *The Forest Rose*.

Cut and Come Again. Authorship unknown. November 5, 1840, New York (Hill's Theatre). Return Strong: George Hill.

Day in France, A. By Charles Silby (or Selby). April 17, 1838, New York (Park). Josh Higgins: George Hill.

Diamond Cut Diamond; or, The Wolf of Brazil. By Joseph S. Jones April 1, 1840, New York (Chatham). Peleg Rowan: George Hill. Hill played a character named Peleg in *Fall of the Alamo* in 1836. See the entry for that title.

Doom of the Tory Guard, The. Authorship unknown. April 26, 1845, New York (Chatham). [Unknown]: George Hill.

*Down East; or, The Militia Training. See *The Militia Muster.*

Down East Bargain, A; or, Love in New York. By J. Moncrieff. May 18, 1837, New York (Park). Zephaniah Makepeace: George Hill. Who is J. Moncrieff? Could the author possibly be W. T. Moncrieff, who wrote *Tarnation Strange; or, More Jonathans* for London performance in July–October, 1838? L.C.C. No. 42948. None of the Yankee-theatre actors performed this play, but Moncrieff possibly wrote it for Hill, who was in London at the time the license was granted. Odell (*Annals*, IV, 129) suggests that *A Down East Bargain* is a rewriting of Samuel Woodworth's *Foundling of the Sea.*

East and West. By "a gentleman of Philadelphia." October 1, 1833, Philadelphia (Chestnut). Josh Horseradish: George Hill. Hill later played this under the title *Josh Horseradish; or, The Lying Valet.*

Ephraim Smooth. Authorship unknown. November 14, 1835, New York (Park). Ephraim Smooth: George Hill.

Fall of the Alamo. Authorship unknown. May 26, 1836, Philadelphia (Arch). Peleg: George Hill. How much of a Yankee play this may have been is questionable. It was undoubtedly whipped together very quickly to celebrate the news of the victory in Texas over Santa Anna, which had just been received. Other characters besides the Mexican general in the sketch were William Travis and Davy Crockett.

Family Ties; or, The Will of Uncle Josh. By J. M. Field and J. S. Robb. June 19, 1846, New York (Park). Josh Sims: Dan Marble.

Forest Rose, The; or, American Farmers. By Samuel Woodworth. October 7, 1825, New York (Chatham Garden). Jonathan Ploughboy: Alexander Simpson. This was first played by a Yankee-theatre actor on November 24, 1832, when George Hill acted it at the New York Park.

*New York, 1825.

*Boston: William V. Spenser, n.d. [c. 1855]. Acting edition.

*L.C.C.: License granted September 17, 1851. This is Silsbee's version for London performance.

Fortune Teller, The; or, The Pedlar of Saco. Authorship unknown. April 12, 1843, Boston (Tremont). Uriah Doo: Joshua Silsbee.

Foundling of the Sea. By Samuel Woodworth. May 5, 1833, New York (Park). Zachariah Dickerwell: George Hill. *Mirror*, X (May 18, 1833), 363, has a detailed summary.

Foundling; or, Yankee Fidelity. By R. C. McLellan. September 7, 1840, Cincinnati. Obediah Whitaker: Joshua Silsbee.

Free Trade! or, The Yankee in Tripoli. See *The Adventure.*

Green Mountain Boy, The; or, Love and Learning. By Joseph S. Jones. February 25, 1833, Philadelphia (Walnut Street but performed by the Chestnut Street Company). J. Homespun: George Hill. The name was altered for the New York (Park) performance on March 19, 1833, to Jedediah Homebred; this name was used in all subsequent billings.

*New York: Samuel French, n.d. [c. 1860].

Home in the West, A. By Colonel Bradbury. 1847, Boston (Athenaeum). [Unknown]: Dan Marble. Falconbridge (*Dan Marble*, p. 189) identifies Colonel Bradbury as "a talented editor, printer, etc. of Cincinnati, an intimate friend of Marble's."

Honest Roguery. Authorship unknown. November 13, 1843, New York (Chatham). Jabez Crampton: George Hill.

Hue and Cry. See *Yankee Land.*

Indian Wife, The; or, The Falls of Montmorency. By Henry J. Finn. May 27, 1830, New York (Park). Sergeant Peletiah Peabody: James Hackett. Clapp reports that this play, which Finn wrote in 1825, was dedicated to Daniel Webster. Hackett probably adapted it for his own playing.

Inquisitive Yankee, The; or, A Peep in All Corners. Authorship unknown. December 4, 1832, New York (Park). Joel Peep: George Hill. The character is listed as Joe Peep for a Philadelphia performance on October 8, 1833.

Job Fox; or, The Yankee Valet. By W. Bayle Bernard. October 1, 1834, New York (Park). Job Fox: James Hackett.
    *L.C.C. 42937. Hackett apparently cleared this for London production but never played it. License granted August 1, 1836.
    *Enthoven Collection: Manuscript copy with some deletions marked. Hackett's signature is on the front cover.

John Bull at Home; or, Jonathan in England. James Hackett's adaptation of George Colman's *Who Wants a Guinea?* December 3, 1828, New York (Park). Solomon Swap: James Hackett. This play was subsequently performed in America under the alternate title.
    *L.C.C. 42919. This manuscript copy bears the following notation on the front cover: "The Character of Solomon Swap altered from the original, Solomon Gundy, in Who Wants a Guinea?" This manuscript is an acting side for Solomon Swap. Hackett probably assumed that the play was acceptable and only the alterations would need new approval. License granted November 17, 1832.
    *Enthoven Collection: This is a promptbook of the play, New York: Samuel French, c. 1860, dated August 17, 1831. Changes have been inserted in a printed edition of Colman's play—detailed cuttings, new lines, a few stage directions. Colman's play is cut heavily throughout. Several other copies of marked scripts are in this collection.

Jonathan Doubikins; or, Jonathan in England. By Richard B. Peake. September 18, 1833, New York (Park). Jonathan Doubikins: James Hackett. This play was written originally for Charles Mathews in 1824, and first performed by him on September 3, 1824, in London (English Opera House). Both Hill and Silsbee played it.
    *London, n.d. [c. 1830].
    *L.C.C. 42868. License copy. Permission granted September 1, 1824.
    *Enthoven Collection: Hackett's promptbook, corrected and with calls inserted. May, 1838. By J. C. Ferrer, National Theatre, New York. A property list is included on the first page.

Jonathan in England. See *John Bull at Home.*

Jonathan in New York. Authorship unknown. June 19, 1826, New York (Park). Jonathan: James Hackett. This is the title given to Hackett's third New York appearance. The "Uncle Ben" story was included.

Josh Horseradish; or, The Lying Yankee. See *East and West.*

Kasper Hauser; or, The Down Easter. See *Casper Hauser.*

Knight of the Golden Fleece, The; or, The Yankee in Spain. By John Augustus Stone. September 10, 1834, New York (Park). Sy Saco: George Hill.

Lafitte, the Pirate of the Gulf. Authorship unknown. October ?, 1840, St. Louis. Hezekiah Homespun: Dan Marble.

Lion of the East; or, Life in New York. Authorship unknown. June 10, 1835, New York (Park). Major Jack Downing: George Hill. A version of this piece was performed in Philadelphia on May 15, 1835; was this actually the première? This play was also known as *The Yankee Lion.* Note also that Gates acted Jack Downing at the Bowery on May 21, 1834, under the title *Life in New York.*

Maiden's Vow, The. See *The Yankee in Time.*

Major Jack Downing; or, The Retired Politician. Authorship unknown. May 10, 1834, New York (Park). Jack Downing: James Hackett. This play was definitely based on Seba Smith's *The Life and Writings of Major Jack Downing of Downingville,* 1833.

Militia Muster, The; or, Down East. Another alternate title is *The Militia Training.* Original version (*Down East*) was probably composed by James Hackett. Revised version in 1832 by S. Beazley. April 17, 1830, New York (Park). Major Joe Bunker: James Hackett.

    *L.C.C. 42924. Manuscript credited to S. Beazley.

    *Enthoven Collection. MS. On cover: as altered by S. Beazley from "Down East." License granted November 19, 1833. This is an error. The date should read 1832.

    *Enthoven Collection. MS. "The Skeleton of the Ludicrous Scene of the Militia Training." This copy has cast, properties, and full stage directions.

Moderns, The; or, A Trip to the Springs. By a Gentleman of New York. April 18, 1831, New York (Park). Melodious Migrate: James Hackett.

    *Enthoven Collection: Manuscript actor's side (probably Hackett's) for the principal character. It begins with Act I, Scene 3. Dated 1831 on the cover.

New Notions. See *Speculations; or, Major Wheeler in Europe.*

Nick of Time. Authorship unknown. May 8, 1843, Philadelphia (Arch). Obediah: Joshua Silsbee. The title is also an alternate for *Sam Patch in France,* but the characters are different.

Of Age To-Night; or, Natur's Nature. Authorship unknown. January 22, 1842, New York (Chatham). Jubal Judex: George Hill.

O.K. Authorship unknown. November 4, 1840, New York (Hill's Theatre). Sober Second-thoughts: George Hill.

Old Times in Virginia. See *The Yankee Pedlar.*

Oregon. Authorship unknown. March 17, 1846, New York (Park).

Oregon; or, the Disputed Territory. By Joseph M. Field. March 17, 1846, New York (Park). Uncle Sam: Dan Marble. This "musical" was first performed in Mobile on January 26, 1846. See Ludlow, *Dramatic Life*, pp. 623–624 for details of cast and contents.

*Our Jedidiah; or, Great Attraction. By O. E. Durivage. February 28, 1849, New York (Olympic). Curtis Chunk: Dan Marble. This play was published and later played under the title: *The Stage-Struck Yankee.* This last title was used by Marble as an alternate for a version of *All the World's a Stage,* which he performed at the New York Park on April 14, 1847. The principal comic character in *All the World's a Stage* is Diggory; how much of a Yankee Marble made him we do not know.

*New York Drama. Vol. 4. New York: Wheat and Garnett, 1878.

*New York: Samuel French, n.d.

Ovid and Obid; or, Yankee Blunders. Authorship unknown. April 30, 1834, Philadelphia (Chestnut). Ovid Bigelow: George Hill. *The Two Ovids* was the title Hill used in Philadelphia for the first performance, but he altered it for the New York Park on September 24, 1834.

Paul Pry from Down East. Adapted from *Paul Pry* by J. Poole. March 24, 1831, Philadelphia (Chestnut). Paul Pry: James Hackett. Apparently another attempt by Hackett to alter an established English comedy to a Yankee play. Paul Pry is available in manuscript: L.C.C. 42879.

Peaceful Pelton; or, The Vermonter. By H. A. Buckingham. November 4, 1837, New York (Park). Peaceful Pelton: George Hill.

*People's Lawyer, The. By J. S. Jones. December 17, 1842, New York (Park). Solon Shingle: George Hill.

*Boston: William Spenser, 1856.

*This play has been published also under the title of *Solon Shingle,* probably John Owens' version, in *The Drama,* ed. Alfred Bates, Vol. 20, London, 1903.

Pilot, The. Authorship unknown. September 25, 1843, New York (Chatham). Sergeant Drill: George Hill.

Rebellion in Canada, The; or, The Burning of the Caroline. By Silas S. Steele. June 10, 1843, Boston (National). Hector Grizzle: Joshua Silsbee. Quinn (*Beginnings to the Civil War,* p. 477) notes a first playing of the play at Baltimore in 1841 but no Yankee is mentioned. Silsbee played it at the New York Chatham on June 16, 1843, as *The Yankee at Niagara.* Did he intend to confuse audiences with Marble's *Sam Patch?*

Redwood; or, Connecticut Curiosities. By J. P. Addams. September ?, 1842, St. Louis. Josh Doolittle: Joshua Silsbee.

Sam Patch's First Visit to Europe. Authorship unknown. September 5, 1850, Philadelphia (Arch). Sam: Joshua Silsbee. Is this an alternate title for *Sam Patch in France?*

Sam Patch in France; or, Nick of Time. By J. P. Addams. April 16, 1840, New York (Bowery). Sam: Dan Marble.

*Sam Patch the Jumper. Authorship unknown. October 26, 1844, London (Adelphi). Sam: Dan Marble.

　*L.C.C.: License granted October 22, 1844. This play was probably put together in London especially for Marble's appearance there.

Sam Patch, the Yankee Jumper. By E. H. Thompson. November ?, 1836, Buffalo. Yankee Sam: Dan Marble. It was first played in New York (Park) on July 31, 1838.

Sam Slick. Authorship unknown. April 24, 1844, New York (Chatham). Sam: Joshua Silsbee. This was probably an attempt to adapt Haliburton's character, Sam Slick the Clockmaker. Silsbee played it under that title in St. Louis in June, 1846.

*Seth Slope; or, Done for a Hundred. By Joseph Sterling Coyne. July 22, 1839, London (New Strand). Seth Slope: George Hill.

　*L.C.C.: License approved July 15, 1839.

Shabby Gentility; or, Sailors on a Lee Shore. Authorship unknown. April 10, 1840, New York (Chatham). Peter Funk: George Hill. Was this a rare attempt by Hill to play a nautical Yankee?

*She Would be a Soldier; or, The Plains of Chippewa. By Mordecai Noah. First playing by a Yankee actor: March 20, 1832, New York (Chatham). Jerry Mayflower: Dan Marble. This is not a Yankee-theatre play, but was written by Noah in 1819 and played frequently for several years. It is included because of its use by Marble.

　*New York: Longworth's Dramatic Repository, 1819.

*Solomon Swap. See *John Bull at Home.*

*Speculations; or, Major Wheeler in Europe. Also titled *New Notions.* By W. Bayle Bernard. September 4, 1837, New York (Park). Major Wheeler: George Hill.

　*L.C.C.: License granted July 21, 1838.

Speculations; or, The March of Intellect. Authorship unknown. September 26, 1843, St. Louis. Freeze-Up-Wrinkle: Joshua Silsbee.

Spy in New York, The. Authorship unknown. November 6, 1843, New York (Chatham). Content Jones: George Hill.

*Stage-Struck Yankee, The. See *Our Jedidiah.*

*Sylvester Daggerwood. By James Hackett. July 6, 1826, New York (Park). Sylvester Daggerwood: James Hackett.

　*L.C.C. 42883. License granted March 31, 1827.

*Enthoven Collection: Manuscript promptbook with notes in Hackett's hand.

*Times, The; or, Life in New York. By a Gentleman of this city [New York]. December 10, 1829, New York (Park). Industrious Doolittle: James Hackett. An alternate title is *Travellers in America*.
 *Enthoven Collection: This is only a fragment, possibly a "side" for Industrious Doolittle.

Times That Tried Us, The; or, Yankees in 1777. By H. Conway. October?, 1840, St. Louis. Uzzial Putnam: Dan Marble.

Tourists, The. Authorship unknown. March 19, 1840, New York (Chatham). Ebenezer Fish: George Hill.

Trip to Niagara. By William Dunlap. First played by a Yankee actor: December 30, 1831, Philadelphia (Arch). Doolittle: George Hill. First performance December 12, 1828, New York (Park).
 *New York: E. B. Clayton, 1830.

Turn Out. Authorship unknown. September 8, 1837, New York (Park). Gregory: George Hill.

Vermonter, The; or, Love and Phrenology. Authorship unknown. January 17, 1842, New York (Chatham). Zephaniah Twang: George Hill.

Vermont Wool Dealer, The. Alternate titles: *The Yankee Traveller, The Wool Pedlar, The Vermonter*. By C. A. Logan. April 13, 1840, New York (Bowery). Deuteronomy Dutiful: Dan Marble.
 *New York: Samuel French, n.d.
 *L.C.C.: 42978. License granted September 28, 1844.

Veteran of Seventy-Six, The. Authorship unknown. October 31, 1840, New York (Hill's Theatre). Colonel Slimmerkins: George Hill.

Wag of Maine, The. See *Yankee Land*.

Western Heir, The. Authorship unknown. June 15, 1846, New York (Chatham). Joel Dean: George Hill.

Wife for a Day. By Bayle Bernard. March 18, 1839, London (Haymarket). Nathan Tucker: George Hill.
 *L.C.C.: License granted March 15, 1839.

Yankee Abroad. Authorship unknown. May 5, 1843, Philadelphia (Arch). [Unknown]: Joshua Silsbee. This may be an alternate title for a play already identified, perhaps *Sam Patch in France*.

Yankee in China, The. See *The Celestial Empire*.

Yankee in 1776. Authorship unknown. June 16, 1843, New York (Chatham). [Unknown]: Joshua Silsbee. This may be an alternate title for a play already identified.

Yankee in Time, The; or, The Maiden's Vow. By J. P. Addams. January 2, 1838, Philadelphia (Walnut). Jacob Jewsharp: Dan Marble.

Yankee Land; or, The Foundling of the Apple Orchard. Original title: *The Wag of Maine.* By C. A. Logan. April 16, 1834, New York (Park). Mischievous Joe: James Hackett. This play appears in three versions: *The Wag of Maine.* Enthoven Collection: The names of the characters in this manuscript version differ from the other versions but the plot is the same.

Yankee Land. New York: Samuel French, n.d. This is Logan's redevelopment of the original. Marble first played it at the New York Bowery on November 19, 1842.

Yankee Land. L.C.C.: License granted October 7, 1844. This version is a rewriting of Logan's second version. Marble subsequently played it under the title *Hue and Cry.*

Yankee Lion, The. See *Lion of the East.*

Yankee Magnetism. See *Bumps.*

Yankee Pedlar, The; or, Old Times in Virginia. First-version authorship unknown. May 8, 1835, Philadelphia (Walnut). Hiram Dodge: George Hill. Could this have been a revision of *Foundling of the Sea?*

*L.C.C. 42937: License granted October 29, 1836. This version is probably a rewriting by W. Bayle Bernard of the first version. It was first played at London's Drury Lane November 1, 1836. Hill played this version widely.

*L.C.C. 42944: This version, submitted to the Licencer in 1837, seems to be a corrected copy of the 1836 version. Why this copy was filed is unexplained.

The New York Drama. New York: Wheat and Garnett, 1876. This is a revised version by Morris Barnett. It was apparently rewritten for Dan Marble.

Yankee Preacher, The. Authorship unknown. June 16, 1843, New York (Chatham). [Unknown]: Joshua Silsbee.

Zekiel Homespun. Authorship unknown. April 11, 1840, New York (Chatham). Zekiel: George Hill. Was this a Yankee adaptation of Colman's *The Heir at Law* or a new sketch? Joseph Jefferson played Zekiel Homespun to the Pangloss of Charles Mathews at the Chestnut Theatre, Philadelphia, in 1823.

B. Yankee-Theatre Stories

Amos in the Stage Coach; or, The Yankee in the Lard Tub (Hill).

Bunker Hill Back, The; or, The LaFayette Dinner at Faneuil Hall (Hill).

Hiram's Courting Scrape with Nancy Slocum and Sal Barter (Hill).

How to Sell a Fox Skin (Hackett).

Jethro R. Dutton's Journey to the Genesee Country (Hill).
Jonathan's Visit to Buffalo, Seneca Village, etc. (Hill).
Misfortune with the Pumpkin Pye, The (Hill).
Soap Tub and the Ugly Aunt, The (Hill).
Solomon in the Pantry; or, Custard Pudding No Seat for a Man (Hill).
Three Chances for a Wife and a Visit to Zeb Hamkins (Hill).
Uncle Ben (Hackett).
Wild Animals (Hill).
Yankee in Trouble, The; or, Zephaniah in the Pantry (Hill).

For additional stories and lecture material used by George Hill the reader is referred to the two volumes on Hill's life: *Scenes from the Life of an Actor* and *Life and Recollections of Yankee Hill*. The first contains the "Lecture on New England," which Hill used extensively in solo platform appearances. The second includes not only this "Lecture" but several other anecdotes and incidents. This is the only extensive repository of Yankee materials other than plays used by Yankee-theatre actors.

C. OTHER PUBLISHED PLAYS MENTIONED IN THE TEXT

Aiken, George L. *Uncle Tom's Cabin*. New York: Samuel French, n.d.
Barker, James Nelson. *Tears and Smiles*. Philadelphia: Printed by T. & G. Palmer for G. E. Blake, 1808.
Herne, James A. *Shore Acres*. In *Shore Acres and Other Plays*. Revised by Mrs. James A. Herne. New York: Samuel French, 1928.
Humphreys, David. *The Yankey in England*. [Connecticut, 1815].
Lindsley, A. B. *Love and Friendship; or, Yankee Notions*. New York: D. Longworth, 1809.
Mathews, Charles, and James Smith. *Mathews in America; or, The Theatrical Wanderer*. London: Hodgson & Co., n.d.
————. *Sketches of Mr. Mathews's Celebrated Trip to America*. London: J. Limbard, c. 1825. The authorship of this narrated version has also been attributed to Anne Jackson Mathews.
Pratt, W. W. *Ten Nights in a Bar-Room*. New York: Samuel French, n.d.
Smith, W. H. *The Drunkard; or, The Father Saved*. Samuel French: New York, n.d.
Thompson, Denman. *The Old Homestead*. In *S.R.O.*, compiled by Bennett Cerf and Van H. Cartwell. Garden City, New York: Doubleday, Doran, & Co., 1944.
Tyler, Royall. *The Contrast*. New York: Dunlap Society Edition, 1887.

D. Archival Materials

Albert Davis and Messmore Kendall Collections. Hoblitzelle Theatre
    Arts Library. University of Texas, Austin, Texas.
Enthoven Collection. Victoria and Albert Museum. London
Genesee County Court Records. Batavia, New York.
Harvard Theatre Collection. Widener Library. Cambridge.
Lord Chamberlain's Collection of Plays. British Museum. London.
Theater Collection. New York Public Library. New York, N.Y.

E. General Sources

The works cited in this list are selected source materials used in the
preparation of this book. The student should consult other basic bibli-
ographies for the wider range of early American-theatre and general
cultural materials available for the period of this study.

Books

Alger, William R. *Life of Edwin Forrest*. 2 vols. Philadelphia: J. B.
    Lippincott, 1877.
Bagster-Collins, Jeremy. *George Colman, the Younger*. New York:
    King's Crown Press, 1946.
Baker, Henry Barton. *English Actors from Shakespeare to Macready*.
    2 vols. New York: Holt, 1879.
Bates, Alfred (ed.). *The Drama*. 20 vols. London: Athenian Society,
    1903–1909.
Beecher, Henry Ward. *Lectures to Young Men on Various Important
    Subjects*. New York: Saxton and Miles, 1846.
Berger, Max. *The British Traveller in America, 1836–1860*. New York:
    Columbia University Press, 1943.
Bernard, John. *Retrospections of America, 1797–1811*. Edited by Mrs.
    Bayle Bernard. New York: Harper & Brothers, 1887.
Birdoff, Harry. *The World's Greatest Hit*. New York: S. F. Vanni, 1947.
Blair, Walter. *Native American Humor (1800–1900)*. New York: Amer-
    ican Book Company, 1937.
Botkin, B. A. *A Treasury of American Folklore*. New York: Crown
    Publishers, 1944.
Brooks, Van Wyck. *The World of Washington Irving*. Philadelphia:
    Blakiston Co., 1844.
Brown, T. Allston. *History of the American Stage*. New York: Dick and
    Fitzgerald, 1870.
Bunn, Alfred. *The Stage: Both Before and Behind the Curtain*. 2 vols.
    Philadelphia: Lea and Blanchard, 1840.

Butler, Frances Anne. *Journal*. 2 vols. London: John Murray, 1835.

Carson, William G. B. *Managers in Distress: The St. Louis Stage 1840–1844*. St. Louis: St. Louis Historical Society, 1949.

———. *The Theatre on the Frontier: The Early Years of the St. Louis Stage*. Chicago: University of Chicago Press, 1932.

Chittick, V. L. O. *Ring-Tailed Roarers*. Caldwell, Idaho: The Caxton Printers, 1941.

Clapp, William W., Jr. *A Record of the Boston Stage*. Boston: James Munroe and Company, 1853.

Clayton, W. W. *History of Steuben County*. Philadelphia: Lewis, Peck and Co., 1879.

Clements, Samuel, and Charles Dudley Warner. *The Gilded Age*. 2 vols. Hartford: The American Publishing Company, 1903.

Coad, Oral S., and Edwin S. Mims, Jr. *The American Stage*. Vol. 14 of "The Pageant of America Series." New Haven: Yale University Press, 1929.

———. *William Dunlap*. New York: The Dunlap Society, 1917.

Cooper, James Fenimore. *Gleanings in Europe*. Edited by Robert Spiller. 2 vols. New York: Oxford University Press, 1928.

———. *Notions of the Americans*. 2 vols. New York: Henry Colburn, 1828.

Cowell, Joe. *Thirty Years Passed among the Players in England and America*. New York: Harper & Bros., 1844.

Crawford, Mary Caroline. *The Romance of the Theatre*. Boston: Little, Brown and Co., 1913.

Curvin, Jonathan W. *The Realistic Tradition in American Art and Drama*. Unpublished dissertation. Ithaca, New York: Cornell University, 1941.

———. "The Stage Yankee." In *Studies in Speech and Drama in Honor of Alexander M. Drummond*. Ithaca, New York: Cornell University Press, 1944.

Dickens, Charles. *American Notes for General Circulation*. London: Chapman and Hall, 1850.

Dictionary of American Biography. Edited by Allen Johnson and Dumas Malone. 7 vols. New York: Charles Scribner's Sons, 1931.

Dimmick, Ruth Crosby. *Our Theatres To-Day and Yesterday*. New York: H. K. Fly Co., 1913.

Dunlap, William. *Diary of William Dunlap*. 3 vols. New York: The New York Historical Society, 1930.

———. *History of the American Theatre*. New York: J & J Harper, 1832.

Durang, Charles. *History of the Philadelphia Stage between the Years*

1749 and 1855. Arranged and illustrated by Thompson Westcott, and clipped from the Philadelphia Sunday Dispatch. University of Pennsylvania Library.

Duyckinck, Evert A., and George L. Duyckinck. *Cyclopaedia of American Literature*. 2 vols. New York: Charles Scribner, 1855.

Dwight, Timothy. *Travels; in New-England and New-York*. 4 vols. New Haven: Published by Timothy Dwight, 1822.

Falconbridge (Jonathan F. Kelly). *Dan Marble: A Biographical Sketch*. New York: DeWitt and Davenport, 1851.

Field, J. M. *The Drama in Pokerville*. Philadelphia: T. B. Peterson and Brothers, 1847.

Finn, H. J. (ed.). *American Comic Annual*. Boston: Richardson, Lord & Holbrook, 1831.

Firkins, Ina Ten Eyck (comp.). *Index to Plays, 1800–1926*. New York: H. W. Wilson Co., 1927.

Fitzgerald, Percy. *Samuel Foote*. London: n.p., 1910.

Forster, John. *The Life of Charles Dickens*. Edited by J. W. T. Ley. London: C. Palmer, c. 1928.

Foust, Clement E. *The Life and Dramatic Works of Robert M. Bird*. New York: Knickerbocker Press, 1919.

Goldberg, Isaac. *Major Noah*. New York: Alfred A. Knopf, 1937.

Graham, Philip. *Showboats: The History of an American Institution*. Austin: University of Texas Press, 1951.

Great Metropolis, The. 2 vols. London: Saunders and Otley, 1837.

Hackett, James Henry. *Notes, Criticism, and Correspondence upon Shakespeare's Plays and Actors*. New York: Carleton, 1863.

Haliburton, Thomas C. *Traits of American Humor*. London: Hurst and Blackett, Ltd., n.d. [c. 1866].

——. *Judge Haliburton's Yankee Stories*. Philadelphia: T. B. Peterson and Brothers, n.d. [c. 1880].

Hall, Basil. *Travels in North America*. 3 vols. Edinburgh: Cadell and Co., 1829.

Hamilton, Thomas. *Men and Manners in America*. Edinburgh: W. Blackwood, 1834.

Hazlitt, William. *The Collected Works of William Hazlitt*. Edited by A. R. Waller and Arnold Glover. 12 vols. London: J. M. Dent and Co., 1902–1904.

——. *Dramatic Essays*. London: Walter Scott, 1895.

Herold, Amos L. *James Kirke Paulding, Versatile American*. New York: Columbia University Press, 1926.

Hewitt, Barnard. *Theatre U.S.A., 1668–1957*. New York: McGraw-Hill, 1959.

Hill, Frank. *American Plays Printed 1714–1830*. Stanford: Stanford University Press, 1934.

Hill, George. *Scenes from the Life of an Actor. Compiled from the Journals, Letters, and Memoranda of the Late Yankee Hill by Cordelia Hill*. New York: Garrett and Co., 1853. See also W. K. Northall, *Life and Recollections of Yankee Hill*.

Hone, Philip. *The Diary of Philip Hone*. Edited by Allan Nevins. 2 vols. New York: Dodd, Mead and Co., 1927.

Hoole, W. Stanley. *The Ante-Bellum Charleston Theatre*. Tuscaloosa: University of Alabama Press, 1946.

Howard, Leon. *The Connecticut Wits*. Chicago: University of Chicago Press, 1943.

Huneker, James G. *The Philharmonic Society of New York*. New York: Privately printed [c. 1890].

Hunt, Leigh. *The Autobiography of Leigh Hunt*. London: Smith, Elder and Co., 1870.

―――. *Critical Essays on the Performers of the London Theatres*. London: Printed by and for John Hunt, at the office of the *News*, 1807.

Hutton, Laurence. *Plays and Players*. New York: Hurd and Houghton, 1875.

Ireland, Joseph. *Fifty Years of a Play-Goer's Journal, 1798–1848*. 2 vols. New York: Samuel French, 1860.

―――. *Records of the New York Stage from 1750–1860*. 2 vols. New York: T. H. Morrell, 1866–1867.

―――. *Records of the New York Stage from 1750–1860*. 9 vols. Cornell University Library, Ithaca, N.Y. Extra illustrated edition. T. H. Morrell (New York, 1886) is the publisher of the text.

Irving, Pierre. *The Life and Letters of Washington Irving*. 3 vols. New York: G. P. Putnam's Sons, 1883.

Jackson, George Stuyvesant. *Early Songs of Uncle Sam*. Boston: Bruce Humphries, 1933.

James, Reese D. *Old Drury of Philadelphia*. Philadelphia: University of Pennsylvania, 1932.

Jefferson, Joseph. *Autobiography*. New York: Century Co., 1889.

Jordan, Philip, and Lillian Kessler. *Songs of Yesterday*. Garden City: Doubleday, Doran and Co., 1941.

Kendall, John. *The Golden Age of the New Orleans Theatre*. Baton Rouge: Louisiana State University Press [c. 1952].

Kittredge, George Lyman. *The Old Farmer and His Almanack*. Boston: W. Ware and Co., 1904.

Krapp, George Philip. *The English Language in America*. 2 vols. New York: The Century Co., 1925.

Leman, Walter M. *Memories of an Old Actor*. San Francisco: A. Roman Co., 1886.

Logan, Olive. *Apropos of Women and Theatres*. New York: Carleton, 1869.

————. *The Mimic World and Public Exhibitions*. Philadelphia: New World Publishing Co., 1871.

Longstreet, Augustus B. *Georgia Scenes*. New York: Harper & Bros., 1840.

Lord, Clifford L., and Elizabeth H. Lord. *Historical Atlas of the United States*. New York: Henry Holt and Co., 1944.

Lowell, James Russell. *The Biglow Papers*. New York: Houghton, Mifflin Co., 1894.

Ludlow, N. M. *Dramatic Life as I Found It*. St. Louis: G. I. Jones, 1880.

McCullough, Bruce W. *The Life and Writings of Richard Penn Smith*. Philadelphia: University of Pennsylvania, 1917.

McKay, Frederic E., and Charles E. Wingate. *Famous American Actors of To-Day*. New York: Thomas Y. Crowell and Co., 1896.

MacKay, Charles. *Life and Liberty in America*. New York: Harper & Bros., 1859.

MacMinn, George R. *The Theatre of the Golden Era in California*. Caldwell, Idaho: The Caxton Printers, 1941.

Macready, William Charles. *The Diaries of William Charles Macready, 1833–51*. Edited by William Toynbee. 2 vols. London: Chapman and Hall, 1912.

————. *Macready's Reminiscences*. Edited by Frederick Pollock. New York: Macmillan & Co., 1875.

McVicker, J. H. *The Theatre: Its Early Days in Chicago*. Chicago: Knight and Leonard, 1884.

Martineau, Harriet. *Society in America*. 2 vols. New York: Saunders and Otley, 1837.

Mathews, Charles. *Memoirs of Charles Mathews*. Edited by Mrs. Mathews. 5 vols. London: Richard Bentley, 1839.

————. Same. 6 vols. Extra-illustrated edition.

————. *The Life and Correspondence of Charles Mathews, The Elder Comedian*. Edited by Mrs. Mathews. Abridged by Edmund Yates. London: Routledge, Warne, and Routledge, 1860. Illustrated edition of the work of Charles Mathews the Elder. See Moreau, Charles C.

Matthews, J. Brander, and Laurence Hutton (eds.). *Actors and Actresses of Great Britain and the United States*. 5 vols. New York: Cassell, 1886.

Matthiessen, F. O. *American Renaissance*. New York: Oxford University Press, 1946.

Mayorga, Margaret G. *A Short History of American Drama*. New York: Dodd, Mead and Co., 1943.

Mesick, Jane Louise. *The English Traveller in America, 1785–1835*. New York: Columbia University Press, 1922.

Minningerode, Meade. *The Fabulous Forties*. New York: G. P. Putnam's Sons, 1924.

Moody, Richard. *America Takes the Stage: Romanticism in American Drama and Theatre, 1750–1900*. Bloomington: Indiana University Press, 1955.

Moreau, Charles C. (collector and arranger). *Charles Mathews (The Elder)*. Illustrated with portraits, playbills, etc. New York, 1891. This unique collection is available only in the Hoblitzelle Theatre Arts Library, University of Texas.

Morris, George P. *Poems by George P. Morris: With a Memoir by the Author*. New York: Charles Scribner, 1860.

Morris, Reverend M. C. F. *Yorkshire Folk-Talk*. London: Henry Frowde, 1892.

Moses, Montrose J. *The American Dramatist*. Boston: Little, Brown and Co., 1925.

———. *Famous Actor Families in America*. New York: Thomas Crowell, 1906.

———. *Representative Plays by American Dramatists*. New York: E. P. Dutton, 1925.

Mowatt, Anna Cora. *Autobiography of an Actress*. Boston: Ticknor, Reed, and Fields, 1854.

Munden, Joseph S. *Memoirs of Joseph Shepherd Munden. By His Son*. 5 vols. Extra illustrated. London: Richard Bentley, 1844.

Murray, Charles Augustus. *Travels in North America*. 2 vols. London: R. Bentley, 1839.

Mussey, Barrows. *Yankee Life by Those Who Lived It*. New York: Alfred A. Knopf, 1947.

Muzzy, David Sayville. *History of the American People*. New York: Ginn and Co., 1927.

Neal, John. *American Writers*. Edited by Fred Pattee. Durham: Duke University Press, 1937.

———. *The Down-Easters*. 2 vols. New York: Harper & Bros., 1833.

Nicoll, Allardyce. *A History of Early Nineteenth Century Drama, 1800–1850*. 2 vols. Cambridge, England: The University Press, 1930.

———. *A History of the English Drama, 1660–1900*. Cambridge, England: The University Press, 1959.

Northall, William Knight. *Before and Behind the Curtain*. New York: W. F. Burgess, 1851.

————. Same. Extra-illustrated edition. Hoblitzelle Theatre Arts Library, The University of Texas, Austin.

———— (ed.). *Life and Recollections of Yankee Hill*. New York: W. F. Burgess, 1850. See also George Hill, *Scenes from the Life of an Actor*.

Odell, George C. D. *Annals of the New York Stage*. 15 vols. New York: Columbia University Press, 1927–1949.

Opinions of the British Press on the Performances of G. H. Hill. Collected by a Friend. New York: John F. Trow[bridge], 1837.

Orbeck, Anders. *Early New England Pronunciation*. Ann Arbor, Michigan: George Wahr, 1927.

Orians, G. Harrison. *A Short History of American Literature*. New York: F. S. Crofts and Co., 1940.

Owens, Mrs. John E. *Memories of the Professional and Social Life of John E. Owens*. Baltimore: John Murphy, 1892.

Page, Eugene R. (ed.). *Metamora and Other Plays*. Princeton: Princeton University Press, 1941.

Parrington, Vernon L. *Main Currents in American Thought*. 3 vols. New York: Harcourt, Brace and Co., 1927–1930.

Paul, Howard. *Dashes of American Humor*. New York: Garrett and Co., 1853.

Paulding, James Kirke. *The Backwoodsman*. Philadelphia: M. Thomas, 1818.

————. *The Diverting History of John Bull and Brother Jonathan*. New York: Harper & Bros., 1835.

———— and William I. Paulding. *American Comedies*. Philadelphia: Carey and Hart, 1847.

Paulding, William I. *Literary Life of James K. Paulding*. New York: Charles Scribner, 1867.

Peake, Richard B. *Memoirs of the Colman Family*. London: R. Bentley [c. 1845].

Phelps, H. P. *Players of a Century*. Albany: Joseph McDonough, 1880.

Phillips, Mary E. *James Fenimore Cooper*. New York: John Lane, 1913.

Power, Tyrone. *Impressions of America*. 2 vols. London: Richard Bentley, 1836.

Quinn, Arthur Hobson. *A History of the American Drama from the Beginning to the Civil War*. New York: Harper & Bros., 1923.

————. *A History of the American Drama from the Civil War to the Present Day*. New York: F. S. Crofts and Co., 1937.

————. *Representative American Plays*. New York: D. Appleton-Century Co., 1938.

Reed, Perley Isaac. *Realistic Presentation of American Characters in*

Native American Plays Prior to 1870. Columbus: Ohio State University Press, 1918.

Rees, James. *The Dramatic Authors of America.* Philadelphia: G. B. Zieber, 1845.

———. *The Life of Edwin Forrest.* Philadelphia: T. B. Peterson and Brothers, 1874.

Rejected Addresses, The. "Opening of the New Park Theatre." New York: Nathaniel Smith, 1821.

Rice, Charles. *The London Theatres in the Eighteen-Thirties.* Edited by Arthur Colby Sprague and Bertram Shuttleworth. London: Society for Theatre Research, 1950.

Roarbach, O. A. *Catalogue of American Publications, 1820–1852.* New York: Orville A. Roarbach, 1852.

Robson, William. *The Old Play-Goer.* 2 vols. Extra illustrated. London: Joseph Masters, 1846.

Roden, Robert F. *Later American Plays, 1831–1900.* New York: Dunlap Society, 1900.

Rourke, Constance. *American Humor: A Study of the National Character.* New York: The Macmillan Co., 1931.

———. *The Roots of American Culture.* New York: Harcourt, Brace and Co., 1942.

Scheinman, Walter. *Copyright Influence on British and American Drama.* Unpublished thesis, Cornell University, 1947.

Schick, Joseph. *Early Theater in Eastern Iowa.* Chicago: University of Chicago Press, 1939.

Schlesinger, Arthur M. *Political and Social History of the United States, 1829–1925.* New York: Macmillan Co., 1925.

Schlesinger, Arthur M., Jr. *The Age of Jackson.* Boston: Little, Brown and Co., 1946.

Seilhamer, George O. *History of the American Theatre.* 3 vols. Philadelphia: Globe Printing House, 1888–1891.

Series of Old American Songs. Edited by S. Foster Damon. Providence: Brown University Library, 1936.

Sherman, Robert L. *Drama Cyclopedia.* Chicago: privately printed [c. 1944].

Shipman, Louis Evan. *A Group of Theatrical Caricatures.* New York: Dunlap Society, 1897.

Smith, Seba. *Letters of Major Jack Downing.* New York: Bromley and Co., 1865.

———. *The Life and Writings of Major Jack Downing.* Boston: Lilly, Wait, Colman, and Holden, 1833.

————. *My Thirty Years Out of the Senate.* New York: Oaksmith and Co., 1859.

————. *'Way Down East; or, Portraitures of Yankee Life.* Philadelphia: The Keystone Publishing Co., 1854.

Smith, Sol. *Sol Smith's Theatrical Apprenticeship.* Philadelphia: T. B. Peterson and Brothers, 1854.

————. *Theatrical Management in the West and South for Thirty Years.* New York: Harper & Bros., 1868.

Smither, Nelle Kroger. *A History of the English Theatre at New Orleans, 1806–1842.* Philadelphia: University of Pennsylvania, 1944.

Sonneck, Oscar George T. *Report on "The Star-Spangled Banner," "Hail Columbia," "America," "Yankee Doodle."* Washington: Government Printing Office, 1909.

Stedman, Edmund C., and Ellen M. Hutchinson. *A Library of American Literature.* 11 vols. New York: Charles L. Webster, 1891.

Stone, Henry Dickinson. *Personal Recollections of the Drama or Theatrical Reminiscenses.* Albany: van Benthuysen, 1873.

Stowe, Harriet Beecher. *Uncle Tom's Cabin, or Life among the Lowly.* 2 vols. Boston: Houghton, Mifflin and Co., 1896.

Stuart, James. *Three Years in North America.* 2 vols. Edinburgh: Printed for R. Cadell, 1833.

Tandy, Jennette. *Crackerbox Philosophers in American Humor and Satire.* New York: Columbia University Press, 1925.

Toqueville, Alexis de. *Democracy in America.* Translated by Henry Reeve. New York: George Dearborn and Co., 1838.

Tompkins, Eugene. *The History of the Boston Theatre, 1854–1901.* New York: Houghton Mifflin, 1908.

Towse, John Rankin. *Sixty Years of the Theatre.* New York: Funk and Wagnalls, 1916.

Trollope, Frances. *Domestic Manners of the Americans.* Edited by Donald Smalley. New York: A. A. Knopf, 1949.

Turnbull, Robert. *The Theatre in Its Influence upon Literature, Morals, and Religion.* Boston: [privately printed?] 1839.

Turner, Frederick Jackson. *The Frontier in American History.* New York: Henry Holt and Co., 1920.

Vandenhoff, George. *Leaves from an Actor's Note-Book.* London: T. W. Cooper and Co., 1860.

Vernon, Grenville. *Yankee Doodle-Doo.* New York: Payson and Clarke, 1927.

Wegelin, Oscar. *A Bibliographical List of the Literary and Dramatic*

Productions . . . by Samuel Woodworth. New Orleans: Heartman's Historical Series No. 18, 1953.

———. *Early American Plays, 1714–1830.* New York: Dunlap Society, 1900.

Wemyss, Francis. *Chronology of the American Stage from 1752–1852.* New York: W. Taylor and Co., 1852.

———. *Twenty-six Years of the Life of an Actor and Manager.* 2 vols. New York: Burgess, Stringer, and Co., 1847.

Whitman, Walt. *The Gathering of the Forces.* New York: G. P. Putnam's Sons, 1920.

Wilson, Arthur Herman. *A History of the Philadelphia Theatre, 1835 to 1855.* Philadelphia: University of Pennsylvania, 1935.

Winter, William. *The Jeffersons.* 2 vols. Extra illustrated. Boston: James R. Osgood and Co., 1881.

———. *Shadows of the Stage.* New York: Macmillan and Co., 1893.

———. *The Wallet of Time.* 2 vols. New York: Moffet, Yard and Co., 1913.

Wittke, Carl. *Tambo and Bones.* Durham: Duke University Press, 1930.

Wood, William B. *Personal Recollections of the Stage.* Philadelphia: Henry Baird, 1855.

Woodworth, Samuel. *Melodies, Duets, Trios, Songs, and Ballads.* New York: Elliot & Palmer, 1831.

Yates, Edmund (ed.). *The Life and Correspondence of Charles Mathews.* See Mathews, Charles.

JOURNALS

Adams, Henry W. "The Montgomery Theatre, 1822–1835." University of Alabama Studies, No. 9 (September, 1955).

Coad, Oral S. "The Plays of Samuel Woodworth," *The Sewanee Review,* XXVII (April, 1919), 163–175.

Davis, L. Clarke. "At and After the Play," *Lippincott's Magazine,* XXIV (July, 1879), 57–63.

Dorson, Richard M. "The Yankee on the Stage—A Folk Hero of American Drama," *New England Quarterly,* XIII (September, 1940), 467–493.

———. "The Story of Sam Patch," *American Mercury,* 64 (June, 1947), 741–747.

"Dramatic Literature," *American Quarterly Review,* VIII (September, 1830), 134–161.

"Dunlap's American Theatre," *American Quarterly Review,* XII (December, 1832), 509–531.

Durand, John. "Souvenirs of Hackett the Actor," *Galaxy*, XIV (October, 1872), 550–556.

Eaton, Walter Pritchard. "Our Humble Dramatic Origins," *Literary Digest*, LII (March 11, 1916), 641–642.

Farmer's Almanac, The. Edited by Robert B. Thomas. 1806–1836.

Free, James M. "The Ante-Bellum Theatre of the Old Natchez Region," *The Journal of Mississippi History*, V (January, 1943), 14–27.

Hazlitt, William. "Mr. Mathews at Home," *London Magazine*, 5 (May, 1820), 179–183.

Hodge, Francis. "Biography of a Lost Play," *Theatre Annual* (1954), 48–61.

Hubbell, Jay B. "The Frontier in American Literature," *Southwest Review*, X (January, 1925), 84–92.

Hunt, Douglas. "The Nashville Theatre, 1830–1840," *Birmingham Southern College Bulletin*, XXVIII (May, 1935), 3–89.

Hutton, Laurence. "The American Play," *Lippincott's Magazine*, XXXVII (March, 1886), 289–298.

Kernodle, Portia. "The Yankee Types on the London Stage, 1824–1880," *Speech Monographs*, XIV (1947), 139–147.

Killheffer, Marie. "A Comparison of the Dialect of 'The Biglow Papers' with the Dialect of Four Yankee Plays," *American Speech*, III (February, 1928), 222–236.

"List of American Dramas in the New York Public Library," New York Public Library *Bulletin*, 19 (1915), 739–786.

Matthews, J. Brander. "Americans on the Stage," *Scribner's Monthly*, XVIII (July, 1879), 321–333.

"Mr. James Hackett," *Tallis's Drawing-Room Table Book* (1851), 36–37.

"Mr. Joshua Silsbee," *Tallis's Drawing-Room Table Book* (1851), 43–44.

Nethercot, Arthur H. "The Dramatic Background of Royall Tyler's *The Contrast*," *American Literature*, XII (January, 1941), 435–446.

"Review of the Biglow Papers," *Atlantic Monthly*, XXIV (January, 1867), 124–125.

Spotts, Carle Brooks. "The Development of Fiction on the Missouri Frontier (1830–1860)," *Missouri Historical Review*, XXIX (1935), 17–26, 86–96.

Tallis's Drawing-Room Table Book (1851). London and New York.

X.Y.Z. "Speculations of a Traveller Concerning the People of the United States," *Blackwoods*, XVI (July, 1824), 92 ff.

"Yankee Notions," *Museum of Foreign Literature, Science and Art*, XXVI (January–June, 1835), 27–31.

NEWSPAPERS, AND LITERARY WEEKLIES

Buffalo, New York
Commercial Advertiser: November 15, 1836.
Daily Courier: May 21, 1849.

Cincinnati, Ohio
Advertiser and Journal: 1840.
Daily Gazette: 1837–1840.

London, England
Age, The: November, 1832.
Athenaeum, The: November, 1832.
Atlas, The: April, 1827.
Bell's Life in London: April, 1827.
Courier, The: April, 1827; November, 1832; November, 1836.
Court Journal, The: November, 1836; 1844.
Drama, The: November, 1832; November, 1836.
Era, The: 1851–1852.
Examiner, The: April, 1827; November, 1832; 1844; 1851.
Figaro in London: November, 1832; November, 1836; 1838–1839.
Globe, The: November, 1832; November, 1836; 1844; 1851.
Globe and Traveller, The: April, 1827.
Illustrated London News: 1851.
Journal of Belles Lettres: November, 1832.
Literary Gazette, The: March 27, 1824; 1836.
Morning Advertiser, The: April, 1827; November, 1832; 1838–1839; 1844; 1851–1852.
Morning Chronicle: April, 1827; November, 1832; November, 1836; January, 1837; 1838–1839; 1844; 1851–1852.
Morning Herald, The: April, 1827; November, 1832; November, 1836; 1838–1839; 1844.
Morning Post: November, 1832; January, 1837; 1838–1839; November, 1844; 1851–1852.
New Monthly Magazine, The: November, 1832.
Observer, The: 1844.
Spectator, The: 1838–1839; 1844; 1851.
Sunday Times: November, 1836; January, 1837; 1838–1839; 1844; 1851.
Standard, The: September–October, 1844; October–December, 1851.
Sun, The: April, 1827; November, 1832; 1844.
Theatrical Observer, The: April, 1827.
Times, The: April, 1827; November, 1832; November, 1836; 1838–1839; 1845; 1851–1852.

True Sun: November, 1832; November, 1836; January, 1837.
Weekly Dispatch: 1844.
New York, New York
  Knickerbocker, The; or New York Monthly Magazine: 1833–1842.
  New York Evening Post: 1828; 1830.
  New York Mirror: 1823–1844.
  New York Times, The: July–September, 1853.
  Spirit of the Times: 1838–1844.
San Francisco, California
  Alta: 1855.

INDEX

Absolute, Sir Anthony: 129

Acadia, the: 236

actors, American: effect of Yankee theatre on, 7, 256, 258, 263; effect of westward expansion on, 37–38; in stock companies, 38; problem of material of, 39–40; in Yankee roles, 58, 256–257, 256 n.; appearing in London, 82, 129, 137, 190; and acting as a profession, 158; and incidence of star comedians, 257–258. SEE ALSO actors, Yankee; names of individual actors

actors, English: American audiences' reaction to, 14; theatre reports of, 17; in American theatre, 37, 38, 103, 129, 256, 262. SEE ALSO Dowton, Wm.; Kean, Edmund; Kemble, Charles; Kemble, Fanny; Macready, Charles; Power, Tyrone

actors, Yankee: significance of work of, 3–5 passim; theatrical functions of, 7; social status of, 7; stature of, as actors, 7; relation of, to English travelers, 14–15; in afterpieces, 22; problem of material of, 89; and female impersonation, 92 and n.; and story-situation plays, 123. SEE ALSO Hackett, James; Hill, George; Marble, Danforth; Silsbee, Joshua

actresses: in Yankee plays, 257

Addams, J. P.: and *Sam Patch in France*, 228; and *The Maiden's Vow*, 232; as actor, 256–257

Adelphi Theatre: Silsbee at, 240; audience of, 241; company of, 250

Adventure, The, or The Yankee in Tripoli: 174, 181

Advertiser and Journal (Cincinnati): 245

Agamemnon: in *Jonathan in England*, 73–76 passim

Age, The: on *Militia Muster*, 134

Albany, New York: and English travelers' itinerary, 15; as Simpson's birthplace, 58; Mathews in, 66 and n.; Logan in, 142, 143, 145; Hill in, 156, 161, 204; mentioned, 85, 162

Albany Museum: Hill at, 161

Albany Theatre: 58 n., 161

Albion, The: 32

Allegheny River: 244

All Well at Natchitoches: 70

America: nationalism in, 4, 7; refinement in, 4, 135; English travelers on, 6, 13–17 passim; criticism in, 28–29, 31–32; growth of cities in, 29, 37, 38; developments in, 1820's–1830's, 29–30; the arts in, 16, 39. SEE ALSO democracy, American; West, the

American Comic Annual: 182, 226

American Farmers, or the Yankee in Jersey: Forest Rose as, 57

American Monthly, The: 32

American Opera House: 106

American Quarterly Review: 32, 36

"Amos in the Stage Coach, or the Yankee in the Lard Tub": 169

Anderson, W. E.: 105

Apprentice's Library: Hill at, 160

Arch Street Theatre: stature of, 18; Logan at, 143; Hill at, 161, 163, 164, 165, 171 n., 213; Silsbee at, 246; mentioned, 163

Arnold, Richard: 90

Astor Place Riot: 14

Athenaeum, The: 132

Athenaeum National Museum: 248, 248 n.

At Home with Charles Mathews: 61, 72, 89

audience, American: English travelers on, 17, 23–27; placement of, in theatre, 21; and the Negro, 24; criticism of, 33–34, 36; effect of westward expansion on, 37, 38; effect of

Yankee in, 221–222; effect of middle
class on, 260–261. SEE ALSO Bibliography A, Yankee Theatre Plays;
Hackett, James, Yankee stage character of; Hill, George, Yankee Stage
character of; Jonathan; Marble,
Danforth, Yankee Stage character
of; Mathews, Charles, Yankee stage
character of; Silsbee, Joshua, Yankee
stage character of
"Yankee Doodle": audience calls for,
18 n., 26; playing of, in theatres, 22;
and personification of New Englander, 43; composition of, 43 and
n.7; verses to, 43 n. 7; version to
tune of, 43 n. 8; banning of, 43 n. 7;
in *The Disappointment*, 46 and n.;
in *The Contrast*, 47; in *Love and
Friendship*, 51; in *Jonathan in England*, 74
Yankee in England, A: 256 n.
Yankee in France: played by Silsbee,
247 n.
Yankee in Time, The: 232, 247
Yankee in Tripoli, The. SEE *Adventure,
The, or The Yankee in Tripoli*
"Yankee in Trouble, The, or Zephaniah
in the Pantry": 166
Yankee Land: and *The Wag of Maine*,
142, 144, 235; played by Silsbee, 247
and n.; plot of, 235–236; played by
Marble, 235; Western feeling of,
236; London reviews of, 237. SEE
ALSO Lot Sap Sago; *Wag of Maine,
The*
Yankee Pedlar, The. SEE *Old Times in
Virginia, or the Yankee Pedlar*
Yankees: western migration of, 45, 85,
160
Yankee story: in *Love and Friendship*,
50–51; and shrewd Yankee develop-
ment, 51; in *Sylvester Daggerwood*,
88, 91 and n., 92–96; in *The Times*,
108, 109; in *Down East*, 112; in *The

Moderns, 119–120; in *Wag of Maine*,
145; of Marble, 223, 225. SEE ALSO
Hackett, James, Yankee stories of;
Hill, George, Yankee stories of;
Mathews, Charles; Uncle Ben story
Yankee theatre: definition of, 1; folkloristic motifs in, 4–5; English response to, 5; realism in, 5; and
common-man theme, 5, 256; and
English-actor tradition, 7; favorable
circumstances for, 39; stimulation
for, 45; Mathews' influence in, 60;
Hackett's contribution to, 81;
launched by Hackett, 102; decline of,
123; first playwright of, 143; Hill's
contribution to, 217–218; relation of
Silsbee to, 240; close of era of, 252;
summary of development of, 252–
253; as "lower-order" comedy, 255–
256; and middle-class comedy, 260,
261
—, significance of: historical, 3–5; in
defining national character, 4–8 *passim*, 255–256, 262; and American
product in theatre, 7, 23, 262–263; to
native actors, 7, 256–258, 263; to native playwrights, 7, 263; and other
American plays, 8, 258–262; in
American comedy, 89, 255.
— plays of: popularity of, 148, 257–
258; definition of, 258. SEE ALSO
alphabetized listing in Bibliography
A, Yankee Theatre Plays; actors,
Yankee; Yankee character
Yankey in England, The: effect of, on
Yankee theatre, 52; first performance
of, 52 n., 54; glossary of, 52–54, 73;
Doolittle in, 53, 54 and n.
Young, Miss (actress): 248 n.

Zekiel Homespun: Hill in, 212
"Zephaniah in the Pantry, or the
Yankee in Trouble": 169